Notes from an
Incomplete Revolution

ALSO BY MEREDITH MARAN

What It's Like to Live Now

Notes from an
Incomplete Revolution

REAL LIFE SINCE FEMINISM

Meredith Maran

BANTAM BOOKS
New York   Toronto   London   Sydney   Auckland

Some names and identifying details have been changed for privacy's sake, but the people in this book and the events it depicts are real.

NOTES FROM AN INCOMPLETE REVOLUTION
A Bantam Book / May 1997

All rights reserved.
Copyright © 1997 by Meredith Maran.
Book design by Donna Sinisgalli.

Library of Congress Cataloging-in-Publication Data

Maran, Meredith.
Notes from an incomplete revolution : real life since feminism / Meredith Maran.
p.   cm.
ISBN 0-553-09952-3
1. Maran, Meredith.   2. Feminists—United States—Biography.
3. Women—United States—Biography.   I. Title.
HQ1413.M335A3   1997
305.42′092—dc20
[B]   96-44806
CIP

Published simultaneously in the United States and Canada

Bantam Books are published by Bantam Books, a division of Bantam Doubleday Dell Publishing Group, Inc. Its trademark, consisting of the words "Bantam Books" and the portrayal of a rooster, is Registered in U.S. Patent and Trademark Office and in other countries. Marca Registrada. Bantam Books, 1540 Broadway, New York, New York 10036.

PRINTED IN THE UNITED STATES OF AMERICA

BVG   10 9 8 7 6 5 4 3 2 1

For Jesse and Peter

This, and everything—
now, and always.

"As we go marching, marching, we are standing proud and tall,
for the rising of the women is the rising of us all . . ."

From "Bread and Roses,"

THE ANTHEM OF THE STRIKING WOMEN TEXTILE WORKERS

Lawrence, Massachusetts, 1912

CONTENTS

INTRODUCTION:
THEN AND NOW

I remember exactly where I was and what I was doing the first time I heard the words *women's liberation*. It was 1970. I was kneading whole wheat bread on the kitchen table in the house my boyfriend Paul and I had built, with a little help from our friends, on a mountain in New Mexico. Paul was reading me a letter from Eddie, a friend from New York. He wanted to know if he could come stay with us for a while. "There's a new movement happening here," he wrote. "It's called women's liberation. And it just wrecked my life."

Paul, Eddie, and I had worked together for years at *Rat,* an underground newspaper on the Lower East Side. Even after our escape from New York, Paul and I stayed on the *Rat* masthead and in the *Rat* family, filing stories from Taos about the hippie communes and the Chicano land-grant movement, hosting and hiding our city comrades when they were running from the FBI or just needed a week or two of rural R & R. But now, Eddie wrote, *Rat* as we'd known and loved it was dead.

A group of women had burst into the *Rat* offices, denounced *Rat* as a "tool of the patriarchal left," kicked out all the men, and declared the paper "liberated in the name of women." The invaders were led by Robin Morgan, a poet we knew from the antiwar movement, now the founder of WITCH: Women's International Terrorist Conspiracy from Hell. Eddie's old lady Joanie was with them. One after another the women spoke bitterly. They said *Rat*'s coverage of the blossoming women's movement had been as hostile as the straight media's. They said they knew why: nearly all the writers and editors on the *Rat* staff were men; the shitworkers were all women. They said the men used their positions of power to get sex from the women. They said men were the problem, and women were the solution. As she pushed Eddie out the door, Joanie told him their relationship was over. She was moving into a women's collective. She was going to be a woman-identified woman. She was through with men forever.

"What the hell is wrong with those chicks?" I sputtered, pounding my fist into the dough. I'd worked on that paper; worked with and slept with those men. Being female had never been an issue for me. If anything, it gave me an advantage, an easy way to get close to the guys who made all the decisions. Sure, the weaker chicks got treated like slaves—Kathleen, the receptionist, was a human doormat: making the coffee, answering the phones in that chirpy voice of hers, sleeping with the (married) editor-in-chief. Jackie, the office manager, was always whining about wanting to be a writer, but she'd never even turned in a story. And Joanie had been complaining about Eddie as long as I'd known her. She said he slept around, wouldn't marry her, wouldn't do his share of the housework—but she'd stayed with him for five years.

"Those chicks are crazy," I told Paul. "I can't believe they brought the whole paper down just to get their names on the masthead." Paul nodded and rolled us each a cigarette. "We got out of the city just in time," he said, lighting my cigarette with his. "I'm glad we're not caught up in all that mess."

But of course that mess came to get us, even on our mountain. One year after Paul and I moved into our dream house, I found myself alone in it, with nothing but an ax, a pile of firewood, and my copy of *Sisterhood Is Powerful* to keep me warm. Even on our mountain we couldn't escape the seismic shift between the sexes, the earthshaking realignment of gender relations, the questioning that began then and hasn't stopped yet: What it means to be a woman; what it means to be a man; what it means to love one, or the other, or both; what equality might look like; what power is and who should have it and how it should be wielded.

Twenty-five years later I sit on another mountain, on retreat from another city, from a very different life, still pondering those same questions. At home in Oakland, an hour's drive from the Zen monastery where I've come to celebrate finishing my first book, my lover Ann is living her woman's life: Driving our teenage sons to school and herself to work; managing a staff of eight and a two-million-dollar budget; rushing home to order half-pepperoni, half-goat-cheese pizza; going to therapy to deal with a childhood of physical and sexual abuse; fielding phone calls from the five or six teenage girls who call Peter and Jesse each night; checking in with our friend Wendy to see how her breast cancer support group went; practicing karate kicks and *katas* on our driveway in preparation for her second-degree black belt test. And thanks to Ann's gift to me of three days' leave from all that, I am free to perch on a rocky outcropping half a mile above the ocean, thinking about the next book I want to write—about how and why a quarter-century of feminism has and hasn't accomplished what it set out to do.

"More than it matters that I am a mother, a bisexual, a forty-four-year-old, an American, a Jew," I write on the pad I pull from my backpack, "it matters that I am a woman."

I've come a long way from believing that being female is irrelevant, that I don't need other women, don't need a movement, only need men. I've spent most of my adult life (after overcoming my initial resistance) as a feminist health care worker, a feminist union organizer, a feminist writer, a feminist mother. Still, the differences between the ideals of feminism and the realities of my life are as significant now as they were in 1970.

I've marched for reproductive rights, but I still mourn the baby I aborted when I was twenty. I've picketed beauty pageants and refuse to wear makeup, but I've been secretly dieting for fifteen years. Terrified when I discovered a lump in my breast, I vacillated hourly between demanding control of my own treatment and begging my (male) doctor to take care of me. I feel "masculine" when I chop wood and "feminine" when I bake cookies, mortified but still subjugated by the power of those labels. I seek out strong, successful women for friends, then sour our relationships with competitiveness and envy. If the personal is indeed political, what does my real life say about my politics?

Out in the world, these contradictions (and others) have sparked a raging debate. Feminists are at war—not only with the enemies of women's rights but, with each other. Twentysomething women are denouncing their feminist mothers' legacies. Veteran feminists are bemoaning young women's naïveté and ingratitude. Lesbian foot soldiers battling AIDS and breast cancer are accusing "glamour feminists" of selling out. Women of color are leaving mostly white groups to form their own.

"Power feminists" accuse "victim feminists" of sitting around in women's studies classes and incest support groups wallowing in self-pity, disempowering themselves and other women with exaggerated statistics about wife-battering, eating disorders, and sexual abuse.

Meanwhile, the majority of American women are going about their business—applying to law school, waiting tables, escaping to battered women's shelters, buying pantyhose, buying BMWs, having affairs, having babies, having mastectomies—as estranged from this debate, and as profoundly affected by its outcome, as they were when it began a quarter-century ago.

A hawk circles lazily below me. I watch, wondering what it's after. Does it fly just to find food—or for the pure, powerful pleasure of stretching its wings, of doing what it was born to do?

I want to write a book about feminism because this is where the women of my generation have made our deepest impression on history, and I am proud to be counted among them. Despite the limitations and failings of feminism; despite the daily differences between how feminism says women's lives should be and how our lives actually are; despite the many mountains yet to be moved—we have moved quite a few.

And I want to write a book about what it is to be a woman because I have witnessed, have lived with, have suffered from the suffering of the two women I love most, my lover and my best friend. What wounded Ann, what wounded Wendy came from being female in a world that devalues females. What has helped Ann become whole, what has helped Wendy heal came from feminism.

"This is not a movement one joins," Robin Morgan wrote in 1970, in her introduction to *Sisterhood Is Powerful,* the anthology that became the manifesto of feminism—inspiring women, and ending marriages from coast to coast. "It exists in your mind, and in the political and personal insights that you can contribute to change and shape and help its growth. It is frightening. It is very exhilarating. It is creating history, or rather, herstory. And anyway, you cannot escape it."

Who would want to? We might miss the chance to change the world—for ourselves, for our daughters, and yes, for our sons. We might miss the chance to finally see who a woman might be, who a man might be, set free from the confines of gender rigidity. And what better way to begin than the way women have always begun: by telling the truth about our lives?

Here, I begin by telling the truth about mine.

Woman to Woman

"I nurtured a secret contempt for other women who weren't as strong, free and respected (by men) as I thought I was. Especially threatening were the women who admitted that they were simply unable to cope with the miserable situation we were all in, and needed each other and a whole movement to change that. Well, somewhere during the last year I became such a woman."

—FROM THE INTRODUCTION TO
Sisterhood Is Powerful
by Robin Morgan

We are seven middle-aged women—thirty-nine to fifty-two, five straight and two bisexual, four of us mothers, one a grandmother, all feminists— away for a weekend writing retreat. This is how we are with each other.

At breakfast the first day we talk about food as we cook and eat together: swapping recipes, confessing attachments to fat and sugar, savoring the crunch of grains between the teeth and the sweet pucker of persimmon on the tongue.

After breakfast we read our poems and stories to each other, telling our secrets face-to-face: the incestuous stepfather, the full moon in the rain, the crack dealer on the corner, the baby's first smile. I can see it all on the other women's faces, the range of emotions I know must be evident on mine—empathy, admiration, envy.

At lunch we talk about being our children's mothers, and being our mothers' daughters.

In the hot tub, later, we talk about writing and how it can and can't change the world. I see I'm not the only one sneaking surreptitious glances at the others' naked bodies, sucking in my stomach, kicking air bubbles up around my thighs. I'm sure I'm not the only one thinking, *I look better than that one, not nearly as good as she does; I wonder if I'll look like her in ten years.*

At dinner we argue vehemently and loudly about pornography and erotica, and what it means that some of us use porn—or is it erotica?—in our own sexual lives, and whether we should be fighting for or against antiporn legislation.

Over dessert we talk about how we argued at dinner. Were we acting like men—interrupting, competing, polarizing, connecting from the neck up? Or were we exploring a strong new way to be strong new women: challenging each other's intellects instead of shielding each other's sensitivities?

As we get up to clear our plates, a man approaches us and asks what kind of group we are. "The way you were arguing," he says, "I thought you must be sisters."

There was a moment, a quarter-century ago, when the rage of the women spiked like a fever, and we came out from behind the men and spoke to each other.

In that moment it became our task to question everything we'd believed about what it means to be a woman, and what women could mean to each other. Maybe we weren't our own, or each other's, worst enemies after all. Maybe there was power, not weakness, in sisterhood. Maybe our mothers were oppressed, not dull. Maybe the lines between masculine and feminine, gay and straight, had been too sharply drawn. Maybe we didn't need men to protect or define us. Maybe we didn't need men at all.

Twenty-five years later our daughters are standing on new ground, and we're still questioning. We know now to consider the impact of our actions on our women friends, on younger women, on womankind. We know the cost of stepping over other women on our way to a man, or a promotion. We have brought our womanly values—collaboration instead of competition, attention to process as well as outcome, integration of spirit, mind, and body—into the family, the workplace, the world. But powerful though we may well have proved it to be, in real life sisterhood is still a thorny proposition. . . .

THROW LIKE A GIRL

Today I beat Bridget at racquetball.

Today *I* beat *Bridget* at racquetball.

Today *I beat Bridget at racquetball!*

In those final moments—when it was 18–16 mine, then 19–18 hers, then 20–19 mine, and then I lost the serve and got it back again without giving up a point, and lost it again and got it back *again*—I wasn't thinking about beating Bridget. I wasn't thinking, even, of winning. I wasn't thinking about meeting Bridget every Tuesday at 9:30 A.M. for the past year on Court 2 of the downtown Berkeley Y—trudging through the gym, past the tidy row of tiny sneakers and the squealing and huffing three-year-old girls and boys, gender-indistinguishable in their OshKosh coveralls and miniature velour jogging suits, heaving Nerf basketballs as big as half their bodies into hoops three feet off the ground. I wasn't thinking about pushing open the door to Court 2 every Tuesday morning wondering if today Bridget would finally tell me that it was too boring for her to play with me—or if this would be the day I'd get five . . . okay, three—three would be a triumph! Three points to her twenty-one.

No, all I was thinking about—not thinking about, really, but *focusing on*—as I was serving for the third time with the score still 20–19 mine, was getting the point. I was completely focused on serving the ball to

Bridget and then hitting it back to her in such a way that she couldn't hit it back to me. I certainly wasn't counting on getting the point on the serve, as Bridget almost always does, racking up four, seven, sometimes thirteen points in a row just serving the ball to me and me falling all over myself trying to hit it back. I don't have a strong serve. I'm resigned to not having a strong serve. I just wanted to get through the serve, then hit the ball to Bridget so she couldn't hit it back to me.

I served. I heard the crack of Bridget's racquet against the ball like a gun exploding in my ear. She smashed the ball against the front wall of the court, her usual killer return, a fraction of an inch off the floor. I dove for the spinning blue blur, and in the last instant before *you'll never hit that ball* took over, I willed myself to override that message. *Just try to hit the ball,* I told myself. *You don't have to hit it well. Just hit the ball. Really* try. And then a voice I didn't recognize, a voice I hadn't summoned and didn't know existed chimed in, strong and clear. *Strategize!* it said. *Don't just hit the ball. Strategize.* Win!

Suddenly I believed I could reach the ball in time. I believed I could hit the ball. I believed I could hit the ball to the exact spot on the wall that would make it land behind Bridget, out of her reach. So I did it. I swear that in that moment my racquet, my arm, my torso, my legs did more than stretch toward the ball; they *grew,* and I hit the ball, hard, and right where I wanted it to go. Bridget wasn't about to give away the game, even if it *was* the first time in a year of beating me that I'd come within ten points of beating her. She lowered her head and charged after the ball like an Olympic sprinter bursting toward the finish line. I heard her racquet and then her body crash into the back wall. But I didn't hear her racquet hit the ball. I turned and saw the ball dribbling limply toward the corner, unhit.

My point. My game.

Bridget walked toward me, rubbing her shoulder. "You did it," she said. We stared at each other in stunned silence. And then a grin spread slowly across her face like a crack in a thick piece of glass. "You did it," she repeated, shaking her head. "Congratulations." I realized that was the first time I'd ever seen Bridget smile.

I felt embarrassed. I don't know why. I didn't want to see Bridget smile. I didn't want her to act friendly or supportive. In fifty-some Tuesdays she'd never acted friendly or supportive, and I didn't want her to start now. It took me a long time to get used to Bridget, to the way she treats me. The first few times we met—silly me!—I thought we might exchange a few pleasantries before she started wiping the walls with me. I thought it might be acceptable to comment on the game as it progressed. Nothing overly chatty, just an occasional "Nice shot," or "Wow! I actually got a point!" There was even a time, early on, when I hoped Bridget might share a pearl or two of racquetball wisdom with me.

Silly me. For the first few weeks, I'd push open the door to Court 2— Bridget always gets there early so she can stretch before we play—chirping some inanely cheerful greeting. Bridget would barely glance up at me, would duck her head with obvious annoyance. Then she'd go back to stretching, her face a mask of concentration, and I'd stand there watching her, feeling like a dumb, overeager little . . . *girl.* Bridget is twenty years younger than I am; my height, about my weight. But unlike mine, her body is solid muscle. Her arms look like Popeye's after a can of spinach; cartoonish sinewy swells pop up every time she clenches her racquet. When she bends to do her stretches, when she coils down low, then leaps up to hit a ball that should, by rights, have soared beyond her reach, her calves look like topographical maps, each muscle set a jagged mountain range. Her hair—what's left of it—is usually kelly green or royal blue and so stiff with gel that it doesn't even quiver when she leaps around the court.

Once I saw Bridget naked in the locker room. It was a terrible mo-ment. I was already dressed in my consulting outfit—silk shirt, linen vest, flowered leggings, silver-buckled boots—on my way to work in the city. She was striding toward the showers, nothing to her but flesh, a skimpy white Y towel clutched in her hand. Her unexpected beauty—the soft, pale roundness of her breasts, the virginal pink of her nipples, the modest patch of pubic hair between her chiseled thighs—took my breath away. Bridget ducked her head as we passed each other, but not before she'd seen me in my Betsey Johnson leggings and my dangling silver earrings; not before I'd seen it in her eyes, the contempt she felt for me, the contempt of a dyke for a dumb-shit straight woman: *Femme! Wimp!* Girl!

Because of course I knew that Bridget was a dyke. It was obvious. But Bridget, despite my repeated efforts to reveal to her our common sexual orientation, seemed unshakable in her belief that I was a married straight professional woman, me with my long hair and spiffy court shoes and occasional mention (in the early days, before I realized I wasn't supposed to talk to her) of my previous racquetball partners: my two sons. Once I got a few points that way. Talking about kids. I'd taken one of my frequent "water" breaks—the water wasn't the point, really, I just needed to walk out of the court once or twice during the hour, away from Bridget, away from my humiliation, to remind myself that there was more to me than was evident in my losing physical and psychological contest with Bridget. This time I came back into Court 2 chuckling. "They're so cute," I said. Bridget glared at me. She *never* took a break, for water or for anything else. Even when I hit the ball into her eye socket from two feet away and her face swelled up right then and there, all she did was yell "Ow!" about five times, punching the wall with each exclamation. Then she was right back in her crouched stance, swollen face and all, ready to beat me some more.

"Cute?" she snarled.

"Those kids in the KinderGym class," I said. "Did you ever notice their teensy little shoes?"

"I hate kids," Bridget snapped. *Of course,* I thought, ashamed. *She's a separatist. She hates kids, and she hates me.* Then we started the next game, and I got five points in a row, my best score ever. "Just *thinking* about kids throws me off," Bridget muttered. "Now I've got a secret weapon!" I twittered, made heady by her uncharacteristic talkativeness. The threat of interaction seemed to help Bridget regain her concentration; she quickly finished me off, 21–5.

At the end of our first few sessions, I'd collapse onto the floor, mopping torrents of sweat off my face while nervously hoping Bridget would agree to meet me again. "Sorry I'm not better at this," I'd simper. "I hope it's worth it for you. . . ." Finally Bridget put me out of my misery and suggested a regular Tuesday morning game. "It's good for me to play you," she explained. "I know I'm gonna win, so I can try out all my new moves. As far as getting a workout," she added, convincingly if cruelly, "I just jump on the rowing machine for an hour after we play."

Six months or so after Bridget and I started playing every Tuesday, I knew I had to make a choice. Either I had to stop playing with Bridget—the punishment she dished out had crossed the line from motivational to demoralizing, and the social benefits package wasn't worth sticking around for—or I had to improve my game. For the first time in my life, I decided to work at getting better at something I wasn't good at. I stopped going to aerobics classes—they'd started to seem boring and pointless anyway—and started playing racquetball once or twice a week with women whose names I copied off the "Partners Wanted" section of the locker room bulletin board.

Debbie, an eighth-grade schoolteacher, quickly became my favorite opponent. Debbie always beat me, but not by much. She would go in for some light conversation before and after (but not during) our games, congratulated me warmly for every reasonably decent move, and said "Let's take it over" when we weren't sure whether a shot was good or not. (Bridget was *always* sure.) But Debbie had plenty of other partners (better partners, she didn't need to say) so she wouldn't commit to a weekly game with me. With Debbie, I had to take what I could get, which wasn't nearly enough.

Willow told me over the phone, when we arranged our first meeting, that she was a body worker, a Pisces, and that she liked to "play hard but have fun." She needed to "check in with me" to make sure I wouldn't mind if she made some "strange noises" when she got excited. I said I was fine with playing hard, fine with fun, fine with noises. *I* needed to "check in with Willow" to confirm that we would be playing racquetball, not having sex. As it turned out, we would be doing neither. Willow was conspicuously silent throughout our first game, and I thought I knew why. She was playing hard, and she was beating me by a landslide, and she wasn't having fun. No fun, no strange noises. Halfway through our second game, Willow put her racquet down and dropped to her knees, peering at the floor. "Did you lose a contact lens?" I asked helpfully, standing perfectly still so as not to antagonize her further. Willow popped something into the little velvet bag she wore around her neck and resumed her playing stance. "Dropped my garlic," she explained, and went on to beat me 21–6. After our third game Willow sidled out of the court without a word, thereby avoiding compromising her spiritual integrity by uttering polite hypocrisies about doing this again sometime.

Judy, a small, attractive family therapist, lost to me for weeks as badly as I used to lose to Bridget, narrating her misses with a steady stream of self-deprecating commentary that annoyed me more even than her half-hearted efforts to get to the ball. She insisted on attributing every questionable point to me; she predictably hit the ball to me instead of away from me, the way I used to hit it to Bridget until she broke me of that habit. *Doormat! Wimpy straight woman,* I would mutter to myself. *Don't be so damn nice! Compete!* At the end of our third session, Judy looked at me tentatively and asked, "Would you be willing to play with me every week? I mean, I know it's not much of a workout for you, but I think if we keep playing I'll get better. . . ." I nodded curtly, sadistically watching the relief wash over her face. Little did Judy know how secure her position with me was: beating her on a regular basis had become the balm that soothed my Bridget-ravaged ego. With Judy, *I* was the one who squelched conversation. I wanted her to concentrate on her game, on getting better at it, so she'd be a better partner for me. Eventually that's what happened.

I played with Martha only once. She appeared in a shocking pink sweat suit, planted herself in the center of the court, her heavy body and huge breasts heaving with exertion almost from the start, and hit only those balls she managed to reach without moving from that spot. Although I was desperate for partners, I gave Martha up because playing with her drove me nuts. I was mad at her every single second of the hour we were on the court together, crashing into her semideliberately every once in a while just to see if I could make her *move.* It was like trying to nudge a mountain into getting up and going for a walk. As I ran in circles around Martha, I struggled to transcend my anger, to summon up more empathic emotions. I did admire Martha for showing up at all: for her determination to be athletic in a body that clearly wasn't designed for fast moves and agile action. I tried to imagine what I'd do with a body like hers, who I might be if fate had assigned me a body like hers, what immobilities and possibilities might have been bequeathed to me along with fifty extra pounds and a pair of size 38-D breasts. But the truth was—physical differences notwithstanding—what infuriated me most about Martha was that she reminded me of myself.

"Wake up, Mom!" Jesse used to snap at me when he and Peter and I started playing racquetball together three years ago. "Mom, you're playing like a stereotype of a woman," Peter said. I thought my preadolescent sons were just being age-appropriately critical of their mother: I honestly had no idea what they meant. "I'm doing my best," I defended myself. Within weeks both of my smaller, younger *male* children became much better players than I was. As Peter and Jesse grew more and more frustrated with me, their critiques became more specific. "You're standing *still!*" "You serve to the exact same spot every time!" "You're waiting for the ball to come to you!" "*Try,* Mom! You're not even *trying!*"

Sometimes I'd sit out a game and watch the two of them playing each other: sweat flying, racquets slamming, feet pounding, the court walls shaking—pondering the difference between these young boys and me. The red-faced all-outness of them; the gently perspiring restraint of me. The competitiveness, the winningness of them; the tentativeness, the uncommittedness of me. Since they were toddlers, Peter and Jesse had always played at sports the way they were playing now. I couldn't remember or imagine myself ever playing at a sport that way.

My earliest sports memory: walking with my father to play catch in Bennett Park on summer Saturday mornings, my mother still asleep in her twin bed, my infant brother in his crib, the horsey leather fragrance rising from my mitt when I punched at it with my five-year-old fist, trotting to keep up with my handsome, competent father as he walked along punching at his. The old men playing chess at the cement tables in the park would glance up at us between moves of pawns and rooks, watching curiously as my father positioned me on the paved playing field. As soon as he wasn't looking, I'd sneak back toward him, closer than he wanted me to be.

When he was eighteen, my father had almost made it to the minor leagues; when he was twenty, he accepted his limitations, married my mother, and went to work in a Manhattan advertising agency. But still he considered himself a baseball expert. What he wanted me to do was learn the "basket catch," the catch we'd watch Willie Mays make when we went to Giants games at the Polo Grounds, just the two of us. To teach me this, in Bennett Park on Saturday mornings, my father would bark, "Ready?" and then, before I had time to answer, he'd toss the baseball a mile or more straight up into the sky. I'd scurry to get beneath it as it fell too fast to earth, its red stitching spiraling dizzyingly down, down, down, while my father shouted, "Keep your eye on the ball, Meredith! Watch the ball!"

One out of five times, then one out of three, then almost every time the ball would land in my mitt with a satisfying thump, my gloved hand curled against my stomach: the basket catch. When I'd caught enough fly balls, it was time to practice throwing. My father would edge himself away from me, farther and farther, and I learned to swallow the lump in my throat that said *you'll never throw it that far; Daddy will be mad and everyone will see* and just swing my arm back and pitch the ball as hard and as accurately as I could. If it bounced in front of him, my father would bend down, pick the ball up, hurl it into his mitt with a sharp *thwack,* and shake his head at me. "You're throwing like a girl, Meredith," he would say impatiently. "You've got to stop throwing like a girl."

My baby brother became a little boy, and soon he took my place at Bennett Park. He had a great basket catch, my father said, and an even better pitching arm. And my brother had something no daughter could ever have: a future in baseball. By the time he was seven, my brother was a Little League pitching star and my father was his coach. On Saturday mornings my father and my brother packed up their mitts and their uniforms and drove off to suburban baseball fields, leaving Bennett Park and me behind. But I'd learned my lessons well on those Saturday mornings with my father: the lessons of success and failure that shaped me. Unlike most little girls, I learned to keep my eyes on the ball, to expect from myself more than it seemed I could do. And I learned that the worst way to do anything was to do it like what I was: a girl.

Abandoned by my first love, I began a romance with horses. On Saturday mornings I pulled on my soft beige jodhpurs and stiff brown leather boots and rode the ferry to a stable on Staten Island, where I pressed my thighs around power and galloped away my grief until finally the burning blisters on the insides of my knees turned to calluses and the power became mine. From two-thousand-pound horses named Sunny and Blackie and Boo, I learned to harness energy, to rein it in, to let it go, to surrender to it. I learned to fly. Soaring over wooden hurdles, I won yellow and red and sometimes blue satin ribbons I brought home and hung in glistening rows on the wall where I could see them from my bed. I imagined myself National Velvet, teamed with my own mighty stallion. No jump would be too high for us, no course too rocky; we'd be inseparable, unbeatable. Compared to playing catch with my father, horseback riding was easy—and lonely. But I was good at it. And no one ever accused me of riding like a girl.

Racquetball was the next sport I took up, thirty years later.

Not long after I started playing with all those different women, it became clear—to me, to Bridget, and even to my sons, who now had to break a sweat in order to beat me—that my efforts were paying off. I was getting better at racquetball. And it wasn't just my game that was changing. Playing with Bridget, and then playing with Debbie and Willow and Judy and Martha, I saw before me the range of possibilities—the range of ways to be a woman engaged in sport. The range of ways to be a woman engaged. The range of ways to be a woman. *And I wanted to be like Bridget.* Okay, a friendlier version of Bridget—but Bridget nonetheless.

I wanted to play as hard as I could. I wanted to know the rules and play by them, no matter who was winning or how either partner was feeling. I wanted to do my best, to throw my whole body and soul into my racquetball game. I wanted to stop throwing like a girl, and I wanted to stop believing it was bad to throw like a girl, and *I wanted to win.*

I knew the person who ought to be the first to know: my friend Mariah Burton Nelson. Mariah had been a professional basketball player in the seventies, during the brief moment in U.S. history when a women's pro team was allowed to exist. Now she writes passionate books and travels around the country giving passionate talks about women changing sports and sports changing women. I've always loved Mariah, but during all my years of stuffing myself into Lycra bodysuits and doing apathetic lunges and leg lifts in aerobics studios in hopes of losing a few pounds, I never understood her books or her passion. *Women. Sports. Big deal.* Now I felt like Helen Keller at the water fountain. "I get it!" I told Mariah. "I feel like I've been playing racquetball wearing a tight dress and high heels— tiptoeing around the court, being careful not to rip my seams or break a heel. It's not just about racquetball, either—now that I'm putting out a hundred percent on the court, I see all the ways I've been holding back, not going for it, since I was a little kid." "Bingo," said the ever-patient Mariah.

Racquetball still had much to teach me.

A few weeks after my conversation with Mariah, near the end of a game with Bridget, I dove for a ball—went all-out to hit a ball, ended up face-first on the floor with my racquet clattering across the court, but successfully returned a ball I normally would have watched whiz by me. Bridget leaped over my prostrate body to make the winning point, then stood with the ball in her hand, staring down at me. "You never would have done that before," she said flatly. I lifted myself onto my elbows to look up at her, past the tightly bound breasts that, naked and bobbing, had made me gasp; past the punk-rock T-shirt with the torn-off sleeves that she wore every single Tuesday; at her expressionless, freckled face. This was as close as Bridget had ever come to complimenting me. I realized that she was beginning to respect me. I knew I deserved it. And by now I knew how to receive it. I said nothing, tried to look apathetic. Bridget continued, "You know, my partner gets jealous when I play with you. Isn't that stupid?"

Oh my God, I thought. *As mean as she's been to me all this time—she's* hitting *on me now?* I struggled to keep my face blank. "I told him he had nothing to worry about, but . . ."

"Him?" I gasped. Bridget nodded calmly. "My husband," she said. I wondered if I was having an injury-induced dream. "You're *straight?*" I blurted. Bridget nodded again. "Far as I know," she said. "But Bob keeps worrying I'll go gay. There's all kinds of lesbians at work, and now you. . . ."

I didn't know what shocked me most: the fact that Bridget was talking, or what she was saying. I could barely absorb the news. Bridget, straight. Bridget, married. Bridget stepping outside the bounds of traditional femininity—*Bridget refusing to throw like a girl*—without stepping outside heterosexuality. *I couldn't manage to do that, as a straight woman or as a lesbian.* Snapshots from the past year flashed through my mind. Me getting furious at Bridget when I asked if she was going to the gay march on D.C. and she asked uninterestedly, "What march?" *(Damn young lesbians, don't even know how they got their freedom.)* Ann and the kids insisting I was being homophobic, just because I listed as proof that Bridget was a dyke these characteristics: her insensitivity, her competitiveness, her unfriendliness, her muscular physique, her swagger. The smug certainty and utter inaccuracy with which I had categorized not only Bridget but myself and virtually every interaction that had ever transpired between us.

"Sorry," I mumbled. "I just assumed you were gay." Bridget shrugged. "Happens all the time," she said.

I went home that night with my self-righteous tail between my legs and confessed Bridget's revelation to my hooting and jeering sons and lover. But apparently my education wasn't yet complete. The week after Bridget came out to me as straight, my other weekly partner—Judy, the wimpy straight woman—walked into Court 2 wearing a T-shirt from Rainbow Services, an all-gay-and-lesbian counseling agency. Had Rainbow hired Judy as their token straight therapist, or what? I gaped at Judy until she cleared her throat meaningfully, apparently in hopes of dislodging my eyes from her chest.

"Are you . . . um . . . do you—work at Rainbow Services?" I stammered. Judy shook her head. *Of course she doesn't*, I thought, my faith in my own gaydar restored. *She must have bought the T-shirt at the flea market without realizing what it was. Typical naïve straight woman.* "My lover works there," Judy said. "My ex-lover, now," she added, her mouth twisted into an unhappy grin. "She left me two weeks ago. I'm still getting over it. Racquetball is great therapy for all that anger."

Judy—a lesbian? This time—seasoned, no doubt, by my recent experience with Bridget—I managed not to blurt, "But I thought you were straight!"

"Yeah, breakups are rough," I mumbled instead. Judy nodded. "We were together four years," she said eagerly. I felt my old impatience with Judy clenching in my gut like an angry fist. *Now don't start trying to make a friendship out of this,* I thought. *I'm here to play racquetball.*

"Ready?" I barked, and before Judy had time to answer, I smacked the ball against the front wall, as hard as I could.

Sisterhood Is . . .

My writing buddy Meg and I are meeting tonight at an espresso joint near my house. While we're waiting in line for our drinks, Meg says, "My new agent is incredible. We talked on the phone for two hours. When we were done, he said, 'You've just spoken your book proposal.' Then he faxed me five pages of notes. It was just what I needed—finally I had my outline."

"Wow," I say. My *agent never faxes* me *notes,* I think.

"He says he's sure it'll be a really big book. He can barely keep himself from telling editors about it while he's waiting for me to finish the proposal."

"I'm really happy for you," I say, and this is mostly true. Meg has been wanting to write a book forever; wanting to write this particular book, an exposé of the media's treatment of battered women, for years. The world will be better—more the way Meg and I want it to be—for having her book in it. Our drinks are served to us and we sit down at a shaky little round table.

Meg and I are friends as well as writing partners. Although we wouldn't be friends if we didn't share writing, and we wouldn't be writing partners if we didn't like each other—well, if we didn't *trust* each other, in all the complicated ways that writing partners need to trust each other: to be market-savvy and editorially skilled and candid and demanding, *and* kind, tactful, and encouraging. The very mix of qualities that make Meg and me so compatible—we're both in our mid-forties, writing about similar issues from a shared perspective, fired by equally fervent passions and ambitions—evokes in both of us not only respect and admiration, but also, at times, ferocious competitiveness.

On some of our nights together, I slip into a sensual trance, watching Meg's mouth caressing the soft curves of her words, stunned by the gale force of her talent. On other nights, the dark nights, I sit stiffly, my limbs and heart held apart, secretly snarling. As Meg reads, I hear only my own bitter voice, listing all the reasons it would be better to be Meg than Meredith: Envying her the prestigious agents who call begging her to write a book, her clips from *The New York Times* and *The Washington Post,* the dollar-fifty that each word she writes commands in the freelance market in which I'm paid a dollar, the brand-new car she bought with the proceeds of a controversial cover story. When I confess—which I do periodically, when my covetousness threatens to render me useless as editor *or* friend— Meg thanks me for my candor, tells me how glad she is that we can talk about these sticky feelings, then admits she's jealous of me, too. She says she envies how easily and prolifically I write (every paragraph is a struggle for her); how single-mindedly I proceed from start to finish (procrastination is her nemesis); the freedom my book contracts have given me to write and garden and raise my kids—although she doesn't have kids, doesn't want kids, but still: she is required to pitch story ideas to editors and haggle over late checks, and I am not. Sometimes it seems that Meg and I spend as much time critiquing our relationship as our writing. But when Meg reads me an article she's written for a national magazine, an article I know will draw outraged letters from misogynists and grateful letters from abused women; or when Meg says a story I've written is one of my best and I know that because she said it, it must be true—in those glory moments I know it's worth the effort it takes to be writing partners with Meg. So we keep at it.

"You go first. Mine's really long," she says. "No way," I say. It's clear there's one main event tonight, and Meg's proposal is it. "Go." "Oh God oh God," Meg moans. "I'm so nervous about showing you this thing." And then she turns to the manuscript in her hands and starts to read. *It's good,* I think. *Really good.* I jot down my comments on a lined pad as she

reads. Good subtitle—title isn't sexy enough. Clever play on words. Perfect tone—expresses militant feminist ideas without sounding (Goddess
forbid!) militant. Meg looks up at me. "It's good, isn't it?" she says.
There's a spot of crimson in each of her cheeks. "Very," I say. "I'm so
happy with it," she says, and goes on reading. As the book's shape unfolds,
I recognize the structure I suggested at our last meeting. I continue taking
notes: Nice comparison; reference obscure; opinion needs documentation.
This book has New York Times *bestseller written all over it,* I think. Argument too rhetorical; blaming the victim; one point contradicts the other.
"Wait till you hear how it ends," Meg says. She reads me the outline for
the last chapter. It takes my breath away. Although actually I've noticed
that my breath has been a bit labored for the past several minutes. I
swallow the lukewarm, chocolatey dregs of my latte. Meg puts her manuscript down and turns to me. "Well?" she asks.

"It's brilliant," I say. "I'm so proud of you." She beams and waits for
more. "I can tell how good it is by how jealous I am. It was actually
painful to listen to—that's how envious I am that it's yours and not
mine."

"That's *great!*" Meg exclaims. "That's a *fantastic* sign!" *Well, yes it is,* I
think. *But could I get maybe a millisecond's worth of empathy here?* "I can
just picture it on the *Times* bestseller list," I say. *Where my books will never
be,* I think. Meg nods excitedly. "I know, I know! I showed it to my friend
Jade and she's written a bunch of books, and she asked me if I'd still love
her when I'm famous!"

Meg gulps down the last of her orange juice, we talk about her proposal for an hour or so, and then it's my turn to read. But Ann's at karate
tonight, so I need to check in on Peter and Jesse. Meg and I head back to
my house. She's never been there when my kids are home. They're watching a basketball game on TV. "Mom!" Jesse says as we walk in. "You won't
believe the shot Jordan just missed!" "Guys—this is Meg," I say. Peter
nods in her direction. "Mom! It's the playoffs!" Jesse yelps. "I know," I
say. *Can't you guys act a little more . . . impressive?* I think. "Meg and I
are going up to Ann's room to work on our writing. I'll watch the tape
with you later, sweetie, okay?"

Meg doesn't say a word about my kids. We sit across from each other
on Ann's white wool rug. I look at her expectantly, giving her a chance to
say how handsome they are, at least. She looks at me expectantly; I read

her my story. The irony is not lost on me: The story is called "Winning"; it's about how women cope with success. My words feel like cotton balls in my mouth. Compared to Meg's proposal, my story—my whole book— suddenly seems trivial. Meg laughs as I'm reading a section I'd hoped was funny. Instantly I feel more connected to what I've written. Maybe it isn't so trivial after all. I read the last line, a bit of advice from my friend Mariah: "There are many ways to keep score, and many ways to win." I look up at Meg.

"It's very poignant," she says. *Poignant?* "I felt like I moved right into your depression with you. I have a few nit-picks—the usual stuff." As she's told me before (apparently to no avail), I should use about half as many adverbs and adjectives. She especially hates the words *prestigious* and *ritzy*. I should try to get into the larger theme earlier. And do I really believe that women's low expectations are simply the result of self-devaluation? "Women writers and accountants are *paid* less, whether we have good self-esteem or not," she says. "You make it sound as though we could just *visualize* our economic conditions away." "Yeah, but if we can't make progress psychologically, get comfortable with success," I say, "what good will economic progress do us?" "It's a balance," Meg says. "I'm just saying both aspects should be in there." "I'll think about it," I say, scribbling her comments on the back of my manuscript, word for word, as fast as I can.

"It's nine o'clock already," Meg says. We've been together three hours. *Two hours for her, one hour for me,* I think. At the end of our last meeting, Meg was upset, angry, and then crying, because we hadn't yet come up with a structure for her book proposal and at ten o'clock I'd said I was too tired to keep trying. "I just don't feel like you're giving me the kind of attention I've given you," she said. "I want it back." A few days later she left a message on my answering machine. "I'm sorry I was so blamey the other night. I was feeling desperate about my proposal, but I shouldn't have taken it out on you. I'm using one of the ideas you gave me in the new draft. There's hope yet! I love you. Call me."

We gather up our papers and pens and go downstairs. Peter and Jesse are in their rooms with their doors closed. Meg and I hug at the door. I tell her again how proud of her I am. I wait, again, for her to say some-thing about Peter and Jesse. She says nothing. "You hung in there through all that confusion and ambivalence. Now you have a great book proposal," I say. "This is actually a book I want to write," she says. I watch her cross the street until she's safely inside her shiny new car. Then I go back upstairs and knock on Jesse's door. "You missed it, Mom," he reproaches me. He starts recounting the game for me, play by play. While he's talking, I think about what else Meg didn't say: that she liked my story. Only that it's poignant. And depressing. Is the story that bad? I wonder. Or was Meg too caught up in her own triumph to focus on me? Or is that just my jealousy talking?

"Are you listening, Mom?" Jesse asks. I must have sighed out loud. "Of course. Pippin passed it to Jordan for the lay-up in the third quarter. Then what happened?" Jesse resumes his narration.

It's complicated, this business of women supporting women. Challenging each other without demoralizing each other. Rooting for each other while facing down our own demons. Nurturing without infantilizing. Taking care of ourselves while taking care of each other. Being tough, but not too tough. Nice, but not too nice.

Too tough is the problem between Meg and me. We question each other's every idea and motivation, dole out attention to each other as if we're rationing grains of rice in a famine, hurt each other's feelings on a regular basis and talk about it nearly every time it happens. After a session with Meg, I often feel exhausted. Our relationship is too hard on me, I think; she's too hard on me, *she's too good a writer for me to keep up with.* But in the six months we've been writing partners, my writing has improved. Stretching to reach Meg's standards makes my muscles ache, and it makes me stronger. All that friction doesn't always feel good. But it works.

Too nice was the problem with Elizabeth, my writing partner before Meg. Elizabeth and I lived a bay and a bridge apart, too, but somehow she ended up coming to my house a lot more often than I went to hers. We'd get together at eight—Elizabeth couldn't leave her young son and daughter until her husband got home from work. When we were settled on the couch (my house) or the king-sized bed (her house) with our cookies and tea, she'd say, "You go first. I only need a few minutes." Sometimes I'd protest, insist on dividing the time in half, tell her to talk about her ideas even if she didn't have anything on paper. Most times I'd capitulate to Elizabeth's generosity, to my own self-interest. Elizabeth and I never argued about our relationship. She never said, "I want it back." I never offered to give it back. She listened to my stories, told me all the things she liked about them, gently suggested changes. She told me often how helpful my suggestions were. She told me she hoped she'd be as good a mother as I was when her kids were teenagers.

I felt soothed after sessions with Elizabeth, bathed in her admiration. Yet between times I worried: Could I trust Elizabeth's praise? Was she being tough enough on me? And—should I be pushing past Elizabeth's selflessness, driving to her house when she offered to drive to mine, refusing to take my hour until she'd had hers? Was it up to me to look after her needs when she wasn't looking after them herself? I felt increasingly guilty about the inequities in our relationship; ashamed of myself, angry at Elizabeth.

I finished writing my book. Elizabeth was offered a juicy magazine job and she took it. Neither of us needed a writing partner anymore. I stopped calling her; then, finally, she stopped calling me. My book came out. Months later I still hadn't spoken to her or given her a copy. I started my second book, started being writing partners with Meg.

One day I got a letter from Elizabeth. She said she felt used and hurt. She wanted to get together and talk. This time I drove to her house. Her husband was curt. Elizabeth didn't hug me. Her kids were due home soon from their play group, so we walked to an espresso joint in her neighborhood. On the way there she told me about the book idea she'd come up with. We sat down with steaming cardboard coffee cups between us. I found myself wishing for a small earthquake, a customer choking at the next table, so I wouldn't have to hear what she was about to say. "I knew I was giving you more time than I took," she said. "I assumed my turn would come, that someday I'd need more from you, and you'd be there to reciprocate. Now I need your help, and you've moved on."

Elizabeth said even though I'd hurt her, she still admired me. "You're kind of a selfish person," she said. "You know what you want and you go for it. I wish I could be like you in that way." I said I wished I could be kinder, more giving, more like her in that way. "But if I were a man," I asked her, "would you call me selfish, or determined?" "Whatever you want to call it," she answered, "you look out for yourself."

I told her that the balance of power is an issue in *all* my working relationships with women. "It's true with my men friends, too," I said. "But I *expect* to deal with that stuff with men."

I waited for her to agree, for some sign of softening. None was forth-coming. "This should be easier for us," I went on. "We're feminists! We're not supposed to be having power struggles. We're supposed to *know* things that can keep this from happening to our relationships!" "I guess we can only be who we are," Elizabeth said. "Not who we wish we were."

"I have this picture in my head of how women should be together," I said. "Self-confident, not insecure. Collaborative, not competitive. Direct, not passive. I just can't seem to make that picture come to life."

Elizabeth regarded me impassively. The warm, nurturing friend and writing partner I'd taken for granted was gone. "Those are good ideals," Elizabeth said. "But I don't think ideals can override the way we were raised, our conditioning, and our personalities. I don't think we should expect ourselves to turn into model feminists overnight."

Hardly model feminists. Hardly overnight, I thought as I drove sadly home. My relationships with Meg and Elizabeth felt like flip sides of the same tarnished coin. Too much competition or too little; too much pro-cessing or not enough: neither was true to the vision of sisterhood all three of us—the legions of us—went to war for, with stars in our eyes and our fists clenched in the air, a quarter of a century ago.

I was a reluctant convert to the cause. From birth I'd identified with my father: what he had, what he was allowed to do and be—not, God forbid, my mother and her shrunken housewife's life. As a child in the fifties I played with boys; as a teenager in the prefeminist sixties, I allied myself with men. By 1969 I was the only female writer at *Rat*. I kept my distance from the other "chicks"—their jobs were to make the coffee, roll the joints, pay the bills. Rumor had it that the editor of the paper, a married man, had been fucking several women on the staff. One night during one of my breakups with Paul, as we were putting the paper to bed, Mike beckoned me into a corner. "I want to come home with you," he said. He'd noticed me at last! I'd never been especially attracted to Mike, but I didn't want to miss out on whatever goodies might come from his being attracted to *me*. He put his arm around me and led me toward the door. Kathleen stepped out from behind her desk. "Mike—please," she said. She looked stricken. At that moment it occurred to me for the first time that what I was about to do with Mike—what I'd already done with several other Mikes—was going to hurt someone. Hurt Kathleen. And Mike's old lady Mary. But was it up to me to protect Kathleen and Mary from Mike's desires? Was I supposed to refuse Mike, put my ambitions aside, just to spare their feelings?

"Lock up, Kathleen, okay?" Mike said. Kathleen turned to me, her eyes dark with pain. Mike and I pushed past her and through the door. All night while Mike did what he'd come to do, I thought about Kathleen, and Mary, about what it meant, what I had done.

Soon after that I moved to the mountains of New Mexico and got back together with Paul. A few months later we heard that *Rat* had been "liberated" by the WITCH collective. Kathleen broke up with Mike and became an editor. Mary broke up with Mike and wrote a chapter for *Sisterhood Is Powerful.*

I was glad I'd escaped the chaos and confusion. I hated this new "women's movement." Why would I, why would anyone want to join up with a bunch of women when it was so clear all the power came from men? The movement's; my own. No matter what those uptight city women said, I wasn't oppressed by my "old man." We had an equal relationship, an open relationship. I did whatever, and whoever, I wanted.

Then I went after Lee—Paul's best friend, and my best friend Trippy's boyfriend—and suddenly all that chaos and confusion were right there on our mountain. One night Trippy asked to talk to me alone. She sat facing me on the bed she shared with Lee. "Haven't you ever wondered why you don't have any women friends?" she said. "All you care about is men— flirting with men, fucking men, getting attention from men." She started crying, her tears splotching onto the Indian print bedspread. "You say you love me. But you're competing with me! If you weren't trying to get Lee into bed, if I wasn't in your way, you probably wouldn't even know I exist."

Looking into Trippy's eyes, I saw Kathleen's. I cried and told her I was sorry, told her I would change, told her now I understood what sisterhood was all about. I didn't tell Trippy I had the hots for her, too. But that felt like a minor omission: having the hots for a woman never felt as urgent, as significant, as full of possibility as having the hots for a man. Six months later I was fucking Jim, a guy from a commune on the next mountain, while his girlfriend was in the hospital having their baby. I still didn't have any women friends. I still felt most powerful when I was rubbing up against power—rubbing up against a man.

It was lust for a man that brought me to Berkeley a year later, but what I found when I got there was women. The women's movement wasn't optional or escapable anymore, not in Berkeley, not in 1971. The women in the house Danny and I moved into were going to meetings several nights a week. I'd planned to go to nursing school and have Danny's baby; instead I joined the Women's Health Collective and got a panting crush on a lesbian. Mostly women were leaving their men, but Danny, disgusted by my "perversion," left me.

I was devastated. Laura was just a crush—Danny was my *life*. I couldn't sleep; couldn't eat; cried all the time; couldn't even work up an appetite for my usual heartbreak remedy: finding another man. I collapsed, and women caught me. The women in the house gave me Valium and bubble baths. The women in the Health Collective invited me over for dinner and told me to go ahead and cry. All these women I barely knew moved in around me like a sisterhood SWAT team. They told me it was okay to be alone. They showed me that I wasn't. I'd always had a boy-friend and no women friends; now I had no boyfriend and a life full of women. We went to speak-outs and rap groups and movies about mastur-bation; we treated each other's venereal warts and fixed each other's cars, and even those of us who were still dealing with men—working for them, or sleeping with them—pledged our primary allegiance to each other.

My world view, my goals, my emotional life, and my daily life were transformed by the same paradigm shift that was shaking the world around me. I stopped seeing women as second-best. I started envisioning a future unlike my father's *or* my mother's—not as a housewife but as a women's health care activist; not as a victim but as a warrior. I stopped competing with women for men, or for a place on the masthead. I started seeing women as the subjects, not the source, of oppression. I joined the movement to end that oppression. For the first time in my life I drew power from women. At twenty-one, at last, I cast my lot with my own gender.

At forty-three, my house is often full of teenagers; some of them female, many of them daughters of feminists like me.

One afternoon I heard three of them, Alexis, Amelia, and Justina, making plans with Peter and his friends Kiko and Marcus. They wanted to try out Amelia's mom's new hot tub. "You guys come over at nine, okay?" Amelia told the boys. "We want some girl-time alone before you get there." "Sure," the boys said, and went off happily on an adventure of their own. The next day I asked Alexis if they'd had fun. "Way fun," she said. "The best part was before the guys got there, when it was just us women. The guys are cool, but—you know how great it is, just girls together." I do, I said, and I thought: *now I do.* But I didn't when I was walking past Kathleen with Mike's arm around me.

A few weeks later I took Peter and Marcus to Family Day at Zen Center, where we met up with Alexis, Heather, Emma, and their mothers. After harvesting potatoes all morning, we were walking through the garden together—Alexis, Heather, and Emma leading the way in their dirt-stained jeans and sweaty T-shirts, their shiny hair glistening in the sun, holding hands and singing; Marcus and Peter behind them with their arms slung around each other's shoulders; us moms bringing up the rear—when Heather's mom said exactly what was going through my mind. "The girls are more focused on each other than they are on their boyfriends," she whispered. "I wasn't like that at sixteen. Were you?" "I always *liked* my girlfriends better," Alexis's mom said. "But if there were boys around, it was understood: they got all the attention."

Later I talked to Heather about what her mom had said. "My female friends are my most important people, my support system," Heather said. "I'm a feminist. When I have a boyfriend, I make a strong effort not to dis my friends for him. I don't want to spend all my time with a boy anyway." She laughed. "In seventh grade my best friend was dissing all her friends for her boyfriend. I wrote this poem to her—'You can't throw me like a used sponge in the garbage. I mean more to you than that.'

"Last year," Heather went on, "my friend Jasmine, who lives with us, had a boyfriend and I didn't. She'd come home all bubbly and in love. She had him over all the time, so it was right in my face. I didn't want to be all pitying myself, but I was hurting. Finally I said, 'Jas, I'm happy for you, but I need you to share this with someone else. I need to spend time with friends who can pay attention to me, tell me I'm a good person, tell me I look beautiful today.' She understood. We got through it."

I asked Heather if she ever felt competitive with her friends. "Sure—all the time," she said. "Over grades, over looks, over clothes." Hard to believe, I thought, knowing that Heather's grades are mostly A's and B's, looking at her tall, strong, svelte body and the innocent beauty of her face. "Mostly over boys. A couple of months ago, me and my friend found out we both liked the same boy. Some girls in that situation say, 'May the best woman win.' Both me and my friend said, 'Okay, you can have him—our friendship isn't worth it.' Then we figured out she liked him better. So I said, 'Go for it.' "

I wondered if what I'd seen between the teenage girls in my own little living-room sample—skewed as it was, having been selected by my feminist-raised son—was typical or exceptional. I asked Peter's history teacher, Susan Groves, who teaches women's studies and advises the NOW chapter at Berkeley High. "Most girls I see," she told me, "make assumptions that we would call feminist. They assume they're basically independent. They're self-confident, less denigrative of other girls than when I was a teenager in the fifties. They're *talking* about these issues: jealousy and envy and competition. Girls' conversations are so different now. They have this new superstructure—feminism—that gives them a language to talk about the old, messy things."

Why, I asked Susan, have the language and assumptions of feminism been so readily accepted by these teenage girls—and boys—when those same ideals have been so hard for adults to incorporate into our hearts, brains, relationships, and legislatures?

"It comes from their families, and from the way the image of women has changed in their lifetimes," Susan said. "Plus the girls at BHS today have inherited the programs set up by the activists who came before them—the women's studies department, self-defense classes, the NOW chapter. And sports . . . in my generation athletics wasn't in the picture unless you were a cheerleader. The funding of girls' sports has had a very healthy effect on girls' psyches. Sports creates a model of bonding and loyalty among women, instead of rivalry and envy."

I came away from my talk with Susan Groves wondering if my friends and I—impaired by our prefeminist childhoods—have passed on to the next generation a torch that's too hot for us to handle.

I thought about my relationships with other women writers—not just Meg and Elizabeth but the web of women who have comforted and contained me, advised and encouraged me.

My many-times-published friend Rochelle called me from her Palm

Beach vacation, screaming with excitement, when she opened *The New York Times* one Sunday and found my book reviewed in it. Despite—or maybe because of—the clear difference between her level of experience and success and mine, Rochelle manages to advise me without condescending, to be my guide while respecting me as an equal. When I worry that my book will compete against someone else's, she says, "No one else can write your book." When I worry that Rochelle's book and mine will compete against each other, she says, "There's room for both of us on the shelf." When I tell her how envious I feel, driving from my house in the flatlands up the narrow, treelined streets to her house in the hills, she sighs and says, "You have your mountain to climb—I have mine."

And also there are the strangers, the women writers who have offered their support unbidden—a nineties sisterhood SWAT team. The nonfiction writer whose work I've long admired, who took me to lunch to tell me she was sending an angry letter to the reviewer who'd compared my book unfavorably to hers. The columnist who interviewed me for a magazine and bared her soul to me in the process. The best-selling novelist I've never met who left a Mother's Day message on my answering machine, telling me exactly how few copies of her first book had sold, offering her heartfelt hope that mine might sell a few more.

As once we marched forth into battle declaring, "The personal is political!" twenty-five years later we aging soldiers fight on, fortified by the young ones who march behind, inventing feminism as we go. Now that our movement has created opportunities that we once had to sleep with men to get; now that we're married or monogamous or driven to celibacy by HIV or disinterest or despair; now that our careers have replaced sex as the driving determinant of our lives—my friends and I don't compete for men anymore. But we're still competing for a place on the masthead. If Meg and Elizabeth and I were teenagers today, if feminism were embedded in our DNA instead of tacked on to the outer, learned layers of our consciousness, would we be crying into our coffee about men, or the masthead, or both? Would our relationships be less polluted by all that fearful measuring and comparing?

Before I go to sleep I reread my story and Meg's comments. *It is poignant,* I think, *but thought-provoking, not depressing.* I delete a few adjectives and adverbs, leaving in the words *prestigious* and *ritzy. She's right,* I decide. *I should mention the material obstacles that get in women's way.* I write a few new sentences, reread the whole piece. It's better for the changes, the writing more concise, the ideas more convincing.

I'm lucky to have Meg's help. I think about her book proposal, now, with more enthusiasm than envy. No wonder her agent's so excited: that new structure really works. *And Meg's lucky to have my help, too.*

WHAT IS FEMALE?

The first time I went to see my brother after his wife moved out of their house, it felt like a cold, cold wind had blown through before I got there. It wasn't just Roberta who was missing. There were holes in the rooms where the nicest things in them had been: the whitewashed armoire and walnut sleigh bed Roberta had been given by the decorator she'd worked for during one of her employment episodes. The pine sideboard and fiddleback flatware, wedding gifts from her grandmother. The antique sewing table she'd stripped and oiled, oiled, and oiled again, rubbing till she raised the lustrous wisdom in the wood. It wasn't just the dust bunnies in the bedroom where the old oak dresser had been, the shadows of the missing iron sconces on the wall, the happily married photos in their tarnished pewter and distressed fir frames turned facedown on the mantel. What chilled me to the bone was the flowers on the dining room table.

Same old vase: a glass brick. It must not have been one of Roberta's favorites; she'd taken the hand-painted pitchers, the tin flower buckets, the granite kenzos with her. Same old cherry wood dining room table—maybe she hadn't been able to find a place for it in the $1,200-a-month cottage my brother had just added to his monthly expenses, or maybe Drew had asked her to leave it. Same fabric-covered warehouse lamp suspended from the ceiling, spotlighting the center of the table, where—in each of the low-rent apartments and suburban houses where Roberta and my brother had lived, in the years when Drew was earning four dollars an hour in factories and the years when his contracting business was taking in a million; in the deep freeze of winter and in the wilting heat of summer—there was always a bouquet of flowers. Crazy clusters of gerbera daisies. Dutch iris unfurling among bare willow branches. Ripe white tulips, their long stems drooping elegantly like the arched necks of Thoroughbreds. In the twenty years I'd known her, Roberta had probably spent as much on flowers as I'd spent on furniture. It was one of the mysteries of Roberta, one of the many things about her that made me admire her resourcefulness and envy her artistry and disdain her priorities and her dependence. Even as her seventeen-year marriage was unraveling, even as her friends and her children were choosing sides and she and her husband were choosing therapists, then mediators, then lawyers—Roberta's flowers had still bloomed, each stem in place, each blossom intact, in the center of her dining room table.

But not today. The vase was there. There were flowers in it. But the unkempt, balding bunch of Japanese anemones, gathered as proof that Roberta was replaceable, instead proved just the opposite. I knew the anemones had been cut from the back garden, where Roberta had planted them the third year she and Drew lived here, the same year she planted tulip bulbs in a sidewalk bed of river rocks and trained espaliered apple trees along the patio wall. I looked at the pitiful bouquet, at the yellowing petals that littered the table, and I pictured my brother wandering through his wife's gardens, her Smith & Hawken pruning shears, if she'd left them behind, or maybe just a kitchen knife in his hand, looking for something—anything—that would fill the vase in the center of the dining room table. And I thought, *She's really gone.*

It was like a little death, and I was flooded with memories. Roberta at seventeen when I met her: apple-cheeked, vivacious, and voluptuous—perfect, I thought, for my eighteen-year-old, handsome, too-thin, too-serious brother. Roberta at their wedding eighteen months later, in the white lace dress she'd sewn by hand, reading vows I'd written in her mother's sun-drenched garden, abloom with the pansies Roberta's sister had planted there. Roberta redecorating the bathroom of my Hayward house in one day for one hundred dollars, in time for a last-minute party. Roberta throwing up in the Kaiser hospital parking lot in her third hour of labor with Josie. Spoon-feeding me scrambled eggs in the bathtub in my twenty-eighth hour of labor with Peter. Draping her babies and then mine across her knees like rag dolls, humming as she rubbed the air out of their gassy bellies. Cooking cream of crab soup and homegrown artichokes for my birthday dinners. Baking "emergency cakes" from whatever she could scavenge from her pantry and, later, baking whole wheat raisin bread in a three-hundred-dollar machine, a birthday gift from her husband and children.

But my strongest memory of Roberta, the event that bonded me to her—for life, I thought—was one I'm sure my brother never even knew about. It was 1979; Peter was four months old. I'd been forced back to work at my fifty-eight-hour-a-week assembly-line job. For the first few days I tried leaving Peter with a sitter, but our separation was as wrenching for him as it was for me. Both of us were crying all the time. Then he started running a fever and vomiting up his formula. "I'll take him," Roberta said, just as I was about to lose my job, my mind, or both. I called her from every break, then rushed to her house after work. She greeted me at the front door with Peter in her arms. He was cooing, smiling, and fever-free. "The numbers on his jacket were peeling off," she said, handing him over. "I sewed them back on while he was napping." I looked at the little red numbers on Peter's $4.99 Kmart baseball jacket. The 2 and the 3 were now neatly outlined in tiny, perfect red stitches. I fell into Roberta's arms, squashing Peter between her big breasts, dizzy with relief and gratitude.

"We're meeting Michelle in fifteen minutes," Drew said. I was staring at the anemones, thinking about driving to the florist and buying him a Roberta-quality bouquet. But I knew I couldn't pull it off, either. "We'd better go." On the way to the restaurant, Drew told me he'd met Michelle at the gym. They'd started dating a few weeks ago. "Is it serious?" I asked. "It could be," he said. "I can't wait to hear what you think of her."

When Drew pointed Michelle out in the restaurant, I almost laughed out loud. What else was there to think of her besides this: she was Roberta's polar opposite. Her body was as angular and lean as Roberta's was soft and rounded. Her haircut was androgynous, chic, and short, framing the sharp features of her face. Roberta's auburn hair fell in waves around her shoulders. She'd come from work, and she looked it in her silk, nylons, and pumps. Mostly Roberta wore cotton. Roberta had always seemed, and looked, a few years younger than Drew; Michelle seemed and looked—and was, it turned out—a few years older. *A real grown-up,* I thought as I watched her pick at her spinach salad and sip at her Chablis, crisply discussing the quality of photography in the redesigned *New Yorker.* *A career woman,* I thought, listening to her describe her job as director of software development at an educational publishing company. "I love kids—other people's kids. But it's a good thing I don't want my own." She sighed. "Between the hours I work, and running every morning, and my enneagram classes, and trying to keep up with my reading so I have some idea of what's going on in the world—I wouldn't have time to get pregnant, let alone raise a child."

As we made our way through dinner, Drew kept shooting me meaningful glances. I kept avoiding his eyes. *Why can't I warm up to her?* I wondered, accepting a taste of Michelle's radicchio fettucine, remembering the alfredo Roberta used to make from scratch, rich with egg yolks, soaked in heavy cream and butter. Michelle was smart, well-read, sophisticated. She and I had much more to talk about—the literary scene, marketing schemes, corporate culture—than Roberta and I had had since our babies grew up.

Then why am I feeling so . . . unmoved by her? I asked myself. Was I turning Michelle into the evil stepmother, blaming her for the loss of Roberta, for the rupture in my family, for which she was clearly not to blame? Was it just too soon for me to see another woman sitting in Roberta's place? I watched Michelle watching my brother, smiling at his nervous little jokes, touching his hand reassuringly. *She's crazy about him,* I realized.

My insides thawed a bit. The waiter brought the check, reached past me to hand it to Drew. Michelle intercepted it in midair. "Let me get this," she said. She opened her purse, laid an American Express gold card on the table. "Oh, no," I protested, pulling out my wallet. I looked at Drew, certain I'd find him doing the same thing. But my brother—who, like our father, had always insisted on paying for my meals and my kids', even when I'd invited him, even when I was earning more money than he was—was sitting perfectly still. And he looked perfectly delighted.

"Thanks, Michelle," he said. "Um, thanks, Michelle," I said. I stuffed my wallet back into my pocket.

We walked out to the parking lot to say good night. Michelle beeped off the alarm on her Audi, kissed Drew, and turned to me. We stood there awkwardly for a moment. *For chrissake—you hug your housecleaner and everyone else in the world,* I scolded myself. *Just go ahead and give this woman a hug.* I reached for Michelle just as she put out her hand to shake mine. Our bodies collided briefly. Hers felt firm and unyielding. "It was great to meet you," she said. "Same here," I said. She kissed my brother again and got into her car. I heard the radio come on. It was tuned to NPR.

Is this what feminism hath wrought? The thought surprised me, but there it was, echoing in my head. Michelle was the model nineties woman: childless by choice, mistress of her fate, captain of her career. She was everything that she and I, among many, had spent twenty-five years fighting to give women the right to be. So what was my problem? "Well?" my brother asked as he started the car. "She seems like a good person," I said.

"You don't like her," he said. I told him that wasn't true. But what was? "She's really bright, and attractive . . ."

"But?" Drew prompted me.

"No *but,* really. She's great," I said. *But she doesn't seem . . . womanly,* I thought.

Which made me wonder where that thought had come from. And just what *womanly* might mean.

I'd spent years arguing with Roberta about the old-fashioned role she'd adopted, the choices she'd made. I'd warned her about the pressure that her sporadic employment and extravagant domesticity were putting on my brother, the inevitability of the separate but equal resentments that did eventually divide them. But while I was trying to convince Roberta to reach beyond her domestic domain, I was basking in its glow: sitting in her sweet-smelling kitchen, sipping tea from her beautiful Italian mug, munching on her oatmeal-raisin cookies. Telling her to get a job was like telling a painter to lay down her brushes. In the two decades I'd known her, I'd made judgments about Roberta, had fallings-out with Roberta. But I'd always felt warm, welcomed, at home with her. And I knew that as long as he was with her—even if she maxed out his credit cards creating it—my brother and his children would always have a warm, welcoming, old-fashioned home.

Has Dan Quayle taken up residence in my brain? I asked myself. Do I really believe that Michelle is any less a woman because she doesn't want kids, pays her own bills, deprives and exercises her body to sinew and bone, rents a condo that she only visits for sleep and sex? Is what makes Roberta female the accident and the indulgence of her fleshiness, her eager embrace of all things domestic, the stretch marks on her belly and the darkened nipples of her breasts?

I thought about the other women in my life: the Michelles, and the Robertas. The career-driven women who are single and childless by choice or by default; who eat take-out dinners most weeknights and work most weekends; who live uneasily in their bodies and their apartments but move confidently through the world, changing it forever as they go. Those are the women who stimulate and sharpen my brain, critique my thinking and my manuscripts, invite me out to readings and plays, introduce me to their editors and spur me on to reach for the next higher rung. But those aren't the women I spend my birthdays with, the ones I call when Jesse is two hours late or Ann and I are in the middle of a fight. It's my heart-centered friends I feel softest with, closest to: the women who grow their own lettuce and bake their own cookies; whose houses are homes and whose lives revolve around relationships.

Then there are my young friends, my *girl* friends, the ones I go shopping for sexy underwear with and giggle through soppy girl movies with, the ones whose lacily dressed beds I sprawl across while we braid each other's hair and keep each other's animal bodies warm. Production managers and receptionists and grad students they may be, but wives and mothers is what they want to be, and neither feminist precepts nor divorce statistics can derail them from this path. Thirty-year-old Francesca, who feels empty, aimless despite her corporate ascension, because she hasn't yet met the father of her children. Twenty-six-year-old gorgeous Alicia, who's been sending away for massage school applications for years but keeps getting sidetracked by men she thinks might give her what she *really* wants. Twenty-eight-year-old Jeannie, whose career path is littered with ambivalence, but whose requirements for a husband are clear: the man she marries must (1) want children, (2) be willing to process feelings, and (3) earn enough money so she won't have to work full time.

I feel compelled to argue with these young women as I once argued with Roberta: to question their values and priorities, accuse them of setting back the clock. And so I tell Francesca to call a sperm bank. I tell Alicia to stop investing in men and start investing in a career. I remind Jeannie of what's likely to happen between an unemployed wife and the husband who supports her: exactly what happened to her own embittered housewife mother. I push them to be less like Roberta and more like Michelle, hoping they'll end up somewhere in between—where those of us who are wives and mothers keep hoping we'll wake up one day: in that postfeminist promised land where being a woman means embracing it all, being valued for it all—heart and head, independence and intimacy, career and family.

So what, then, in all these women; what in all the parts of me, is "female"?

Is it social conditioning, biological inevitability, or a combination of the two that makes me feel more "womanly" when I'm planting seedlings in my garden than when I'm chopping wood at my cabin; more womanly when I'm sweating and grunting making love than when I'm sweating and grunting playing racquetball; womanly when I'm sewing a patch on Peter's jeans but "manly" when I'm rewiring a lamp? And why is it that when I'm baking—cinnamon-swirled raisin bread in winter; blackberry cobbler when summer lays the brambles low, melting chocolate and butter, mixing nuts and flour, making the people I love *happy*—I feel most womanly of all?

Appalled by the distance between my instincts and my beliefs, I decided to approach the question the way a studious man (or woman) might: by soliciting some expert opinions. I consult with a man and a woman who walk the gender high-wire every day: James and Thalia, two of the transsexuals I volunteer with on the Pacific Center Speaker's Bureau.

From his unique vantage point, James Green has quite a view of the gender landscape. In the course of his fifty years, he's been a lesbian and a straight man; a lesbian co-parent and a father; a lover and a husband. Born female, James lived most of his adult life as a lesbian. Since his genital reconstruction surgery five years ago, he's been in a heterosexual relationship with a woman. He's also co-parenting the adolescent daughter a long-term lesbian lover conceived with him. After a recent speaker's bureau gig in a college sexuality class, the professor told James that the female students refused to believe he was ever a woman. "But he's such a hunk!" the women said. I understand their dilemma—I can't seem to keep from flirting with James myself. Which makes me wonder: Is it the handsome, masculine James that the heterosexual me is attracted to? Or is the femme lesbian in me drawn to the butch dyke who once lived in that compact, studly body of his?

"I think feminism is valuable," James tells me. "But it's on the wrong track to try and eradicate the differences between male and female."

"Which are . . ." I prompt him. "The differences between in and out," he says. "Psychologically and emotionally, not just sexually. Estrogen's effects are nearly all internal. Testosterone's effects are highly visible. Men act out their emotions. Women take things in. They process things internally."

"They?" I tease him. "How quickly you forget!"

"I'll never forget. But I have balance, now, between my male and female selves."

You sure seem to, I think. A conversation with James is the best of both worlds: he's receptive to my ideas *(like a woman)* but assertive about his own *(like a man)*. He's easygoing, funny, self-reflective, and sensitive; and he's a walking compendium of gender data. *Maybe,* I think, *we'd all be better off with what James has had: half a lifetime as a member of the opposite sex.* "Before transition," he says, "I had this masculine interior that was constantly trying to overcome my female exterior. As a woman I was much more competitive and aggressive. Now I have nothing to prove. By putting the feminine inside where she belongs and the masculine outside, I'm balanced. I'm unafraid of either side."

"Can't say that about too many men," I say. "Or women," he responds. "Even when I had a female body, even when I'd been in a relationship with the same woman for fourteen years, I was never accepted in the lesbian community. The other women could tell there were things about me that just weren't female."

"So you think it's all about estrogen and testosterone?" I ask James.

"Not completely," he says. "Gender as social construct definitely plays a role. We put arbitrary values on people based on their external genitalia.

"It's the patriarchy that's served by rigid gender roles," James told me. "By assigning a person a gender, you assign them a social place. If they move out of that place, it upsets the balance and threatens the power structure. How can we justify devaluing the work of the people who raise and teach our children; how can we justify lowering the pay of phone operators and secretaries when those jobs became female instead of male, if we don't have a gender-based system?

"But I know from personal experience that there's a biological component to gender identity as well. To go too far in either direction—to say that there's only male and female and nobody gets to cross any lines; or that it's all artifice based on social agreements—both positions are too extreme to be true."

I ask James to name what he considers to be his male and female traits. "Male: I won't ask for directions," he says, grinning. "And I don't always like to talk about my feelings. Female: I can back off when someone gets in my face. I'm not the driver from hell anymore. And . . ." He's pensive for a moment. "I was about to mention that I love having fresh flowers in the house. But it's actually my daughter and my girlfriend who care about that. Anyway, I know men who go out and buy flowers every day." "Gay men, I bet," I say, thinking of my brother, and the anemones. "Hmm . . . now that you mention it, that's true," James says, and we laugh together.

"Some cultures consider people like James and me to be shamans because we walk in two worlds," Thalia Gravel, another speaker's bureau member and a male-to-female transsexual, tells me. I remember a gay Apache friend on the bureau telling me the same thing—he's revered in his tribe because he can contact both the male and the female spirits. "It's like living with 3-D glasses on," Thalia says in her lilting voice. "For us, one lens is red and one's green. Most people only get one color or the other."

Thalia (then Thomas) was five years old when he first asked himself what I'm asking her, forty years later. "In kindergarten the teacher told us to line up: boys here, girls there. I had the body of a boy. But I knew I was really a girl. So I stood there between the two lines, asking myself what *boy* and *girl* meant, while everyone else stood there laughing at me. Eventually

I learned how to be a boy. By the time I was twelve, I had it down, so I didn't get beaten up anymore for breaking the rules."

Six feet tall, with the breasts and hips of a woman and the bone structure of a man, Thalia passes for female in all but the most gender-sensitive settings. She feels least safe in gay bars, where men call her "one of *those* things"; and on the streets of gay neighborhoods, where trans-sexuals are a favorite target of gay bashers. I've often heard that male-to-female transsexuals are the most despised sexual minority, even among other sexual minorities, and I notice that I myself have a harder time connecting with Thalia than with James.

Thalia doesn't say she's a woman. She says she's "a kind of a woman." "You don't give Clint Eastwood estrogen and get Gina Lollobrigida," she says. "For me to say I'm a woman would deny the experience of women. If I moved to Ireland, I wouldn't say I'm Irish."

I ask her the same question I'd asked James: what's the difference between being a man and being a woman? "Having grown up in the boy's side of the world, I was conditioned to be less open about my emotions and less receptive to other people's," she says. "As a man I could never say 'I don't know.' As a woman it's okay for me to say that. The emotional responsibility is different, too. As a female I fit differently into the cultural matrix of caregiving.

"If I'm in a store and a little kid falls down and hurts himself he'll look at me like, 'Can you fix this?' Kids wouldn't look to me for that when I was in a male body. Men are expected to take a more managerial ap-proach—they look around for a woman to solve the problem. As a woman I don't say, 'Where's this kid's mother?' anymore. I just pick the child up and comfort him."

For years, Thalia tells me, she walked by a schoolyard on the way to work. One day when she was still Thomas, he stopped to watch the children playing. Within moments, two teachers and a security guard had positioned themselves between him and the children. A few months later, as Thalia, she stopped to watch the children again. This time the same teachers approached her, smiling. One asked her approvingly, "Which one's yours?"

"There's a certain set of behaviors that are approved for female per-sons," Thalia says matter-of-factly. It occurs to me that in her position I'd be a lot more bitter than she or James seems to be. Or maybe not, if I'd done all the self-examination they've had to do. "The extreme is a cartoon-ish femininity—the helpless woman with big boobs and big hair. I got into that when I was younger. Now when I wear a dress, I feel like I'm in drag. It's just a choice of manipulating symbols. I like to play with it both ways. But I still like a nice sequined gown now and then."

Aren't shoes the hardest part? I say. Definitely, Thalia agrees. I wear a size eleven, I tell her. "I can squeeze into an eleven-and-a-half," she sighs.

"Running shoes, cowboy boots, wing tips—no problem. I buy men's," I say. "But for dress-up—"

"Nordstrom's, girlfriend," she says. "I stock up every time they have a sale. Listen: next time you need to borrow a pair of pumps, you just come and see me. I've got every color and hue."

Finally Thalia and I have found our glue—the ultimate girl-talk: shoe-talk. *Now* I know how to be with her. "Do you bake?" I ask. "I've always baked," she answers. "And," she adds quickly, "I've always fixed cars. I set a gorgeous table, and I take out the trash. I'm Betty Crocker, and I ride a big motorcycle.

"I almost sold my bike when I went through transition. I thought it would make me less female. Then I had a revelation: Nobody can make me line up on the girls' line or the boys' line anymore. Other people's definitions of *female* don't have to be mine."

A week after our evening with Michelle, my brother calls to say how happy he is with her. "She's really sweet when you get to know her," he says. "She just has this kind of cool facade."

I say I can imagine that might be true. Lots of people, I say, aren't who they first seem to be. He tells me excitedly that Michelle loves base-ball, that she came to one of his games and cheered herself hoarse, that she's looking forward to meeting his kids this weekend. *Yeah, well, I bet she won't be sewing the numbers back on their jackets,* I think, and then I scold myself. "She wants to spend more time with you, too," he says. "She really likes you. She couldn't believe how much you two have in common."

"We do have a lot in common, don't we?" I say. *And even if we don't,* I think, *there just might be something I could learn here.* "Got your datebook? Let's pick a night."

OBJECTS OF DESIRE

A couple of months ago, Ann called me from work and told me not to make any plans for the night of Saturday, January seventh. She had that fervor in her voice, the seductive intensity I used to hear a lot more often before Peter and Jesse were teenagers—back in the days when our kids' problems were cute, not sanity-threatening; when passion, not parental anxiety, inspired Ann to call me or me to call Ann in the middle of nearly every workday. "I'm taking you on a mystery date," she said. "You won't know where we're going till we get there. Oh, and Mer," she added, "you might want to start planning your outfit. Only sixty shopping days left."

I'm "there" now—on a long line of people in front of a downtown San Francisco building I don't recognize. In keeping with my submissive role for the evening, I let Ann select my outfit: the black washed-silk dress she licked her lips over when I tried it on in the College Avenue boutique; the cowboy boots I found in the men's department of a local thrift shop; the silver choker she gave me years ago for Valentine's Day—suggestive enough of a collar that the cold weight of the metal against my throat keeps a faint sexual current buzzing between my legs. I'm dressed; I'm there; but I still don't know where "there" is.

"Want me to tell you?" Ann asks. I shake my head. I like not knowing, not being in control. At least for tonight. Early in our relationship—

when I was in recovery from my abstinent heterosexual marriage, and lesbian feminism was in recovery from the abstinent seventies, struggling to redefine the politics of power and pleasure, to keep saying no to patriarchy and coercion while opening to the yes of desire—Ann and I used to play seduction games in public places. She'd take the stool next to mine in a gay bar, ask my name, ask if she could buy me a drink, if she could kiss me, if she could come home with me. She'd walk around my living room, thumbing through my books, picking up my pueblo pots, examining the photographs on the wall. She'd ask if we could build a fire, if she could put on a Joni Mitchell album, if I had any candles, if she could make love to me all night long. Sometimes I was shy, sometimes aggressive; sometimes she'd have to talk me into the bedroom; sometimes I'd carry her in there. There was nothing patriarchal or coercive about *this*. "Yes" was the answer to every question.

I notice now that everyone else on line with us is male. On closer inspection I see that the men are wearing cashmere coats, elegantly rumpled linen trousers, Timberland boots; and there's a certain familiar trill to the shreds of conversation that drift like confetti through the night air. "Is this a gay event?" I ask Ann. She smiles. Yes! Now I'm *really* looking forward to the evening.

Ann and I used to hang out in the Castro on weekends—drinking lattes and eavesdropping on the men's dishy café conversations; exchanging knowing smiles with the other lesbian couples in the sex shops and gelato stands on Eighteenth Street; trying on thick, expensive sweaters in the men's clothing stores; holding hands and basking in the gay-and-lesbianness of it all. Or we'd go dancing at one of the women's bars in Oakland or San Francisco, or head up to the Russian River to lie in the sun with the naked men, their fat penises napping against their muscular thighs, and the half-naked women, their pubic hair curling out from under their bikini bottoms and their pink nipples pointed at the sky. I never failed to get a sexual contact high from the men; even in repose they seemed always to be recovering from the last tryst, or tanning and shopping in anticipation of the next. And lying around with lesbians kept my sexual fantasy fuel tank on "full." From behind my sunglasses I'd watch the women teasing, kissing, lying breast-to-breast, throwing each other into the pool, and I would imagine—vividly, lasciviously—what they would do to each other later, in bed. Then AIDS muffled the happy noise of the Castro, and lots of lesbians got clean and sober, so the women's bars closed, and we bought the cabin and started spending weekends there. I love our country life, our family life, but I miss the carnal buzz of gay-and-lesbian ghetto life.

"Why no women?" I whisper. "I was just noticing that," Ann says, glancing at her watch. "This party started an hour ago. Maybe the girls got here early and left early, and the boys are fashionably late, as usual. Or maybe this is just a boy-type event."

The line moves slowly up the marble steps and into the lobby, which is undulating with hundreds of stylishly dressed men and, yes, a good number of stylishly dressed women. Everyone is chatting, laughing, drinking, eating delicious-smelling pasta out of white deli boxes. "Welcome!" a handsome young man greets us. His shocking pink T-shirt says, "We're here/we're queer/we have e-mail."

"Gay people! Yummy food! This is *perfect*! But what is it?" I ask Ann.

"It's a Digital Queers benefit for the Lambda Defense Fund," Ann says. "There's a cabaret that starts in a few minutes, and dancing later on. I didn't really know what I was getting us into when I bought the tickets, but I figured with the boys in charge, at least the food would be great."

The food *is* great: garlicky Caesar salad, artichoke-heart pasta, focaccia topped with sun-dried tomatoes; and for dessert, platters of shortbread cookies and tall Thermoses full of Gay Java. There's also an open bar. Ann and I almost never drink, but . . . "That's why we took BART instead of driving," Ann says. "C'mon, Mer. This is our big romantic night. Let me get you a drink."

Screwdrivers in hand, we wander into the huge back room, lit by swirling magenta strobes, swarming with men and women of all ages, ethnicities, and apparent proclivities. I'm filled with that deliciously excited yet safe feeling I have only when I'm surrounded by men who have no sexual interest in me, and women who just might. "Mm-mm-mm," Ann murmurs, squeezing my hand. I follow her eyes to an androgynous man—or is that a woman?—with sculpted cheekbones and finger-waved, canary yellow hair. "Ooh," I sigh as an unmistakable female in a black Lycra bodysuit weaves through the crowd. "You're so predictable," Ann teases me. "And so happy," I say, brushing a cookie crumb from the corner of her mouth. "Let's cruise."

Ann and I have different tastes in women, men, and nearly everything

else. She likes boyish girls and girlish boys; I like femmy model types and
Jesus Christ look-alikes. She grows more attracted to people as she comes
to know them; I'm turned on by strangers, sexually indifferent to friends.
But on this one point my lover and I agree: we're married, not dead. From
day one we have acknowledged—not always without pain, and almost
always complicated by the limitless reach of bisexuality—that the lust we
cherish in each other, the lust that keeps us drawn to each other, inevitably
also draws us to others. From day one we've chosen the challenge of
monogamy over the challenge of all available alternatives; from day one
we've told each other the truth about our crushes and our more dangerous
liaisons. Ten years of giggly and tearful disclosures have kept us trusting
each other, knowing each other, choosing each other, truly faithful to each
other—and still tempted by others.

After a party a few years ago, a group of friends—all nearing midlife,
all in committed relationships, all straight except for me—got into a
heated all-night dissection of monogamy. By dawn we'd only been able to
name the problem, not solve it: "We want to stay married to who we're
married to—and we don't want to die without having sex with anyone
else." Shanti said what we really need is a safe sex, all-persuasions, socially
responsible brothel. Chris said he wished straight people could have "fuck
buddies" outside their marriages the way gay men do—without deception,
jealousy, or divorce. Before she headed off for morning meditation, Jolene
suggested a more Zen approach: living satisfied in the moment, cleansing
ourselves of irritating desires. Unconvinced, Joel wondered despairingly if
serial monogamy, with its cycles of heartbreak and upheaval, is the only
acceptable way to satisfy his seemingly incompatible needs for sexual diversity, intimacy, and family.

I talked about two couples I know, one lesbian, one straight, both of
whom have found other ways to satisfy those needs. Allison and Miki are
longtime lovers, co-mothers of their two-year-old son, and self-defined sex
radicals, as committed to sexual freedom as they are to each other. Together and separately—but always openly, and always with a latex barrier
in place—they fulfill their fantasies in lesbian sex clubs, with strangers,
with friends. Together and separately they make love with whomever they
please, and whomever pleases them. At their housewarming party last year,
their tiny San Francisco apartment crammed wall-to-wall with leather
dykes, lipstick lesbians, butch boys, and drag queens, Allison and Miki

unwrapped their gifts as we guests cheered: a blender, a vase, assorted Tupperware, two whips, one pair of handcuffs, a lavender silicone dildo, and bread box–sized cartons of dental dams and rubber gloves. A card from the local vibrator store was read aloud: "Whoever said lesbians just like to cuddle," it said, "never met the likes of you!"

Stephen and Maggie met on a commune in the early seventies, and in their twenty years of marriage, they've never deleted the sexual freedom clause from their relationship. When their three kids were babies, Maggie mothered while Stephen exercised his option, flirting and necking with women who knew that he was available only sexually and only in the moment. But when their youngest son started kindergarten and Maggie got around to sex with other men, she didn't go for one-night stands and anonymous encounters in the park. She fell in love. Stephen felt threatened and abandoned, but Maggie was unrepentant, swearing she could love both men and love them well. After a year of separations and reconciliations, Stephen finally accepted Maggie's interpretation of "open marriage" and, in the process, Maggie's lover, who has since become a friend of the family. Stephen's only emotional attachment is to his wife, but he makes love often with women he meets when he goes out dancing alone, or women he meets at work. In their wallets each of them carries a card signed by the other, attesting to their primary relationship and to their approval of each other's sexual autonomy.

At times I've felt envious of Stephen and Maggie's arrangement—incredulous that they've been able to pull it off; jealous because they seem to "have it all"; staid and somehow sold-out by comparison. When I see them, I ask them what's new, how they're getting along, ashamed to realize I'm half-hoping they're in crisis again: that one or the other of them has been seized by possessiveness and insecurity, that even these paragons of sexual liberation can fall prey to the foibles of lesser mortals like me, who opt for the more traditional setup. At other times I wonder not how they do it but why they bother; it's exhausting just *witnessing* the energy their relationship demands.

The founder of Digital Queers steps up to the mike and introduces a comedienne called Lea De Laria. A short, fat woman in a shirtless tux and flopping breasts explodes onto the stage, screaming how happy she is to be in a "room fulla queers."

"You faggots are so lucky," Lea declares. "You wanna have sex—you just go off into the bushes. Lesbians can't just have sex. They have to *work on the relationship*. You have sex with a man, he has a cigarette. You have sex with a woman, she says, 'What are you thinking?' "

Ann pokes me in the ribs. She's always telling me I should have been born a gay man, because I'm always complaining about how women think sex has to be so damn *meaningful,* always wishing women could be more like men and just have some *fun* for once. I say yeah, I'm a faggot at heart (or, more to the point, at genitals). But then I think about how I'd *really* feel about anonymous sex if my lover was out in the bushes having it. And I think about the gay men I know who say they should have been born lesbians, because they long for the kind of intimacy only women seem eager to share. And then I give my monogamous girlfriend who always wants to know what I'm thinking a grateful squeeze.

Once I thought I'd never be able to give it up. When I was still married to Richard but increasingly aware that my next lover would be a woman, I asked one of my new lesbian friends, "What's the difference between sex with a man and sex with a woman?" "With a man it's such a solitary experience," she said. "Neither of you knows what the other is feeling. You're both having sex, but you're not really connected to each other. With a woman—you touch her clit; you know how she feels. She touches your breast; she knows how you feel. You understand each other completely. There's this deep emotional bonding. It's not just sex. It's *merging*."

Uh-oh, I thought. Maybe I wasn't cut out to be a lesbian after all. That's what I'd always *liked* about sex with men: the separation, the autonomy it allowed. Even while we were humping away, I'd have my experience; he'd have his. We'd meet somewhere afterward in a puddle of bodily fluids. Wouldn't deep emotional bonding smooth the rough, exciting edge off sex? Wouldn't *merging* dull the intrigue: square peg fitting mysteriously into round hole?

Yes, it would and it does, for some couples, lesbian *and* straight—enough of them to keep legions of sex therapists—lesbian *and* straight—in BMWs and *New Yorker* subscriptions. That's what happened in my marriage. But that's not what happened, not what happens with Ann and me. It's true: After a decade together, we're less incendiary than we were as new lovers, when every touch turned flesh to molten lava and every kiss was hallucinogenic. We pick each other up in bars less often these days; the pueblo pots belong to both of us now; the photos on the wall are of the two of us with our teenage sons. But still we thrive on the tension of our differences; still we take turns being round peg, square hole. Still she surprises me with mystery dates; still I swoon when she smooths black silk over my hips. Maybe it's the distance we maintain in other areas of our very separate lives, or maybe I was cut out to be a lesbian, after all, but I find I've developed quite a taste for deep emotional bonding—before, during, and after sex.

"When I first strapped on my dildo," Lea says, "my girlfriend wanted to call the penetration police. But then she told me relationships are about compromise. So she got me this thing." Lea brandishes a four-inch-long dildo in the shape of a dolphin. "Isn't this *sweet*? Men: you know how ridiculous this is. I could pick my teeth with this thing!"

"A few years behind the times, isn't she?" I whisper to Ann. She nods. "Very." When I first got involved with Ann, lesbian feminist doctrine equated penetration with patriarchy; critiquing desire took precedence over satisfying it. Thanks to pioneers like Allison and Miki—and the passage of time, and dogma—the post-Stonewall generation of lesbians seems to be enjoying sex more and polemicizing about it less.

"You know why lesbians have pierced noses?" Lea continues. "So they can breathe during cunnilingus. Yeah, we lesbians love our cunnilingus. Those poor straight girls can't get their boyfriends to lick a postage stamp!"

Munching my focaccia, sipping my sour drink, I'm happy as a clam. Why does it feel this good to sit in a room full of strangers, laughing about our sexual predilections? Maybe the laughing, the naming, the *claiming* counteracts, just a bit, what goes on outside this room—out there in the real world, where gay people lose their families, their jobs, their lives because of those predilections. But Jesse Helms and all his clones be damned—I refuse to apologize for my gay brothers and their unfettered sexuality, or for my lesbian sisters, cuddlers and orgy-goers alike. I admire the boys for their hungry sucking and fucking, prowling the streets in their predatory bodies, sniffing out the next sexual feast—keeping the life-force fires burning, even with safe sex guidelines running through their heads; even between funerals, while death snarls in wait. And I admire lesbians for fighting the good fight: prevailing over the woman-hating and dyke-baiting that would snuff or sever us from our desires, pushing through passivity to pleasure, making love in handcuffs or in lace, on flannel sheets or pushed up against a bathroom wall, or not making love at all: saying with every sexual refusal and every sexual act, *this is what I want and I don't need a man to give it to me.* And yes, for nose-piercing in service to cunnilingus.

It seems that homophobia has inadvertently given gay people a gift—that being defined solely by our sexuality makes us necessarily more connected, more committed to it. Has being challenged constantly about our sexual tastes made us more aware of them, more determined to honor and relish what pleasures we can give ourselves and others with our bodies?

Lea leaves the stage amidst riotous applause. Ann and I get on line for another drink. I'm scanning the outfits, hair styles, faces, and bodies of the people ahead of me when the bartender catches my eye. He's a striking man: ebony-skinned, tall, with a shapely shaved head and huge gold hoop earrings. And he's staring at me. Our eyes lock. I feel him, us, *it* in my knees, in my chest, in my cunt. I look away. I look back. He smiles flirtatiously at the man ahead of me, pours him a drink. Then looks back at me. It's my turn now. "Lime Calistoga," I say. *"Please."* He scoops ice into a clear plastic cup, pours bubbling water over it, hands the cup to me. Our fingers touch, hot against the cold wet plastic. A small jolt shudders through me. He smiles. He presses his thumb against mine, then lets go. "Enjoy," he says. He turns to Ann. "What would *you* like?"

"That bartender," I say to Ann as we walk away with our drinks. "He's bi. And he wanted me."

"I know," she says. "I watched the whole thing."

"It's incredible," I say. "How much can happen without words."

For just a moment I allow myself the pleasure of the fantasy. He slips out from behind the bar. We walk out of the party together. We're alone in a hotel room. He takes off his crisp white shirt. I shrug out of my black silk dress. We stare at each other. His body. Naked. My body. Naked. We move toward each other. Stop. Stare. Neither knows who the other is, what the other likes. We are about to find out. We embrace, hot flesh singeing hot flesh. I gasp . . .

"Do you wish you could . . ." Ann asks. Her face, the room full of faces come back into focus. *Do I wish I could . . . ?*

I try on yes. It doesn't feel quite true. And then no—the more reassuring answer. Not quite right either. My truth, my desire, is somewhere in between, as usual. . . .

A couple of years ago, I was having an expense-account lunch in a fancy restaurant with Robert, a potential client. "We could go back to my office," I said, when our negotiations seemed complete, "and write up a contract." Robert pushed aside the remains of his pot de crème and my chocolate decadence and leaned across the table. "Or," he said, "we could take the afternoon off and go fool around."

Robert knew I was in a relationship with a woman. I knew he was in a relationship with a woman. I felt more than a little flattered, more than a little excited. For an instant I considered his offer.

Could I?

No.

Did I wish I could?

Not exactly.

What *do* I wish for, then?

Simpler, more animal relationships, unencumbered by human fears and the rules that are meant to contain them. The elimination of HIV disease from the face of the earth. A pain-free answer to the puzzle: *"We want to stay married to whom we're married to—and we don't want to die without having sex with anyone else."*

"If circumstances were different . . ." I said. Robert nodded. "Maybe in another lifetime," he said.

I declined Robert's offer. We resumed our business discussion. We made a good deal; we both got what we wanted. I paid the check. We parted with a pleasantly charged hug.

A year later, Robert called and asked me to help his stepdaughter get a job. But first, he said, he wanted to apologize for "hitting on me" during our last meeting. I hadn't been offended then, but I was offended now. I thought we'd had the next best thing to a zipless fuck, a mutual attraction between equals; that it could as easily have been I who named the spark that arced between us. His apology made it seem tawdry instead, a modern version of the oldest story in the book. Had I naïvely experienced as consensual a flirtation in which Robert experienced himself as predator and me as prey? Did he want power, or sex—and how could he, or I, or any of us in this culture know the difference? Was this just another case of my bisexuality turning on yet another straight man with "All she needs is a good fuck" fantasies running through his head (and his penis)? If not, what in Robert's wanting of me, in my wanting of him, warranted apology?

And—even if we can't always have it, why do we make ourselves suffer so for *wanting what we want*?

"Yes and no," I answer Ann's question. "In the fantasy—yes, I wish I could go home with the bartender. In the real world, no."

No because it would hurt Ann and our relationship, and because I'd be worried about AIDS, and because I might not even like the guy, or sex with a man, for God's sake, after all these years. But *no, too,* because I've already had my fun with the bartender. I got to do my favorite part. If only for a minute or two, I got to do the dance. Sex—sex is dangerous, unpredictable, volatile. But the dance is safe. It may not satisfy the body, but the dance never fails to rouse the spirit.

"I wonder why it's always men who hit on me," I say. "Never women."

This is an old lament of mine. It took me years to understand what used to happen almost every time Ann and I went to a gay bar: exactly the opposite of what happened everywhere else. The women—as well as the occasional gay man, who mistook her for a cute boy—found Ann, with her short haircut and men's clothes and trim body, utterly irresistible. They'd flirt blatantly with her, ignoring me completely. Then we'd go out into the straight world, where Ann's androgyny made her invisible to straight men—who took my long curls and leggings as evidence that I was available to them.

Ann squeezes my shoulder. "Women flirt with you all the time, Mer," she says. "You just don't notice it. Women are more subtle than men."

"I like the way men do it," I say. "I like to be stared at."

"Well then, stop complaining and enjoy it," she advises me.

Seventies disco music starts blasting from ten-foot-tall speakers. People move onto the floor. Men in kilts dance with men in tight jeans; women in suits dance with women in shorts and T-shirts; women and men dance alone. A chain of mixed-gender dancers snakes across the floor, their hands on each other's shoulders, laughing and recruiting others as they go.

"Look," I say, nodding at two women in the smudgy shadows of the stage. Ann and I watch them for a moment. We can't see what they look like, but we can see how they feel. We can see their desire. They are backed up against the stage, one bent over the other. They are kissing deeply. Their hands are everywhere—tangled in hair, stroking skin, gripping clothes. "Wow," I say. I look around and see others watching them, too. The women pull apart, move onto the dance floor, where they continue their show.

Under the lights we can see them clearly now. They both look no older than twenty. One is wearing theatrical makeup, her Asian features accentuated by white powder and black eyeliner, her hair in a chignon, a spit curl centered on her forehead. She's wearing a skintight red velvet minidress, black stockings, and spiked heels. The other woman is in tux and tails and gleaming black leather shoes, with short, slicked-back hair, no makeup, and an utterly delighted look on her face. They dip and twirl like Fred and Ginger; they clench and kiss like Warren and Annette. When the song ends, they acknowledge the crowd's applause with a curtsey (Ginger) and a bow (Fred). Then they sink to the floor in a corner, where they caress and pant and grope at each other some more.

"Butch-femme just ain't what it used to be," I sigh. Ann smiles.

"Hot, hot, hot," she says. I pull her close, wrap my arm around her waist, stroke the curve of her hip. I still remember the first time. She presses her body against mine. "Hot, hot, hot," I say.

MOTHER-DAUGHTER WOUND

We're sitting around a big oak dining room table in a sprawling brown shingle house way up in the Oakland hills: eight female Berkeley High students, two female Berkeley High teachers, two of the girls' mothers, and me. The girls are unloading their backpacks, spreading Xeroxed articles and maps and vocabulary lists out across the table. The mom who lives here is in the kitchen, arranging whole wheat fig bars on a plate and plunking ice cubes into a pitcher. One of the teachers hands out copies of the agenda. "Berkeley High Young Women's Delegation to the International Women's Conference, Beijing," it says at the top. "Introductions" is the first item on the list.

"I'm Shoshanna," says a tall blond girl with a crystal and a Star of David dangling from a silk cord around her neck. "Phyllis. Shoshanna's mom," calls the woman from the kitchen. "Mayumi," says a chunky Japanese girl. "Susan Groves," says the Berkeley High women's studies teacher. "Meredith Maran," I say. "My sons go to Berkeley High. I'm here to help raise money for the trip." "I'm Pilar," says an olive-skinned girl in tattered short shorts, crimson lipstick, and thick-soled sneakers. The graying woman behind her says, "Margaret. Pilar's mother." Margaret strokes her daughter's gleaming jet-black hair. "And her greatest supporter," she adds.

One after another the girls give reports on the group's fundraising efforts and travel arrangements and presentations on the status of women in China and migration patterns among Third World women. "Are they this serious about school?" I whisper to Susan, who taught Peter's world history class last semester and will teach Jesse's in the fall. "These young ladies are *motivated,*" she whispers back. "They've spent a lot of time and energy—not to mention raising two thousand dollars apiece—to get themselves to Beijing. They're determined to get the most out of it they can." The final topic on the agenda becomes an energetic debate: what should the Berkeley High delegation contribute to the speak-out to be held in the young women's tent at the conference? "Maybe we should talk about incest," says Mayumi. "I have so many friends who've been molested." "What about domestic violence?" says Roxanne. "Or crime," adds Shoshanna. "I think we should focus on Bay area issues," Susan says. "Let the national delegation handle the more general stuff."

As the girls talk and argue, stopping to listen when one of the adults interjects an opinion, then picking up the conversation again, I watch the soft, sweet dance of the mothers and their daughters. Every time Phyllis brushes by Shoshanna to answer the phone or refill a glass, one of them touches the other: a pat, a squeeze, a kiss. Every time Pilar finishes speaking, she leans back against her mother, who keeps a hand resting on her daughter's back. I'm touched, witnessing this evidence of what is possible between a mother and a daughter who share more than DNA. And I can hardly decide who I envy more: these mothers their strong feminist daughters, or these girls their loving feminist mothers. *I don't remember my mother ever touching me like that.* When I was the age these girls are now, my mother and I were having screaming fights almost every day. One night my father came home from work and had to pull my mother and me apart; we were rolling on the kitchen floor, shreds of each other's skin stuck under our fingernails. When I was the age these girls are now I left home. My mother let me go.

The meeting ends. The girls stuff papers and books into their backpacks, hug each other good-bye, thank me and the other mothers for our support. As the others are piling into the cars parked in the driveway, Tina, a fifteen-year-old Latina girl, beckons me aside.

"I read your book," she whispers. She bends her head so the curtain of her gleaming black hair hides her face. Then she looks up at me. "It made me realize something important about myself. I'm bisexual, too. I've never told anyone before. I just had to thank you for being so open and honest in your book."

"Thank *you*," I whisper back. "And let me know if there's anything I can do to help." Tina gives me a quick hug and darts out the door.

Susan Groves and I stay to help Phyllis clean up. "I never knew your last name before tonight. I assumed it was the same as your kids'," Susan says as we're carrying glasses to the kitchen. "Hey—are you related to Rita Maran?"

That again. I nod. "I know your mother! She's a good Berkeley activist," Susan says. "I heard she's going to China." *Yeah, I heard that, too.* I nod again. "You're kidding! Your mother's going to China?" Phyllis says. "That's so cool. My mother hasn't gone farther than the beauty parlor in twenty years."

"Which delegation is she going with?" Susan asks. Phyllis stops washing glasses. "I don't know," I say. The two women look at me, waiting. "I don't talk to my mother very often," I say. "We're not . . . we don't really get along very well."

A drop of water plops from the faucet into the sink. Then another one. "Well, mothers and daughters—that relationship can be so hard," Susan says. "I hardly ever see my mother either," Phyllis says. "All that messy history." Then she looks at me. "But—" I hear what she doesn't say. "But *my* mother's a housewife. We have nothing in common except that messy history. *Your* mother's a feminist."

I don't say what's going through my head, what goes through my head every time this happens—when I sign my name to a check in a Berkeley food co-op or submit a story proposal to a left-wing magazine or introduce myself to a stranger at a demonstration and someone asks if I'm my mother's daughter. Yes, my mother is a feminist. And the main thing we seem to have in common is the pain we cause each other.

Yes, my mother is a feminist, and a model "reentry woman": a divorced ex-housewife who enrolled in grad school in her fifties, commuted two hours each way from Berkeley to U.C. Santa Cruz, and earned her Ph.D.—along with rave reviews from her feminist professors—in "the history of consciousness." Of course we all went to her graduation: my brother, his wife, his kids; Ann, my kids, my ex-husband, me. We dressed up for the occasion, brought her flowers, took photographs, took her out to lunch. Her classmates, most of them younger than my brother and me, looked on admiringly, and I could see the poignant picture we made: a grandmother accepting her Ph.D., dedicating her future to a better world, surrounded by her children, her lesbian daughter-in-law, and her grand-children—a triumphant snapshot of women's gains, seen through the lens of one exemplary woman's life.

That was what I saw. What I *felt* was much uglier. "You'll do anything for attention," the little monster in me snarled at my mother as we stood with our arms around each other smiling into the camera—the very accu-sation she had hurled at me: when I was expelled from Little Miss Muffet's Nursery School for biting; when I came home with yet another "unsatis-factory" in Behavior on my report card; when I jumped onto the back of a strange man's motorcycle, at age twelve, and rode away with him during a summer camp trip to Boston. I smiled and nodded that afternoon when my mother's classmates said, "You must be so proud," and I was. Proud of her; ashamed of myself, because I couldn't keep that old resentment from boiling over.

At lunch, while our kids threw french fries at each other and our mother raved about the keynote speaker's impressive curriculum vitae, my brother and I behaved so badly, we made our children look genteel. Like a mirror, my brother's glacial face reflected back to me what I felt: refusal. Our mother's demands for attention turned both of us to stone. Refusing. It was as though we were filled with lethal gas that would poison everyone around us if we should open our mouths to speak or smile. It was as though we were back in my mother's house, trapped, powerless, in the crazy maze of her unspoken needs. My lips were sealed; my body felt like a block of ice with my heart frozen solid inside—the way I have always felt in the presence of my mother.

Selfish bitch, I berated myself. *Can't you just be nice for once? This is her big day.* Selfish bitch, my mother called me when I dug in the way I was digging in right then: standing my ground, armored by my anger, refusing to acknowledge her needs until she took one step, at least, to meet mine. *I'll stop fighting with you all the time, stop getting in trouble at school, stop sneaking out of the house, start asking you how* your *day was—if you'll look at me, just once, as if you love me.* The more I acted like an unloved child—

wild, incorrigible, unreachable—the angrier she got. The angrier she got, the more unloved, and unlovable, I felt. Desperately, it seemed to me, she needed me to be a good girl, to prove to her and to the world that she was a good mother. Desperately I needed her to be a good mother, to prove to me and to the world that I was a good girl.

On the phone, the day after her graduation, my brother and I tried to ease our shared guilt, reciting to each other the words we'd each paid numerous therapists to recite to us. "With all we've wanted her to give us all our lives, no wonder it's so hard, even now, for us to give to her." I knew, even then, that my problem was the opposite of what it appeared to be: not a lack of empathy for my mother, but too much of it. As long as I could remember, I'd been filled with my mother's pain; as long as I could remember, I'd believed that I was the cause of it. My rage was the purgative I hoped would expel her pain from my body. But understanding why I couldn't be kind to my own mother didn't keep me from hating myself for it—then or now.

My mother is a feminist, yes, and a human rights activist, too. After she got her Ph.D., she founded a nonprofit organization dedicated to ending torture around the world. She corresponded—in Spanish, French, and English—with political prisoners in Chile, Algiers, Northern Ireland, Brazil. When they escaped or were released, she gave them sanctuary, speaking engagements, parties. She'd call to invite me, telling me how interesting the event would be, how courageous the guest of honor, how righteous the cause. Then she'd ask if I would come early to help her get ready.

I thought I knew what she wanted, really. She wanted me to keep my hand resting on her back. She wanted me to be her greatest supporter. She wanted her left-wing daughter at her left-wing side for all her left-wing friends to see; the appearance of the kind of relationship we both wished we actually had. *What kind of a selfish bitch would refuse her mother that?*

The truth was, although I hid my longing behind the fierce mask of my resistance, I wanted a close, loving relationship with my mother at least as desperately as she wanted one with me. I wanted to believe that somehow, someday, she and I would rise together from the sucking swamp of our history, from the morass of our incompatible personalities and dueling deprivations, miraculously unmeshed and unentangled, rejoined at last in love. I wanted this so much—want it so much still—that even all my failed, foolish attempts to make it happen could not convince me that I might as well wish I'd been born into an African tribe or with straight blond hair. It simply was not to be. But I couldn't face this finality, haven't faced it still, and so each time my mother summoned me, I went, ostensibly to avoid her anger, secretly to give my futile fantasy another try.

I met awe-inspiring people at those parties of my mother's; heard their nauseating stories of imprisonment and torture; wondered how they could laugh, drink wine, eat hors d'oeuvres—as if life could just go on after what had been done to them. *Look at all the good she's doing, all the good people who respect her. So what's your problem?* I left my mother's parties angrier at her, and at myself, than at the social injustices they were meant to expose. And I still haven't opened the book she gave me as my Christmas present eight years ago, although the white letters on its blue spine stare accusingly at me from my bookshelf every day. *Torture,* the book is called.

"I feel guilty as a feminist because I don't speak to my mother," my friend Sauda tells me. Talking with Sauda reminds me I'm not the only feminist on earth who can't seem to have a feminist relationship with her mother. But it also summons the punishing voice within me—*whose?*—that says, unlike me, Sauda has a right to her anger. *You didn't have it so bad.*

My mother was a garden-variety, white middle-class woman, one of the legions of frustrated fifties housewives whose untreated abusive childhoods, unrequited longings, and empty lives spawned a whole generation of white middle-class feminists. Sauda grew up in a housing development on the South Side of Chicago with a single mother who took care of her kids when she could and sent them to stay with relatives when she couldn't: the weeks she spent on the psychiatric wards of public hospitals, disabled by depressive breakdowns.

"I struggled for years with my feelings about my mother," Sauda tells me. "On the one hand, I have my feminist analysis. I understand why my mother abandoned me. She had five kids, she had no help, she was poor, and she was sick. Having breakdowns was a response to all that stress. I know she couldn't have done any better." Sauda tugs at the squared-off topknot that rises from her shaved head like a mesa from the desert floor. "On the other hand, it's this simple: I was a kid. I needed my mother. Her oppression as an African-American woman, a poor woman, an emotionally ill woman is real. But my scarring is real, too. And it needs tending to."

What Sauda says conjures up the unflattering picture I keep in my head of how I am, how I always have been, with my mother: stiff-jawed, entrenched in refusal, forever six years old, forever snapping *what about me?*—at her, and at everyone else in my life who's ever come close enough to rouse that old rage. "That's what happens with my mother and me, too," I say. "She was damaged by her parents; I was damaged by mine. We're both hurt, and we're both waiting to be tended to by the other. We've tried everything. We've stayed up all night talking and crying. We've gone to therapy separately and together. We've decided to spend more time together. We've decided to spend more time apart. Nothing works. And I always end up feeling like it's all my fault."

"A friend told me once that a daughter can't heal her mother," Sauda says. "A mother always has power over her daughter. It's not like resolving a problem between friends, between equals. I know if I had a daughter and she said 'You did a horrible thing to me'—it would be awful, but I like to think I'd own it. I'd say, 'I'm the mother. It's my job to make this right.' "

Yes, I say. Accepting that responsibility has been one of the most painful things for me about being a mother. It hasn't always been easy, taking care of my children—it's been wrenching and terrifying, consuming and exhausting, as my mother always said it was for her. But far more than it has caused me pain, loving my children has brought me joy. And I've never questioned, when something's wrong between me and my kids, whose job it is to make it right.

Sauda shakes her head. "I used to think it was mostly up to me to reach out to my mother," she says. "I thought, I'm a feminist. I have tools she doesn't have. And she's had such a hard life. So I tried to fix it all by myself. When I told her I was a lesbian twelve years ago, she told me I was an abomination against God. Even then I said I'd give her time. I kept trying to make her understand who I was. But she couldn't hear me. It was just like being little again—trying to be a good daughter so she'd act like a good mother.

"Finally, a year ago I called her and told her Xochi and I were getting married. I said I'd understand if she didn't want to come to the ceremony, but I did want her to be happy for me. She wouldn't give me her blessing.

I told her I didn't want to have contact with her again until she could accept me as I am and participate in healing our relationship. I haven't spoken to her since."

I was there a month ago when Sauda and Xochi spoke their vows to each other in a flower-filled boathouse beside a lake, their witnesses a hundred people of every age, ethnicity, and sexual persuasion. Along with everyone else in the room, I gulped down tears when Xochi's parents gave their blessings "to our daughter, Xochi, and our new daughter, Sauda"— blessings offered in the absence of Sauda's mother, father, brother, and sisters. And along with everyone else I burst into laughter a few moments later, when Sauda's chosen godmother, an elegant black woman draped in African cloth, stepped out from behind Sauda and Xochi at the altar and instructed the audience in a loud, ringing voice, "If anyone here objects to these two people, these two *women* being joined together, speak now—and then *get out!*"

"The ceremony was a turning point," Sauda says. "I wasn't saying 'Poor me, my mother won't come to my wedding, she thinks I'm an abomination.' I was saying 'I know that's not true. I'm my own person now.' I was taking power. I realized that day I can get nurturing from other people. I don't need to keep experiencing what I experienced as a little girl. I became an adult, finally, at the age of thirty-five—when I accepted that if my mother won't meet me halfway, this relationship is something that's lost to both of us."

"You accept that you'll never be close to your mother? *Really?*" I ask Sauda. I'm always thinking I've reached that point, only to find myself hoping for a miracle again the next time I hear my mother's voice. "What about when you read one of those dedications in a book—some feminist thanking her mother for her love and support? Or when you meet someone who gets along really well with her mother? That always gets me going."

I tell Sauda about the Berkeley High girls' meeting, and about the evening I spent recently with seventeen-year-old Heather and her mother Harriet. As they bustled around the kitchen they've shared since Heather's dad moved out eight years ago—Heather patting the rice that Harriet had cooked into homemade sushi rolls; Harriet drizzling miso dressing over the greens Heather had picked from their garden; the two of them moving easily through the paces of their life together—I grew dizzy with envy. "Is your relationship as good as it looks?" I blurted. They looked at each other and nodded. "We relate to each other and the world in a similar way," Heather said. "We like most of the same things—backpacking, women's fantasy fiction, spirituality. I think we just got incredibly lucky: we happen to be two extremely compatible people who wound up in the same family," Harriet said. Heather crumbled feta onto the salad. "There's a lot of taken-for-granteds between us. We have a bond of recognizing our feminine selves and being proud of that."

"Has it always been this good?" I asked. Dark-haired, brown-eyed Harriet and her fair-haired, blue-eyed daughter answered at the same instant. "Pretty much," Heather said. "Except when she was in junior high," said her mother. They both laughed. "Locked in her room, wouldn't talk to me about anything, hair spray, rolling eyes, the whole bit," Harriet said.

"I *never* wore hair spray!" Heather protested. "You wore hair spray," Harriet said, a smile crinkling into wrinkles at the edges of her mouth. She and I looked at Heather, at her blue eyes and clear skin, her sun-streaked, unsprayed hair cascading down her slim back, her beauty nearly blinding. Harriet turned to me again. "But then in tenth grade she came into her own, so she could come back to me as an equal."

"Instead of me having to fight for more independence as I get older, my mom accepts my changes," Heather said as we sat down to eat. "Like when I told her I wanted my boyfriend to sleep over. A lot of my friends' moms freak out about sex. But she said, 'It's up to you. I've raised you well, you have good values, you're going off into the world now, and I'm not going to undermine you as a person.' "

I asked Harriet what her own mother was like with her. "Very fearful, very conformist, more tied into right and wrong than she was into seeing me as a person. I've been in therapy twenty years with all that." She sighed. "But I couldn't have made that mistake with Heather—she wouldn't allow it. I remember when she was born, I decided I'd never let her wear pink. I dressed her in strong colors—purple, royal blue. Then when she was two years old, she pulled out this pink dress her aunt had sent her. For the next three years, she would only wear pink. I realized then that Heather was born with her own strong sense of who she is. I don't get to put my values on her." The phone rang; Heather sprang up to answer it. "Hi, sweetheart," I heard her chirp. "Luckily," Harriet added, "I adore her *and* her values, so it hasn't been a problem."

"I feel really blessed that my mom's such a strong woman," Heather said when she came back to the table. "She's helped me become a strong woman, too."

"I can't imagine who I'd be if I'd had that kind of relationship with my mother," I tell Sauda. "We have all these ideas and values in common, just like Harriet and Heather. But the chemistry between us has never been good. It's not just the way she treated me when I was a kid, or our family dynamics, or our personality differences. It's much more complicated than that. And it's hard to explain when people ask how I can be a feminist and *not* be close to my mother."

"People ask me that all the time, too," Sauda says. "I say, being a feminist means that even with your own mother, you need to know when enough is enough. I can't go to my grave suffering, trying to understand my mother because I understand the plight of women. Feminism doesn't mean any two women can be close. It means knowing what you want and being in healthy relationships so you can get it."

Sauda seems so clear, so resolved. I wonder aloud if I'll ever feel that way. "I don't long for my mother to love me anymore," she says. "But I still long for some normalcy, for a relationship that's mutually respectful." She's quiet, staring at the floor. Then she looks up and laughs, a flash of white across bittersweet chocolate skin. "I don't know if that's true, really. Maybe if I got that much, I'd revert to—'Gee, now that we have that, won't you hold me?' "

A few days after my talk with Sauda, I get a call from my mother. At first I don't recognize her voice; she sounds different, *old,* and I realize I haven't spoken to her in months. The years of making dates to talk about our relationship are over; the years of "trying to be honest," "trying to use 'I' messages"; even the years of "trying to be civil." We only speak, now, about logistics: when there's a birthday or graduation coming up, or a relative coming to town, or she wants my kids to come for dinner. "How are the boys? How's your job, your writing, your friend who has cancer, your health?" we ask each other. As we exchange our guarded answers, news briefs from our divorced lives, all I hear myself saying is *See how much I've accomplished? See how much other people like me? Have I convinced you yet that I'm a decent person?* And all I hear my mother saying is *See how much I've accomplished? See how much other people like me? Have I convinced you yet that I'm a decent person?*

My mother says she wants to see her family before she leaves for China. She suggests a picnic in the park next Saturday. I say Ann and the kids and I are starting out on our summer vacation that morning. She suggests Ann and I change our plans. I explain that we have twelve hours to drive that day and suggest dinner Tuesday night. She says my brother and his kids can't come to Berkeley on a weeknight. I suggest we get together when she gets back from China. She sighs, says we'll do it Tuesday night without my brother, asks what I want to bring. You *invited us,* my horrible self whines. *Why can't you just* offer *something for once?* "I'll be in the city working all day. I won't have time to cook," I say. "Can I just bring dessert?" She sighs again. "Never mind. I'll get dinner." "Let me bring drinks, at least," I say. I hang up the phone choked with guilt. *Why can't I do better than this?*

After our Tuesday morning game, my racquetball partner, Debbie, says, "I saw your mother's picture in the paper. She's going to China on a human rights delegation—you must be so proud! I recognized the face right away. You look just like her." Proud, yeah, I mutter, but she and I don't . . . "Every woman has issues with her mother," says Debbie, whose white Republican mother disowned her when she married a black man, and has yet to meet her teenaged daughters. "But you should try and honor the parts of her you admire. We only get one mother apiece." I'll try, I mutter.

Driving the two miles from my house to my mother's that night, it occurs to me that this is the last time I'll see her before my birthday a week from now. I feel a familiar flicker. *Maybe she'll bake me a cake.* One year— was I five, or seven?—she made me an ice cream cake shaped like a ship, with rainbow sherbet frosting and different flavors of Life Savers for portholes. I thought I had the cleverest mother in the world. Life Savers for portholes! And I'd never had angel-food cake before; it dissolved in my mouth like a sweet white cloud. *She did try; I know she did. She didn't have much to work with, and she did the best she could.*

In the midst of one of our late-night crying fights ten years ago, when I was accusing her yet again of not loving me, my mother told me this story: When I was eighteen months old, the night after I'd been rushed to the hospital with croup, she went to the neighborhood butcher. "The usual? Three lamb chops?" he asked. "Two. My daughter's in the hospital," my mother answered, and then she burst into tears. "I'd never felt such intense emotion in my life as I did in that moment," she told me. "I couldn't believe I was crying in front of the butcher. I didn't know what to do with all that pain." "Is that all loving me has been for you?" I cried. "Too much emotion, too much pain?" "No, no, no," my mother said, but it was too late for me to believe she'd ever been glad to love me, too late for me to hear whatever it was she was trying to say.

I don't want it to be too late. I don't want my mother to go to her deathbed without the love of her daughter. I don't want to go to my deathbed still angry at my mother. I don't want everything I know about Mother-blaming in misogynist culture to supercede the way I feel. I want to grow up, forgive her, forgive myself. And I don't know if that will happen in her lifetime, or mine.

My mother welcomes us at the door of her apartment. She hugs Peter, hugs Jesse, hugs Ann. She and I don't touch each other. Our bodies are like the wrong ends of magnets. Her dining room table is covered with books and papers, Xeroxed articles, and maps. In the kitchen I see a frozen chocolate cream pie defrosting on the counter. *So much for my birthday cake.*

We can't eat in the dining room, so we sit on plastic chairs on the tiny patio she shares with the other tenants in her building. There isn't room for all of us at the patio table, so we arrange our chairs to face each other as best we can. My mother passes out a stack of color brochures about China. She tells us about the UN documents she's having translated into twelve languages. She tells us how difficult it is to find a translator for the Arabic. She tells us she finally got her visa and hotel reservations, even though the Chinese government is trying to sabotage the conference. *You'll do anything for attention.* If this was anyone else talking about going to the International Women's Conference in Beijing, I'd be animated, engaged, asking questions. My mother is talking, and I've turned into a sullen adolescent.

I get up and go inside. I wander around the apartment. I'm looking for something. I don't know what it is. There's almost nothing familiar in my mother's house, almost nothing I remember from my childhood—just the Shirley Temple pitcher in the kitchen, and the Ella Fitzgerald records beside the stereo. My mother has lived in two different countries and five different apartments since I left home; I guess she left a lot behind each time she moved. I see she's still using the disk drive I gave her when I bought a new computer ten years ago. And sleeping in the bed my brother built for her when she moved to Berkeley from London seventeen years ago, right after her mastectomy, to be close to her children and grandchildren. I leaf through the papers piled on the dining room table. A human rights petition signed by my mother and a bunch of well-known Berkeley feminists. Clippings from last Sunday's *New York Times.* Some thick documents with the UN seal on the cover. I scan the room. I'm looking for something. I don't know what it is. Then, on the dining room shelf, I see myself—Peter, Jesse, Ann, and me, laughing together in our back yard, my arms around my sons' waists, their heads towering over mine—the photograph I framed and gave my mother for her birthday last year. I pick up the photograph, stare at it until my eyes burn and the image blurs, until all I see in the picture is me. *What does she see when she looks at this picture? What does she feel?*

I rub my eyes and go back outside. Jesse's chair is empty; I'm sure he went to play basketball at the park across the street, the way he usually does when he comes to my mother's house. My mother is talking to a woman her age who has a duffel bag in her arms. ". . . And this is my grandson, Peter, and this is Ann," she's saying. Coming up the stairs behind the woman, lugging a gigantic suitcase, is a woman my age. Behind her is a little girl clutching a pink stuffed rabbit. "Meredith! This is Betty, my upstairs neighbor," my mother says. "Nice to meet you," I say, the way a well-brought-up person would. "And this is Maria, her daughter, and her granddaughter Nancy."

I nod at Maria, surreptitiously scrutinizing her face. She looks tired but relaxed, present, not frozen. *Not like me with my mother.* "I'm hungry, Mommy," Nancy whines. "I know, sweetie," Maria says. She puts the suitcase down, puts her arms around her daughter. "We'll just put Grandma's suitcases away. Then we'll take her out for dinner, okay?" "Betty just got back from a month in France," my mother says. "Maria picked her up at the airport." *A good daughter, not like me.* "Well, see you later," Betty says. She climbs the stairs to her apartment, trailed by her daughter and granddaughter. *Who's taking you to the airport, Mom?* I roll the words around in my mouth. *I'll take you to the airport, Mom.*

"Pie, anyone?" my mother asks. "Meredith—you're up. Would you get dessert? And while you're in there, we'll need plates and napkins, too." I take a deep breath and walk into the kitchen. *Frozen pie.* I don't even know where my mother keeps her napkins. And how am I supposed to carry all this stuff back out there by myself? *Why does she always . . .*

"Need help, Mom?" Peter comes up beside me, throws his arm around me, hugs me to him. *How does he always . . .* "Yes," I say, handing him a stack of plates. I kiss his muscled shoulder. "Yes, I do, sweetie. Thanks."

Woman to Man

"I haven't the faintest notion what possible revolutionary role white heterosexual men could fulfill,
since they are the very embodiment of reactionary-
vested-interest-power. But then, I have great dif-
ficulty examining what men in general could
possibly do about all this. In addition to doing the
shitwork that women have been doing for genera-
tions, possibly not exist?"

FROM THE INTRODUCTION TO
Sisterhood Is Powerful

"Some mention, albeit brief, should also go to
three men: [my husband, my son, my editor's assis-
tant]. Without such men, 'this book would not
have been possible.' On the other hand, it would
not have been necessary."

FROM THE ACKNOWLEDGMENTS

It's my friend Sharon's birthday, and her boyfriend, Jeffrey—a forty-year-old SNAG (Sensitive New Age Guy) whose girlfriends have all been strong, successful women—is going to make his specialty: homemade chocolate pudding. (That and stir-fried veggies, Sharon confided to me once, are actually the *only* dishes he ever prepares.)

As Sharon and I are cutting up vegetables for the salad, squeezing lemons for the lemonade, and grating cheese for the pasta, Jeffrey walks into the kitchen. He looks around blankly, as if he's in a stranger's house, not the apartment he's shared with Sharon for three years. He asks her: "Do you have any eggs?"

I wait for Sharon to ask Jeffrey what would make them *her* eggs, not theirs, or why he hadn't shopped for the one part of the meal he'd agreed to prepare. But instead Sharon says, in a tone I haven't dared take with my sons since their ages were in single digits, "If we do, Jeffrey, they'd be in the fridge. Why don't you take a look?"

We had big plans for men, back when feminism was new. Some women could hope for no greater contribution from men than that they would simply cease to exist. The more optimistic among us envisioned a new breed of men, liberated from their gender roles by women's liberation from ours. These guys would cook and cry, go to therapy and diaper babies, assist us in achieving the multiple orgasms we so deserved, then pop up out of bed to go clean the bathroom.

To some extent our plans have been realized. Besides paying two-thirds of the rent and all of their vacation costs (Sharon says she finds this supportive, not sexist), Jeffrey does cry, and he does enjoy giving as well as receiving oral sex, and he does clean the bathroom—even if he still thinks of the kitchen and its contents as "hers." My older son is a better cook than his father is. The girls he dates tend to be more avid athletes than he is. Both my sons spend as much time waiting for girls to call them as I spent, at fifteen, waiting for boys to call me.

Still, when I listen to my single, straight women friends lamenting the shortage of available men, I'm reminded of my grandmother's complaints about the meals at her favorite Catskills resort: "The food is terrible, and the portions are so small!"

Listening to my coupled friends cajoling their boyfriends and husbands to help them make (and clean up after) dinner and—less successfully in most cases, to help them make (and clean up after) babies—it seems like a miracle that it *ever* works between men and women, now that we all know what we know. . . .

LETTER TO MY FAVORITE BOYFRIEND

Dear Oso,

I got a phone call while I was working in my garden today. "Meredith?" said a young, sweet, unfamiliar voice. "This is Sarah. Jim Gold's daughter."

I did the first translation: Jim Gold = Oso. (Remember that day in 1970, when you and I went from not knowing each other in the morning to being lovers in the afternoon? That was the day I started calling you Oso. "Bear," in the language of our New Mexico village; but Oso, too, because that was how you made me feel: *oh, so . . . so, so . . .* And what a bear of a man you were, what a big moaning grumbling screaming lumbering lusty hairy bear of a man.)

Who's Sarah? I wondered then. *Another daughter, one I don't even know about?* "Sarah?" I repeated. "I used to be Rain," she explained wearily, as if she'd explained it a thousand times. I almost chuckled aloud. *Oh. Another hippie name rejected by another child of hippies.*

"Your name doesn't sound familiar to me, either," she said. "Have I ever met you?" I bit back the answer that sprang to my lips. *Your father and I were fucking each other's brains out for the first time at the moment you were born.* "I haven't seen you since you were six months old," I said instead. "How old are you now?" "Twenty-three," she answered. *Jesus,* I thought, *Rain's four years older now than I was when she was born.*

"We got your name and number off my dad's answering machine," your daughter said, and a wave of dread rose up from my gut. I swallowed it back down. *I know:* I told myself. *Oso's far away, on a trip to Europe or something. He got my messages telling him I was coming to New Mexico last month. He asked Rain to call and tell me why he never responded. When he gets home he'll call me and . . .*

"I'm calling to tell you about the memorial service," Rain said.

First there was a whoosh through my body, a blast of comprehension that blew a hole right through me. *Jim Gold is dead.* And then there was a big resounding *NO!* and my mind took off, racing in search of some other explanation. Any other explanation. *A memorial for someone we knew in common. A memorial for . . . for . . .*

"Did your father die?" I asked your daughter. She gasped. "Oh my God!" she said. "You didn't know?" And that's how I found out that you were dead.

Funny how my first instinct was to take care of her, the way I took care of your younger daughter, Rain's half-sister April, when you sent her and her best friend to stay with Ann and me a couple of years ago. You and I laughed a lot on the phone before April came and while she was here: you and me, once the last of the red-hot lovers, now a couple of graying old farts looking after each other's hot-to-trot teenage kids. But the truth is, I got a major kick out of the whole thing: meeting your punked-out, feisty daughter; seeing what kind of a maniac you'd raised (a maniac just like you); watching her talking to you on the phone in my living room; hearing her call you Dad; noticing the way she paid respectful attention—lace body stocking, motorcycle boots, and multiple nose rings notwithstanding—to what you said.

And so as the shock, the fact of your death, was buzzing around my head, I was worrying about Rain. "I'm sorry. I'm so sorry for you," I said, wishing I could picture her face, remembering only her tiny flannel-swaddled body in the cedar cradle you built for her right after you started fucking me, in the old adobe house you shared with her mother, who watched in icy silence as I bent to see if I could recognize my lover's face, your face, in hers. "This must be terrible for you," I said in my comforting mother voice, the voice I use with my own children. "You thought I knew, and now you have to be the one to tell me."

I was proud of your daughter: she started to cry. "I've been okay with this, really," she said between sobs. I was proud of you: even though you'd split up with her mother while Rain was still in that cradle, you'd stayed that connected to your first daughter. She still loved you that much. She was "handling your affairs." *Your affairs!* "He never even got to come home," she cried. How could she show her grief so openly to me—a stranger, someone she'd never even heard of? *(I am grateful for this, at least: to know that my name wasn't bandied about in her family as the cause of its dissolution.)* Did she know that I loved you that much, too? Did she sense somehow the debt I've felt I owed her since the day she was born? Or is it just that Rain is her father's daughter, an *Osita* overflowing with uncontainable raw emotion?

While I listened to Rain—Sarah—crying, the reality of your death started burning through my skin. *Oso is dead. I'll never talk to Oso again. Never make love with Oso again.* "Sarah," I said, "is it okay to ask you some questions?" "Yes," she answered, so I asked her where and how and when you'd died. While you were visiting friends in New York. A terrible headache; a diagnosis of brain cancer; a prognosis of six months. And then, two weeks after the diagnosis, the day before you were scheduled to fly home—*the day I whined onto your machine, "Don't you love me anymore? I'm coming to New Mexico tomorrow and you still haven't called me back!"*—your friends finding you in bed, still and stiff, the life all out of your big empty body.

"Were you close to your dad?" I asked Sarah. "Oh, yes," she said, and as she told me the story of her relationship with you, I drifted back to all the times I said yes to you. And all the times you said yes to me. Starting with the day we met: a hot, late autumn afternoon. A gathering at a friend's house near the A-frame I'd just finished building with my "old man," Paul. You making eyes at me across the crowd, easing me away from Paul, asking me my name. I was intrigued, not attracted—you were too big, too hairy, too old, not my type. Still, I said yes to you when you asked me to give you a ride to your commune, two dirt road miles away. Still, I muttered some excuse to Paul, climbed with you into our Volkswagen bus, drove off with you across the mountain that lay between your home and mine.

And I said yes to you again, a few minutes later, when you turned to me—I don't recall your words, only the determination in your crazy green eyes—and asked me to stop the car and make love with you right then and there.

A girl had to have *some* rules in those days of limitless sexual possibilities, and my only sexual policy was this: if I thought it would take longer to explain to a guy why I didn't want to fuck him than it would take to fuck him, I'd just shoot up some Emko foam and do it. By the time you asked me to stop my car on that mountain, I'd had enough one-shot sexual encounters to know that I had little to gain or lose either way. If I said no, I disappointed a friend, and for no good reason. (Unlike you, most of the guys who came on to me back then were already my friends.) If I said yes, I made the guy happy, enhanced my reputation as a "hip chick," and opened myself up to a new—if almost always sexually unsatisfying—experience.

So I wasn't hoping for much when I said yes to you and stopped my car on that rutted back road. I opened the glove box and took out the can of Emko foam I kept there for just that purpose. I followed you through the dense sage and piñon until we found what passes for a clearing in the high desert. You took off all your clothes: boots, socks, jeans, T-shirt (no underwear)—your eyes fastened on me. I took off all my clothes: boots, socks, jeans, T-shirt (no underwear)—my eyes fastened on you. And then you arranged your shirt and jeans on the scrabbly ground and lay down on top of them, lay down on your back with your whole quivering eager erect self spread out before me. "C'mere," you said, beckoning to me, inviting me to straddle you, so that your body protected mine from the untender terrain as we rocked and rolled beneath the endless turquoise sky. From the first moment we were skin to skin, I felt more with you than I'd expected to feel. As you moved inside me, our eyes still locked, it all started melting together: my apathy into passion, me into you, you into me, our four-legged body into the desert. I hadn't expected to be touched, but you touched me. Your great heaving cries ringing out across the still, silent mesa. The juniper berries popping below. The moans that reverberated through me as they came up through you. The scent of crushed pine needles in my nose. The muchness of you, the suchness of you, the oomph and the passion and the hugeness of you. I didn't come with you, but I . . . went with you. We were good. We were good together. We were good, good, good together. When at last we peeled ourselves apart, broke the suction of sweat and sex, reluctantly untangled toes from toes, hips from hips, cock from cunt, chest from breasts, arms from arms, hair from kinky, matted hair; when we stood at last and faced each other again—

eyes wide, legs shaking, pulling on socks first to keep from scratching up our feet, then T-shirt, jeans, boots—I wasn't who I had been before.

I don't remember what happened next. Even if I could ask you, I know you wouldn't remember, either. (Logistics never interested you; only the feelings mattered.) I don't remember bringing you home, don't remember wondering where your pregnant old lady was, or whether or not you noticed that your truck was missing from in front of your house. I don't remember what we said, what I drove away thinking about how or when we'd ever make love again. I don't even remember how or when I found out that while you were pouring yourself into me, your first child—Rain—was coming into the world at the nearest hospital, fifty miles away.

I do remember telling Paul about what we'd done. I had to tell him right away; that was our deal: no secrets, no lies. So that night, while I was folding the laundry we'd done in town earlier that day, I told Paul that I'd fucked Jim Gold. He wasn't surprised. But he was furious. I was shocked; Paul had never reacted that way before. "This time it's different," he yelled. I didn't understand how he knew that, or what exactly he meant. But I knew he was right. A few weeks later Paul took his typewriter and moved to Santa Fe.

After Paul left, you and I were together as often as you could get away. Sometimes you'd walk the two miles over the mountain to come see me. Sometimes a guy from your commune would drop you off at my house and pick you up a few hours later. You couldn't take your truck—something to do with your girlfriend, with your baby, with secrecy. I never knew when you'd show up (neither one of us had a phone—or a bathroom, or most of the other things we both accumulated over the next twenty years). But I was always ready for you. Always wanting you. Always wanting the next adventure with you. The sitting up, the lying down, the right side up, the upside down, the kitchen table, the couch, the bed, the bed, the bed.

And the big yes you said to me when I said I wanted to have your baby. And the night we cried together until dawn painted the mesa purple, the night the blood came and we knew it would never happen.

I don't know what kept you coming back to me, all those years later, when you were talking dirty to me on the phone or writing me romantic letters or kissing me in a parking lot. But what kept me coming back to you was the look on your face the day you discovered my clitoris. We'd probably made love fifteen times by then, and I'd never yet had an orgasm with you. (As you might recall, I hadn't been registering many complaints—our sexual acrobatics always left me dazed, crazed, and amazed, if not entirely fulfilled.) That wasn't unusual for me, in those days, because fucking was what men wanted to do, and fucking didn't make me come. The guys I'd said yes to before you were easy to please—as long as I just wanted to please them. Unlike me, they came whether they were fucking a stranger for the first time or their girlfriend for the thousandth time. The men I said yes to went home to their old ladies whistling a happy tune, high on vitamin O, relieved because I never hassled them when they said they couldn't spend the night.

I figured something was wrong with me. My women friends never complained about being unsatisfied, so I assumed they were *real* women, the kind of woman I wished I could be: relaxed enough, hip enough, *womanly* enough to have the *right* kind of orgasms. But I only came with guys I'd been to bed with at least a few times—guys I'd explained my problem to, guys I'd trained to help me solve it, guys who were willing to be trained. So far I hadn't found many men like that. I had no reason to believe you'd turn out to be one of them. So I'd decided to enjoy what we had, not risk spoiling it by making unromantic, technical demands.

One day I got a letter from a friend in New York. She'd quit what she now called the "male-dominated Left" and joined a new movement for women's liberation. She enclosed a copy of a book called *Sisterhood Is Powerful.* I was surprised to recognize the names of many of the contributors: women I'd known only as the girlfriends of the men I'd planned demonstrations with, laid out underground newspapers with, spent the night with. Carl's old lady Angela. Bobby's old lady Marly. Rick's old lady Connie. The days and nights I waited for you, I worked my way through the book. All those invisible, silent "chicks" weren't anybody's old ladies anymore. They were *feminists* now. They were putting their relationships with each other, their *sisterhood,* ahead of their relationships with men.

For the first time—for just a moment—I considered the impact of our romance, yours and mine, on your girlfriend, the mother of your new baby. *I don't even know her,* I told myself. *Why should I care more about her feelings than my own, or Oso's? Anyway, she and Jim probably have the same agreement that Paul and I had. Doesn't everyone?* I went on reading. The book was full of boring academic treatises, moving personal "herstories," angry poems. On page 197 I found an essay I read once, then again, and again: "The Politics of Orgasm" by Susan Lydon.

According to Susan Lydon, the "fact" that had undermined my sexual self-esteem, fed my sexual insecurity, inspired my sexual fatalism was nothing but Freudian fiction. According to Susan Lydon, my desire for "direct clitoral stimulation" did not prove that I was frigid, unfeminine, sexually immature, or castrating. All it proved was that I knew what would give me the orgasm (or two, or three, or twenty) to which I was entitled. According to Susan Lydon—and Masters and Johnson, whose research she cited— there was no such thing as a "right kind of orgasm" or a "wrong kind of orgasm" because THERE WAS NO SUCH THING AS A VAGINAL ORGASM!

The next time you appeared at my door, I decided to take a chance on you, to share my revelation with you. We climbed the cedar ladder to my loft bed, assumed our customary positions, commenced our customary precoital nuzzling. Once I was assured of your full attention, I yanked my already-worn copy of *Sisterhood Is Powerful* from beneath my pillow. It fell open to page 197. "Read this!" I instructed you, tracing the all-important words with my fingertip. *". . . the dichotomy of vaginal and clitoral orgasms is entirely false. Anatomically, all orgasms are centered in the clitoris, whether they result from direct manual pressure applied to the clitoris, or . . ."*

I regarded you expectantly.

You regarded me blankly.

"What's a clitoris?" you asked.

I sensed that your question was sincere, and so I devoted myself to teaching you the answer. You were such an eager student that I was inspired to explore the question deeply from every angle—not once but several times that afternoon. And when the lesson was complete, when you had amply demonstrated your retention of all that I had taught you, I opened my eyes and found you beaming from ear to ear. "You came in my hand!" you crowed, your glowing eyes as delighted as a child's. "Just like that! You came in my hand!"

And just like that, my heart was yours.

Incredible, but true: never before you, and never after, did I make love with a man who was as wildly enthusiastic about—as wholeheartedly, wholebodiedly committed to—my pleasure as he was his own. The men before you (who had a passable excuse; even I didn't know any better in those One Giant Leap for Mankind days), as well as the men after you (who had no excuse at all, aside from a lifetime of sexist training), conveyed their annoyance with my sexual preferences in a range of subtle and not-so-subtle ways. The momentary hesitation of the hand. The nearly imperceptible but undeniably repulsed curl of the lip. The rushing through; the dozing off during. The seemingly solicitous inquiries about my need for "more." And, of course, that time-honored, quintessential closing shot in any day's battle between the sexes: the barely postcoital snore. One boyfriend of mine articulated what most men merely enacted, informing me not once but often that my sexual wants were burdensome to him, an unpleasant detraction from the main event. "Anticlimactic," he actually said. If I really loved him, he asserted, I would give up my immature, self-centered focus on my clit, on what I wanted him to do for me, and focus instead on what we could do together: intercourse, "natural sex," sex the way God and man intended it to be.

In the early eighties—ten years after you "discovered" my clitoris with all the naïve pride and excitement of Columbus "discovering" America; six years after I'd stopped saying yes to the many in favor of the one yes of marriage—I was made to understand that a new generation of men was loose upon the land. My friend Diane was dating twentysomething men, men fifteen years younger than you and five years younger than me, men who had somehow grown up unmaimed by the myth of the vaginal orgasm. Men who would never ask what, or where, a clitoris was. Men who knew, and therefore didn't need to be taught, that oral sex could be unisex; that intercourse was one of many main events; that a woman was the best judge of her own sexual satisfaction (among other things). It was difficult to contain my envy as Diane regaled me with tales of her sexual encounters—although I did, intellectually at least, rejoice in the progress her stories reflected. Sisterhood had turned out to be powerful indeed—for those young enough to enjoy its sexual benefits. There I was, trudging off to sex therapy with my well-trained but unenthused thirty-five-year-old husband; renting lesbian porn videos for much-needed inspiration; and having hot phone flirtations with you (remember our little flare-up in 1983?). Meanwhile Diane was having two, three, many orgasms per session with a series of sweet-faced, clitorally conscious young men.

Sex therapy with my husband turned into divorce therapy, and for the first time since 1973, I was back in the sexual marketplace. This time I was taking no chances. My next lover was going to be someone who understood exactly what makes sex great for a woman. Someone who knew everything from Anatomy to Zygote about satisfying a woman. Someone (preferably an HIV-negative someone) who could appreciate—no, *adore*—the heart, soul, and genitalia of a woman. In short: a woman.

You never got to meet Ann. Somehow I just couldn't imagine the two of you in the same room. But trust me on this, Oso: Ann is a woman after your own heart. She's not male, or Jewish, or six foot five, or hairy, or wild, or unavailable, the way you are—*were*. But her sexual energy reminds me of yours. Her delight in offering as well as accepting pleasure, her adventurousness, her attention to detail—you'll be glad to know that even in your absence, for these last ten years, at least, I have been well taken care of.

And so, it seems, have my straight young women friends, the ones who are sleeping with the men of Generation X. It's not that I don't hear plenty of complaints about men from my twentysomething pals—quite the contrary. These women want to stop fooling around, worrying about AIDS, and getting their hopes crushed. Just like all your girlfriends, who bugged you with their demands for commitment, my friends want to get married. But the guys they date or live with don't have stable jobs; won't go to therapy; don't want children; smoke too much pot; talk more than they listen; want to date other women; aren't oomphy enough or sensitive enough or self-aware or *there* enough. Like you—a man ahead of his time!—these dudes aren't husband material, but sexually, they're no slackers. "Except for the occasional jerk," my twenty-eight-year-old friend Francesca tells me, "who knows what to do and just doesn't feel like doing it," my friends' bedmates lick, they touch, they kiss, they wait, they ask, they learn. Some of them, I am told, even offer to sleep in the wet spot. "It's ironic: they've almost turned it into another male ego thing," Francesca says. "Like: I'm so hip and cool and modern, I made this woman come five times." (I hear this and want to ask you, Oso: *Was your delight in my orgasms for my pleasure—or your own?*) Unlike most of the guys I was with before and after you, my friends' men—for whatever reasons—expect to do unto others no less than they want done unto themselves.

Prospects for the next generation—if my sons and their friends are any indication—also appear good.

Recently I was driving Peter and Kiko home from a surfing trip. The car radio was tuned, as usual, to the local hip-hop station; as usual, the three of us were critiquing the songs for sexism, homophobia, or the more general "bad values." A song I'd never heard before came on, a song called "Downtown," which quickly revealed itself to be an ode to oral sex. Nothing surprising there; about half the songs on that station extol the virtues of one (hetero)sexual practice or another. What was unusual about this song was that the singer was a woman. And she was warning her man that if he didn't plan on visiting her "downtown," he'd best not plan to visit her at all.

"Amazing," I blurted. Peter and Kiko looked at me curiously. "What's amazing?" Kiko asked. I searched for an answer that was both honest and nonembarrassingly nongraphic. "I'm surprised to hear a woman being so explicit about what she wants sexually," I said. Still, the boys looked at me uncomprehendingly. "What's so surprising about that?" Peter asked.

"When I was your age," I said, the phrase I swore I'd never say, the phrase that now falls from my lips approximately ten times a week, "girls and women weren't supposed to like sex. Sex was supposed to be something women put up with just to make men happy. So girls and women didn't say much about what they liked—in songs or anywhere else. You never would have heard a woman singing about oral sex."

Peter and Kiko sat silently, trying to make sense of this information. It's always so gratifying to tell my kids these strange-but-true tidbits from the past—to see how shocked they are by inequities our generation took for granted. They were stunned to hear, for instance, that when I was a child, women were teachers, nurses, or mothers; not anchorwomen, firefighters, or CEOs. That while the boys played baseball in the schoolyard, in the girls' gym we stood in a row, safely snapped into our institutional green gym suits, flapping our elbows diligently to the chant, "I must—I must—I must improve my bust—it's better—it's better—it's better for the sweater." When I told my kids I was suspended for wearing pants to my high school, Jesse said he couldn't remember ever seeing a girl wearing a *dress* to his school.

"For real?" Kiko asked, finally.

"Weird," Peter said. "Most of the girls I know are more into sex than I am."

What do you think, Oso? What do you think it means, the way the "politics of orgasm" have changed since your generation of men was raised on "Wham, bam, thank you, ma'am"? Do you think Rain and April and Peter and Jesse will have better sex, better relationships, better lives—even though they may never in their lives experience sex without the threat of death—because girls and women are allowed to want sex, now, and boys and men believe that "making love" means two people (or more) giving each other pleasure?

What do you hope for your daughters, Oso? Do you hope that some-day they'll know a great passion, like the passion you and I shared? Do you hope that someday a man will love Rain or April so desperately, want Rain or April so fiercely, that he'll leave his sleeping wife and baby, make his way to your daughter's bed, moan and thrash and cry with her there, then leave her in a pile of sticky sheets for the wife he still loves and the baby he adores? Do you hope that someday Rain or April will love a man so desperately, want him so fiercely, that she'll pretend his family doesn't exist, beg to bear his child, drive her husband away, then flee the home she loves when this great passion suddenly seems the most traditional of trian-gles, the guilt seeps in, and the pain of remorse and rejection becomes too torturous to bear?

I sit here now crying, knowing that you aren't a living person any-more. I rummage through my old trunk, dig out my big manila "Oso" envelope, surround myself with things you gave me. The note you left in my post office box: *Will be up tomorrow to go on wood run with you—get Clint's chain saw & Gas & Oil—Love Gold.* A poem: "The wind howls/ wondering what it is to be a tree/the wind changes/blowing switching directions/the mama sleeps/the baby coos/the daddy dreams/the wind changes/the baby coos." That baby was Rain; she called me on the phone today. The daddy, you said, was dreaming of me.

Your letters, with postmarks through the decades. 1971, when I ran away from you to Europe. 1983, when you asked me to leave my husband and come back to you and New Mexico. 1985, reminding me to keep writing poetry. 1992, thanking me for looking after April.

"The clouds covering the mountains . . . ," you wrote in your first letter to me, *"worries, possession. Here are the roots, yours, mine, a whole new tribal system, and you are a part of me as much as anyone."* And in the last one: *"It never goes away,"* you promised, *"unless something so bitter and relentless has gone down."*

Some would say, Oso, that what went down between us *was* bitter and relentless. Rain's mother might say that, or maybe even Rain herself. Paul certainly did, and so did my husband.

I want to call you up right now, Oso. I want to talk to you about us then, knowing what we know now. I want to ask you if you see it, now, the way I do: as a great romance, yes—but a great romance shrouded in the rampant sexism of its time. I wouldn't give up a moment of it, Oso; I wouldn't change a thing. But I see this now, too: the great romance that spanned a quarter-century, never failed to quicken my heart and moisten my loins, gave me some of the greatest sex and greatest joy I've known—also broke up two relationships, condemned Rain to a lifetime of joint custody, threatened my marriage, and leaves me, now, feeling invisible and guilty. I loved you for twenty-five years, and we never ate a meal together. Rain had never heard my name. On the list of people to whom your poems will be distributed, my name is unlikely to appear. I imagine Rain telling her mother about her conversation with me; and wonder whether she will ever talk to me again. Not knowing what else to do, I write a condolence card hoping that your ex–old lady will have forgotten—or forgiven—who I am.

I won't be going to your memorial service, Oso. I'll be out of the country that week, on a much-needed family vacation with Peter, Jesse, and Ann. So I won't be standing among strangers in a crowded room, trying to figure out what to say to Rain and her mother, twenty-three years later; or wondering how many of the weeping women in the room have a pile of letters and poems at home, just like mine.

When I got off the phone with Rain today, I wandered into the kitchen. "What's wrong, Mom?" Peter asked me. "You're standing there staring into space." I realized then that my sons have never heard your name, either. "A man I loved died a month ago," I said. "I just found out."

"Who was he?" Peter asked.

Who was he?

"He was my favorite boyfriend," I said.

Love, as always,
Meredith

ABORTION RIGHTS (AND WRONGS)

Lee's phone call is unexpected, out of character, out of the blue. "Meredith? Listen—I've been thinking about some stuff . . . about the old days. I miss you. I need to talk to you. Could you come for a visit sometime soon?"

I don't know what surprises me more: Lee's request, or the fact that he's calling at all. For the past two decades, it's been Lee's wife Sharret who's made the phone calls, sent the birth announcements and baby pictures, kept us all connected. Sharret who notifies me, and the rest of the California branch of our old New Mexico clan, when she and Lee are coming to town. Sharret I've grown closer to throughout the years of disjointedly intimate phone calls and sporadic, chaotic reunions. My knowing of Lee, my love for Lee, has been frozen in time, unchanged by the decades and the distance: no bigger, no smaller, no more or less important than it was when I lived with him—and his girlfriend Trippy, and my boyfriend Paul—on a mountain near Taos, five years before he met Sharret, a few light-years and a hundred and fifty miles from the Albuquerque suburb where he and Sharret and their sons live now.

No more and no less important now than it was for nine weeks in 1971, when Lee's first baby—my first baby—lived, briefly, in my body.

"Please, Meredith?" Lee says. "I really want to see you." I've been working, lately, on learning to say a simple, unqualified yes to people I love—a new and, so far, surprisingly satisfying experiment. It occurs to me now that Memorial Day weekend, the weekend Ann always spends at karate camp near Albuquerque, is just a few weeks away. Each year Ann asks me to go with her, to spend some time in New Mexico with her before and after camp; each year I go to the cabin alone instead, to write and sulk and envy her for being where I could have been, if only I'd said a simple yes. Maybe, I think, this is my chance to say two yesses for the price of one.

"Is Memorial Day soon enough?" I ask Lee.

"Great," he says. "Thanks."

It's Sharret who runs to the door to welcome us when Ann and I pull up in our bright red rental car. Lee, of course, is at work. Since he stopped being a hippie and started being a lawyer fifteen years ago, Lee spends most of his time at work: defending Chicano activists and fired school-teachers and the Constitution. "I missed you," Sharret says, hugging me, then Ann. "I missed you, too," I say. Coming to New Mexico, walking into Lee and Sharret's house, always feels like coming home. "I feel like I saw you yesterday," she says. "But do you realize you haven't been here for seven years?"

I do realize that when a not-so-little boy thunders into the room. A boy whose whirling body emanates energy, whose round brown eyes dart from Ann, to me, to the unfamiliar car in the driveway, to his mother: taking it all in, processing all of it at the speed of light. A boy whose mother is a dark-skinned, dark-haired New York Jew like me; whose father is a fair-skinned, blond man like my sons' father. A boy who could have been . . . "Sam," Sharret says, "this is Ann and Meredith. You haven't seen them since you were really little." "In your high chair," Ann adds, grinning at Sam. "You wanted to wear your blue rubber boots all the time, even when you were taking a bath."

"I can't believe you remember those boots," Sharret says. "You're right: he wouldn't take them off." Sam stares at Ann with those big gleaming eyes. "I *kinda* remember that," he says. Then turns to his mother, tugs at her arm. "Mom: can I go to Walker's? Pleeease?" Sharret rolls her eyes at us over his head. "Sam—you just got home. Don't you ever want to spend a minute in your own house?" "C'mon, Mom. It's my first week of summer vacation." "Okay, okay," Sharret says to Sam. And then, to us, "The world's greatest negotiator." Ann and I exchange a smile. *Just like Peter,* we're both thinking.

"Where are the little guys?" I ask Sharret. She leads the way to the front bedroom, a room that was empty the last time we were here. "Jacob, Isaac," she says to two identical tow-headed boys, "Ann and Meredith are here." Two faces turn toward us, toward Sharret, toward each other, and back down to the sheets of paper spread between them. I feel the same yank in my gut I felt the first time I laid eyes on Sam, seven years ago. *Did Lee feel that way when he met my kids? I've never asked him. I've never felt I could ask him.* "Nothing comes between these boys and their drawing," Sharret says. "They're incredibly talented." Ann and I smile at each other again. *Just like Jesse.*

Sharret, Ann, and I are drinking tea at the kitchen table an hour later when we hear the front door opening. "Lee's home," Sharret says. I stay where I am, look her full in the face. She looks relaxed, pleased, expectant. Smiling, she nods toward the door. "Go on," she says to me. Before I even see Lee—just hearing the sound of his footsteps crossing the threshold, feeling the eagerness with which he approaches me—I know that this visit will be different between us. "You rang?" I smile as Lee folds himself around me. His hug is stronger and longer than any he's ever given me. Before he untangles himself to greet Ann, he looks at me intensely. "Thank you for coming," he says. "It means a lot to me. Really."

After dinner and bedtime stories and several good-nights-for-the-last-time, the four of us settle onto the couches I remember from Lee and Sharret's last house, the house I visited for the first time in 1979, when I was married to Richard and Peter was five months old. We exchange news and gossip about our mutual friends for a while; then I turn to Lee.

"Why am I here, Lee?" I ask. I ask this deliberately in front of his wife and my lover. I want his answer to be one he can give me in front of his wife and my lover. "It's what I told you on the phone," he says readily. "I've been thinking a lot, lately, about our time in Taos. Questioning what it all means. I found myself wanting to talk to you about it. I guess I'm just realizing what our relationship means to me."

I'm astounded by what I'm hearing. And by the fact that I'm hearing it in front of Sharret and Ann. Yet Lee's words resonate with me. *I've always known what our relationship means to me. But I've felt alone with it all these years.* "You're important to me, too, Lee," I say hesitantly. "So . . . what is it about the old days that you want to talk about?"

"Maybe you two should have this conversation some other time," Sharret says, getting up to move a load of laundry from the washer to the dryer. "Why don't you guys drive Meredith's car when we go to Santa Fe tomorrow? I'll take the kids with me so you can have some privacy." Sharret's offer is as unexpected as Lee's forthrightness. She's always been impatient with our endless rehashing of the sixties—she usually sits through those nostalgia-fests rolling her eyes, advising us to get over ourselves already. But this is the first time she's absented herself from the conversation, or encouraged us to spend time alone together. *Either she just can't stand to hear all that reminiscing one more time, or she really wants Lee to have a chance to say whatever it is he has called me here to say.*

And so the subject is changed, and the four of us stay up much too late yakking about kids and karate and friendships and Clinton and crime and the rise and fall of our middle-aged bodies, until our eyelids are drooping and we're yawning more than we're talking. And then we all hug each other good night and Lee and Sharret go off to their bedroom and Ann and I climb into the big brass bed in "our room" in their basement. The next day I drive Ann to karate camp in the mountains, and then I come back to Lee and Sharret's and help them buckle Sam, Jacob, and Isaac into their car seats in Sharret's brand-new Volvo station wagon, and we distribute Game Boys and boxes of juice, and Lee gives each of his sons a kiss and tells them to be good since Mommy will be alone with them in the car. "Do you want a bagel, honey?" he asks Sam, who is already asking where we might eat lunch but now shifts his attention to the choice between plain, cinnamon-raisin, and sesame. *He calls his son "honey." I love that.* We agree to rendezvous at a supermarket in Santa Fe, where we'll buy beer and ice cream to bring to the barbecue Paul is hosting in honor of our reunion. I ask Lee to drive my car so I can feast my eyes on my beloved New Mexico landscape as we traverse it. He climbs behind the wheel, and our little caravan heads north out of Albuquerque.

"So, how's your life?" I ask Lee as we cruise through suburbs and sagebrush, past billboards and mesas. I realize that I'm interviewing him, the way I interview people when I'm nervous, when I'm trying to make them like me. Lee answers my questions, but perfunctorily, distractedly.

Just south of Bernalillo he stops midsentence, looks at me for a long moment, then turns back to the highway that's spinning out ahead and behind. "Meredith: I want to talk about what happened between us," he says. "I want to talk about the abortion."

"Oh," I say. *So that's it, after all. After all these years.*

"I've never gotten over it," Lee says. "I feel like I'm still grieving."

Grieving. I thought he'd forgotten all about it. I drape my arm along the headrest behind Lee's neck, touch his shoulder lightly with my fingers. "Me, too," I say. We both fall silent.

A few miles roll by. Snowcapped mountains, dry arroyos, scrubby piñon trees. This land is more dramatic, and more barren, than I'd remembered. "After Peter was born," I say, "I was happier than I'd ever been in my life. But there was this sadness in me, too. I kept looking at my new baby and wondering what my other baby, what our baby, would have looked like."

I feel tentative, uncertain, but relieved to be talking about this, to be finally saying these things to the only person I can say them to. "I wondered the same thing the first time I met your kids," I say. "And just last night at dinner I was thinking, there could be this twenty-two-year-old person, right here at this table. This person we'd all love, this person who'd be related to all of us: Sharret, Ann, your kids, my kids, you, me."

I tell Lee this much, but I don't tell him all of it. I don't tell him about the despair that gripped me every day of the forty-seven months it took to bring Peter into being. The years of infertility tests and drugs and surgeries, when I wondered if the baby I'd given up had been my only chance at motherhood. When I couldn't shake the fear that my inability to create a new life was punishment—God's, nature's, my own body's—for having ended one. I don't ask Lee, now, what I wanted to ask him when he and Sharret plunged into their own infertility hell, in the years after Peter was born: *When the doctors were telling you and Sharret that you might never have a child, did you ever wonder, the way I did, if our baby had been your only chance?*

"I still don't understand what happened, really," Lee says. He glances at me again, the corners of his mouth unsteady. Not angry. Sad. "Why did you—how did you make the decision to have an abortion, Meredith?"

How did I?

How does any woman make that decision?

"It was really, really hard," I say slowly. "You know how much I always wanted a baby. Paul and I talked about it all the time, but we were so young. After he and I broke up, before you and I were together, I slept with a few guys without using birth control. I had this fantasy: pioneer mama, raising her kid alone on the road in a Volkswagen bus. But nothing happened—until you. Then it was impossible to go through with it."

"Why?" Lee asks me.

What's ready at my lips is the shorthand explanation, the story I've come to think of as the truth. *I thought I was infertile. I got pregnant, I took drugs before I knew I was pregnant, I had to get an abortion.*

But as I open my mouth to tell that story to Lee, now, I wonder: *how true is it?*

"Remember the bladder infection I had while you and I were sleeping together?" I ask. Lee nods. *Six months after Trippy left Lee and Paul left me and I left Oso, on my way out of New Mexico, finishing off an old attraction to an old and dear friend. It was so warm and easy to fall into bed with Lee, to touch with passion the body I'd touched a thousand times in friendship, to be caressed by the hands that once followed along behind me in the corn rows, patting mounds of soil around the seeds as I dropped them into the moistened earth.*

"Before I knew I was pregnant, I took antibiotics," I say. "The doctor told me that if I had the baby, the pills might cause birth defects."

The words ring hollow in my ears. They're true, but not the whole truth.

I drove my bright red Volkswagen bus straight from Lee's house in Albuquerque to Trippy's flat in San Francisco. She was still my best friend; I told her everything. Every morning we'd mark off the days since my last period on the calendar in her kitchen. Finally, she sent me to the Haight-Ashbury Free Clinic for a pregnancy test. I felt too guilty to ask her, or my brand-new boyfriend Danny to go with me, and I didn't have any other friends in San Francisco yet. So I sat alone on the battered couch in the Free Clinic waiting room as the bearded, ponytailed doctor took my hand and said gravely, "You're pregnant."

Before my mind could react, my soul was flooded with joy. A baby! A miracle! "Do you need help?" the doctor asked. "Why don't you say 'Congratulations'? Isn't anyone happy to be pregnant anymore?" I snapped. And then I remembered that Trippy still hoped to be the mother of Lee's first child; that

Danny kept saying he "knew" I wasn't pregnant, and refusing to talk to me about what might happen if I was; that I'd just finished a long course of high-dose tetracycline. "Yes," I muttered, choking back the first of a million tears. "I do need help."

"Even if I'd been willing to take a chance on the tetracycline," I continue, determined now to fully answer Lee's question, and my own, "you were in New Mexico. I was in San Francisco. You were thinking you might get back together with Trippy. Trippy was thinking she might get back together with you. And—I was with Danny. He didn't want to raise . . . someone else's kid."

This, Lee must know, is quite an understatement. Danny was part of our extended New Mexico circle. He and Lee had always detested each other. I'd had a crush on Danny for years; during one of his visits, I'd almost jumped into his car and left Paul and New Mexico to go with him. *Danny knew how much I wanted a child, how hard it was for me to consider an abortion. He said if I got rid of Lee's baby, maybe he and I could make a baby together soon. That never happened—Danny and I fought about it every month for two years, until finally I went looking for a man who wanted to be a father—but I clung to my hope throughout the whole ordeal. The day we broke up I screamed at him, "You tricked me into having an abortion!" But even then I knew that I had tricked myself.*

"I thought about running away from all of you and just having the baby on my own," I say. "But where would I go? I was twenty years old. Everyone in my life was against it. Trippy would have been so hurt, and she was my best friend. I wanted a child, but I guess I wanted my friends—I guess I wanted Danny—more."

I glance at Lee. His jaw is clenched; a nerve in his cheek is twitching. *I can't believe we're just now talking about this. I can't believe how much pain there still is in this.*

"Okay," Lee says. "That explains why you got the abortion. But I still don't understand why you didn't *talk* to me about it. You just called and told me you were on your way to the hospital. Your mind was already made up." His voice catches. "And I didn't even know you were pregnant."

"But we used Emko foam," Lee said, when I called him from the phone booth on the corner of Haight and Ashbury. Through the cloudy glass I could see Danny in the driver's seat of my bright red Volkswagen bus, smoking a

Camel, waiting to take me to the hospital. "Except that one time," I reminded him. After a long silence, Lee said, "You could come back here. We could have the . . . baby together. See how things turn out."

His words brought tears to my eyes. But I had no time for tears. I was due at the hospital in ten minutes. "Listen, Lee: I'm with Danny now. I just have to do this." He exhaled sharply. "Do you need money?" he asked then, sounding weary beyond his twenty-three years, like . . . somebody's father. I couldn't tell him the truth; I assumed, as we all assumed in those days, that the phone might be tapped. I couldn't say that I'd borrowed a friend's MediCal card, that I was going to have an abortion under her name because I didn't have the $350 it cost to have one in my own. "It's taken care of," I said. "This is sad," Lee said after a pause. "I mean, I could have been a father." "I love you, Lee," I said. "I gotta go. I'll call you tomorrow so you'll know everything's okay."

"I knew that talking to you would just make the whole thing harder for me," I say. Harder, even, than it already was. *The anguish, and then the numb resignation, of the decision. The hostile hospital social worker, interrogating me in the windowless basement examining room, trying to extract from me the name of the baby's father. (I said he was a Frisbee player I'd met in the park, that I hadn't caught his name.) The form I had to sign (in my borrowed name) swearing that I would become "mentally unbalanced if forced to bear a child."*

And then: the glare of the operating room lights. The silent, scowling, masked doctor; the icy speculum he thrust punishingly up inside me. The groaning sound and then the clenching ache of the vacuum machine suctioning the life out of me. The moaning and crying of the women in the recovery room; the rhythmic stabbing pain in my womb; the hole in my heart that was torn open again and again, year after year, month after month when the blood came. The hole in my heart that even the twin miracles of my two healthy sons has not yet fully healed.

Lee says, "I just wish I'd had a little more time to think about it before it happened."

"It does seem unfair, now," I say. "But then . . . it was the beginning of the women's movement. Abortion was barely legal in California; it was still illegal most everywhere else. There was an epidemic of abortions among the women in the Haight—as if they had to prove that an abortion was no big deal in order to defend women's right to have one. Lots of the women I knew had had three or four. They used abortion as birth control. The men didn't seem to care; no one wanted to have kids in those days. I felt like I was the only person in the world who thought it was a tragedy."

Danny's ex-girlfriend Jessica, the one with the big wild hair, standing in my bedroom doorway the night I found out I was pregnant, summoned by Danny to help me make the "right" decision. Jessica telling me that she'd had "a bunch of abortions" and that they hadn't been that bad. "No fucking for a couple of weeks afterward, that's the worst part," she'd said, grinning. I wanted to believe that having an abortion wasn't so bad. I wanted to be as cool, as hip, as feminist about my abortion as Danny's other girlfriends had been about theirs. Mostly, I wanted to go on being Danny's new girlfriend.

"Lee," I say to the side of his face, "it did feel like a big deal to me. I wished I could have the baby. Being pregnant was a miracle and a nightmare. It made me feel incredibly connected to you, in a way that I'd never felt connected to anyone.

"The pregnancy felt right, somehow—but nothing *about* it was right. The day I found out, I sat in the park and wrote you a long letter. I cried for hours. I just couldn't mail it. Trippy was so upset, and Danny—you know I'd wanted Danny for so long, and keeping the baby would have meant losing him. I couldn't even deal with my own feelings—there was no way I could deal with yours. So I kept you out of it until the last minute. I'm sorry."

I see that the endless miles of mesa have been violated by endless billboards rising like tombstones from the sand. There used to be seventy miles of distance between Albuquerque and Santa Fe. Now there's hardly any at all. It all seems so long ago, I think. Trippy and I speak on the phone once or twice a year. Danny's married to a feminist activist; their son is in the fourth grade. "Is there anything in this world that hasn't changed for the worse?" I mutter. Lee looks at me sharply, then follows my gaze out the window. "Not much," he says.

"There's something else that's been bothering me all these years," he says. "Pretty soon after you had the abortion, someone—I don't remember who—told me that it might not have been my baby."

"Who said that?" I blurt angrily. *As if I could make the question go away by blaming the person who asked it.* "I honestly don't remember," Lee says. "It could have been any number of our friends. But the point is, I've always wondered. It made me feel a little crazy, to be so upset all these years about a pregnancy . . . about a baby that might not have even been mine."

"It was your baby, Lee," I say firmly. *No one ever understood why I was so sure the baby was Lee's. After all, I'd slept with Danny later that same month. But I was sure then, and I'm even surer now. Three times in my life I've felt the tiny explosion of sperm meeting egg; each of those times I was pregnant. Could Lee believe—could any man believe—that I'd felt our two bodies creating a third body the instant it happened?*

"I was right in the middle of my cycle when I was with you," I say. "By the time I slept with Danny, my period was due. I already had these huge swollen breasts. Believe me, Lee—it was yours. Ours." He nods. "I was pretty sure," he says. "I just needed to ask you."

I slump down into my seat, turn my head to watch the once-familiar landmarks whizzing by. "I did the best I could do at the time," I say quietly, as much to myself as to Lee.

The best I could do—for whom?
  For my baby?
  For me?
  For my best friend?
  For my boyfriend?
I ask myself now what I didn't dare ask myself in 1971, what I've never dared ask myself since. *If I could have kept the baby and kept Danny, too—despite the tetracycline, despite Trippy's pain—would I have given birth to that baby?* Would I have called Lee from that phone booth to tell him that Danny and I were going to raise his child, invoked my rights as a woman to override any objections he might have had?

If I could have kept the baby and kept Danny, too—would that twenty-two-year-old have been at the dinner table with us last night?

Like nearly everything, abortion just doesn't seem as simple now as it did when I was twenty. In 1971 it seemed there were endless possibilities, endless pregnancies in front of me. In 1971 my women friends and I were first taking birth control pills, first claiming our bodies for ourselves, and in that first blush of feminism we felt fully entitled—in fact, politically required—to determine the fate of our pregnancies by ourselves as well.

In 1971 I hadn't yet felt the moist clutch of my own child's hand in mine, so I didn't yet know how much there was to lose to a choice and a curette. I didn't know that as my friends and I aged—even as we marched and picketed and wrote checks to defend what is so bloodlessly referred to as "a woman's right to choose"—our past and future abortion choices would begin to seem more personal and less political.

I didn't know that for twenty-three years I would be haunted by the disembodied soul whose life I chose to end—and now, by the father of that soul, who was deprived, by me and by circumstance, of his own right to choose.

How would I feel, whose rights would I invoke, if some girlfriend of Peter's or Jesse's refused to have, or insisted on having, an abortion—*for herself, for her baby,* not *for her boyfriend?* How would I feel if some girlfriend of Peter's or Jesse's made the same choice that the fifteen-year-old girlfriend of our young friend Ely made, just last week: to have Ely's baby over his objections? How would I feel if some young woman unrelated to me chose to relegate my grandchild to an abortion clinic emesis basin?

How would my life be different today, how would Lee's life be different today, if I'd said no to everyone and everything except my desire to bear a child, and said a simple, unqualified yes to Lee in that phone booth twenty-three years ago?

I'll never know.

We approach the urban sprawl of Santa Fe, its boundary creeping south to meet us miles too soon. Gleamingly new gas stations and motels sparkle in the sunlight where dusky gray chamisa once bloomed. I'm unprepared for the end of this conversation, unprepared to rejoin Sharret and those three little boys.

"You know, Lee," I say hesitantly, as we leave the highway and curve along Cerrillos Road toward town, "I've always felt there was some meaning to that pregnancy, whether either of us knows what it is or not. That's one reason it means so much to me to keep on knowing you, to know Sharret and your kids." I feel self-conscious, afraid of pushing Lee away instead of bringing him in closer. Do I sound too California, too self-serving, too female? If I can convince Lee to forgive me, will that allow me, at last, to forgive myself?

"There *was* meaning to it, Meredith," Lee says intently. "I don't understand it fully, either, but I do know this: neither thing can be undone. We made a baby together. And that child isn't here now. I guess we both have to live with that for the rest of our lives."

Lee pulls my bright red car into the Furr's Supermarket lot and parks next to Sharret's white Volvo. The Volvo's doors are standing open; three lively tow-headed boys are buzzing all around it. "Hi, you two," Sharret calls to us. It feels good to know that Lee will tell Sharret what we talked about—and that this won't be the first she's heard of it. "Lee—Jacob needs to go to the bathroom."

Lee turns off the ignition, pulls the brake on carefully, and turns to face me. This time his gaze is clear and strong. "Meredith—I'm glad we finally talked about this," he says. "And I do want to stay close to you. Closer than we've been."

"Me, too," I say. "Let's try." And then I fold my grief and my regrets and that little spirit back inside my soul, where I keep them. And Lee puts his grief and his regrets and that little spirit away, wherever it is that he keeps them. And then Lee gets out of the car and grabs Jacob up in his arms and strides off across the parking lot to take his son to the bathroom.

A Woman's Work

Seniority determines everything on a union assembly line: how much you get paid, what shift you work, which jobs you're eligible for, how easily you can be fired. But even if I hadn't needed to recite my start date so often, during the four years I worked on the truck line at Ford, I never could have forgotten it. I'd celebrated that day for years, along with good socialists everywhere: it happened to be March 8—International Women's Day.

There were two thousand men on the truck line at Ford when I started there in 1977, and thirty-four women. Two of the women were leftovers from Ford's first equal opportunity era—the World War II years, when housewives were ushered, briefly, into factories because the men were busy fighting fascism—so they had more than thirty years' seniority and "gravy jobs" on day shift. The rest of us worked nights, 5 P.M. to 3:30 A.M. Monday through Friday; 3 P.M. to 11:30 P.M. every Saturday. We'd all been hired within the past three years, when big companies like Ford started worrying about losing their government contracts and facing class action lawsuits if they didn't comply with the new affirmative action regulations and get some women, quick. The women Ford got were all in our twenties and thirties—married and single, lesbian and straight, white and

Mexican and black. Our differences paled in comparison to what we had in common. The thirty-two of us bonded instantly, and fiercely.

I was the first woman, the only woman, and the newest hire in the chassis department, so, as most women were, I was given the worst job on the line. Preparing myself for ten hours in the spray booth—attempting to shield my body from the oily black paint that leaked and dripped and misted onto me all night—required me to arrive at the plant a half-hour before the shift began. There I was issued my evening attire: two pairs of way-too-big white cotton gloves (the first pair would barely last till the line stopped for lunch; the second pair would be tattered and drenched with paint well before the end of the shift) and one pair of way-too-big blue-and-white-striped coveralls, with the Ford logo on the breast pocket and the lingering stink of cleaning fluid and motor oil clinging to the stiff canvas. The company refused to stock smaller sizes.

We complained about it nightly in the women's locker room, as we rolled up our coverall sleeves and cut the fingers off our gloves. Fran said, "I asked my foreman for smaller gloves. He said, 'You shouldn't be taking men's jobs if you can't do men's work.' " Candy said, "They want to make sure we get the message: the government made them hire us, but nobody said they have to make it easy for us."

I'd button my coveralls up to my chin, seal the front closed with a strip of black duct tape, stuff my hair into a bandanna, and smear a thick coat of Vaseline onto every exposed part of my body—wrists, neck, face, ears. Then I'd trudge out to the spray booth, squirt my paint gun a few times to make sure the day shift guy hadn't left it clogged, and wait with my vision blurred by Vaseline and my heart in my throat for the line to start.

Sixty-two trucks per hour, fifty-eight mandatory hours per week. Six hundred and twenty times each night a bare metal truck frame, hanging on thick chains hooked to the overhead conveyor, lurched through my spray booth like a groaning mastodon. My job was to insert cotter pins through the hub of each wheel, tap hub covers onto them with a mallet, then cover every inch of the frame with just the right amount of paint. Too much, and the guys down the line would get paint all over them; too little, and I'd be written up for "bare spots" by the quality control inspec-tor. "Goddammit, Graham!"—my last name was my husband's in those days—the foreman would yell, watching me dangling off the edge of the spray booth, frantically shooting paint at the departing frame just when I should have been finishing the one behind it. "Are you in the hole *again?*" It wasn't so much again as still. I spent most of every shift, most of my first month at Ford, where no autoworker ever wants to be—in the hole, falling further and further behind the pace of the line, running and failing to catch up.

Each night when the line creaked to life, I faced it full of vending machine coffee and conviction. *If a man can do this job, so can I.* Each night within a half-hour of starting time a man—men—*were* doing my job: as I started slipping into the hole, the guys around me would start working ahead on their jobs so they could run into the spray booth and help me do mine. Roy would pluck the cotter pins from my mouth and thread them through the hubs in a flash. Pepper would tap the hub covers on without denting them the way I did. When I came back from my breaks (sometimes I had the strength to make it to the bathroom; usually I just collapsed into a nearby cardboard box of carpets), I'd find that Chico, the relief man, had left me ahead instead of behind, where I'd left him.

I brought doughnuts for the guys every day and fetched them bacon-cheeseburgers and fries from the plant cafeteria every night at "lunch," but that hardly seemed thanks enough. Night after night, week after week, my male co-workers did whatever it took (and it took a lot) to keep me from getting fired. When the general foreman started visiting me in the spray booth, demanding that I go out with him and warning me of the consequences if I didn't comply—as he swore several of my female co-workers had already done—Roy advised me, "Don't argue with him. Paint him. Everyone knows what that asshole's trying to pull on you. If he comes flying out of there with black paint all over that clean white shirt of his, the whole plant'll know exactly what happened. He'll never get away with firing you." The next time the GF came to call, I screwed up my courage, angled my spray gun so the paint would ricochet off the chassis, and splattered him from designer tie to wing-tip shoes. He stomped off dripping paint; the guys on the line burst into hoots and cheers. The GF never bothered me again.

In the bathroom, the locker room, the cafeteria; in our carpools driving up and down Highway 17, the women traded similar stories about the men. There were always a few disgruntled guys—like the one who sent me searching the plant, my first night, for a left-handed wrench; or the one who walked around muttering, "I used to work for Peterbilt. Now I work for Pussybilt." At least once a week one of us was asked, "What's a cute thing like you doing in a filthy place like this?" ("Find me a waitress job that pays seven hundred bucks a week," Fran would answer. "I'll be out of here tomorrow.")

But most of the men were glad we were there. Some had daughters they hoped would work at Ford someday—where else could a woman earn $11.25 an hour for straight time, time and a half for eighteen hours a week of overtime, and double time for Sundays and holidays? Some automatically supported anything the company opposed. Some made it clear they appreciated the improvement in the scenery. "I'd rather flirt with a pretty girl all night than stare across the line at another ugly guy like me," the men would say. Sometimes it didn't stop with flirting. Sometimes marriages were broken when women who'd been dependent on their husbands, earning five bucks an hour in an all-woman office or factory, got a sudden intoxicating dose of that deadly combination: a ready supply of interested men, and economic independence. But whatever their motivations—old-fashioned labor solidarity, old-fashioned chivalry, or plain old lust—the men were our comrades, our suitors, and our protectors; our teachers, our buddies, our knights in greasy armor. They picked up after us and flattered us and covered for us and celebrated with us when we made it through the gauntlet of the ninety-day probation period.

The job was hell. I was gone from home thirteen hours a day, six days a week. My husband worked day shift in a paper mill. I'd creep into bed an hour before he got up, lie there praying for sleep that never came, while birds chirped at the sunrise and an endless assembly line of truck chassis rolled by behind my eyelids. Five or six hours later, every muscle in my body cramped and aching, weepy with exhaustion and dread, I'd drag myself into the shower, eat some scrambled eggs and coffee ice cream, drive down the freeway, and start all over again.

The job was hell—and I loved it. Every time I pushed through the turnstile beneath the sign that said, "The World's Best Autoworkers Pass Through These Gates," every time I punched in at five P.M. and most especially every time I punched out at three-thirty A.M., I felt a kind of pride I'd never known. Despite the company's not-so-subtle efforts to prove that women couldn't build trucks; despite my body's inclination to agree—from day one I had insomnia and painter's cough and tendinitis and head-to-toe bruises that provoked my doctor to ask, during a routine physical, if my husband was beating me—I was making it at Ford.

As the weeks and months went by, it was becoming possible for me to do my job. The cotter pins started slipping effortlessly, somehow, through the hubs. The chassis started sailing out of the spray booth with a perfect coating of paint. Now when the line started each night I felt resigned, not terrified. I knew exactly what I'd be doing for the next ten hours, and I'd performed those motions so many thousands of times that I could (and did) do them in my sleep. I was learning to use tools I'd never heard of and machines that weighed twice as much as I did. I was learning to joke and gossip, in English and Spanish, through mind-numbing boredom and pain. I was growing bulging muscles in places where only flesh had been visible before. I was earning three times the money I'd made on the all-woman assembly lines I'd worked on before Ford—packing cookies, stuffing circuit boards, frying taco shells. I was beating the odds, beating the line, enduring more physically and mentally than I'd ever taken on. I was becoming an autoworker.

I loved how butch, how competent I felt as my skills and confidence blossomed, swaggering around in an auto plant with wrenches in my pockets and grease embedded in the palms of my hands. I loved making my way to the chassis line, ducking under hanging cables and jumping across the pit, chatting with my fellow workers above the cacophony of shrieking air guns, belching forklifts, and triumphant honking as one after another perfect gleaming truck was driven off the end of the line. I loved it that there was a place for me in that monstrous factory, a locker with my lock on it, a time card with my name on it, a spray booth of my own.

I'd been at Ford one year when a miracle happened: after four years of infertility, finally, I got pregnant. I was ecstatic, and frantic: the spray booth was no place for a fetus. I asked for a medical transfer to a job that wouldn't cause a miscarriage or birth defects. My union committeeman told me since I was the plant's first pregnant line worker ever, the company was determined not to "set the wrong precedent." Pregnancy was optional, they said, so a medical placement would amount to "special treatment," "reverse discrimination" against the higher-seniority man whose job I would be taking. They offered two choices: stay in the spray booth, or quit.

"Neither," Fran swore when she found me crying in the bathroom. At lunch she wrote a petition and circulated it among the high-seniority men—friends of her high-seniority husband Chuck, who'd been a painter on day shift for twenty-five years. By quitting time a hundred and fifty of them had signed it, offering to trade their off-line gravy jobs for mine. The next night I was transferred out of the spray booth. The next week Fran and I joined the union women's committee.

When Peter was born, Ford gave me another ultimatum: come back to work after twelve weeks, or be fired. Eight weeks' unpaid maternity leave for a vaginal birth, twelve weeks for a cesarean—that was all state law required; that was all Ford allowed. I left Peter with a neighbor every afternoon and drove down the freeway awash in his tears and mine. My nipples burned; milk meant for my baby left dark wet circles on my coveralls while I cried and tightened brakes, leaked and installed shocks. I'd nurse Peter in his sleep when I got home at five A.M.; Richard would take him to the neighbor's house when he left for work at six. I'd sleep for a few hours and run to snatch him up in my arms until I had to give him up again. Every hour I was awake, I thought about quitting my job. But I just couldn't do it—not after all my fellow workers had done for me, not with all the women in the plant and all the women to come counting on me. I had my own precedent to set. We'd proved women could be autoworkers. Now I had to prove that mothers could be autoworkers, too.

When I got pregnant again eight months later, the company transferred me, without a petition or a fuss, to an off-the-line job cutting carpets. By the time Jesse was born, the economy and the auto industry were in free fall. In 1981 layoffs began; two years later the plant was shut down. One problem was solved: I was home with my babies. But now I had a new one: how would I ever find work as meaningful, as fulfilling, as high-paying as my job at Ford?

In the twenty years since, I've found work that's as lucrative, and work that's as politically challenging, and work that uses muscles I never got to flex in the spray booth. I've been a house cleaner and a receptionist, a technical writer and a journalist, an editor, creative director, and author. I've never had to smear Vaseline on my face again. I've never had to spray-paint a foreman again. I've never had the exhilarating satisfaction and the wearying pressure of being the first woman to hold my job again.

My old friend Fran is fifty-six now, and she still punches a Ford time clock every night. After our plant closed, she transferred to the Ford stamping plant in Buffalo; when she was laid off from there in 1990, she transferred to the parts warehouse in Dallas. Her husband Chuck died of lung cancer ten years ago; the doctors blamed the paint fumes. Fran lives with her mother now, in a little house north of Dallas, close to her younger son and three grandchildren. When she's not out on medical leave with her chronic tendinitis, Fran makes nineteen dollars an hour as a packer on graveyard. She's still a rabble-rouser, still dragging people to union meetings, but she's no upstart new-hire anymore. She's even got a desk and a phone so I can call her at work.

"Can you believe it?" she says, her wild Mississippi twang untamed by a lifetime of relocations. "I've got twenty-two years' seniority in this damn company." She cackles. "Ford never would've let me in the door if they'd known I'd be bothering them this long." In the background I hear the whine of a forklift, the clacking of a computer keyboard. "Although what good it's all done, I don't know," Fran says. "Nothing much has changed—especially where women are concerned. Actually, for me things have gotten worse."

I ask her why. "Being an older woman means double trouble," she says. "I was thirty-four years old when I started at Ford. I got a lot more help from the guys then than I do now. Maybe they were trying to make a move on me—but now that I'm old and ugly, I guess they figure I can fend for myself. They're busy going after the pretty young things."

She sighs. "Plus jobs are scarcer now. So women are more resented. Especially older women. I've heard the young guys say many times, 'She's an old bag. Why doesn't she retire already and give the job to someone who needs it?'"

There's an outburst of voices; then I hear Fran's laughter, and another woman's. "My friend Vaneisha wants to talk to you," Fran says. "Says she wants to give you the younger woman's point of view."

Vaneisha comes on the line. "It's just the older men that can't get used to us," she says. "They're jealous of the women's independence—if it wasn't for the women's lib, blah, blah blah. . . . They resent the women making the same amount of money." A third woman grabs the phone. "Oh, yes. I can guarantee *that*," she says, laughing. "A guy in my area calls all the women babycakes." Vaneisha takes the phone back. "But the younger men came up with a different attitude. They know a woman's got to work and that's that. No disrespect to the older ones, but the younger women came up with a different attitude, too. I was raised to take care of myself. 'Don't depend on no man'—that was my parents' motto," she says.

Vaneisha tells me she's been at Ford eight years, since she was twenty-two and her daughter was three. "I'm teaching my daughter the same thing: be an entrepreneur. Make as much money as you can. Don't let no man stand in your way." I ask how her husband feels about that. "He loves a strong woman who don't need a man for nothing. He loves me working. He's a nineties man," she says.

"Now don't get me wrong," Vaneisha adds. "Sometimes being a woman does get in the way of me doing my job. We pick car parts. That stuff can be heavy. The men won't help us—they say, 'You make the same I make. If I can do it, you can, too.' And if I wanted to have another baby, I couldn't. Picking up these heavy rotors would mess me up.

"One girl here had several miscarriages. They wouldn't give her a lighter job. That's how it works around here: If they like you, they'll accommodate your needs. If they don't, good luck. Finally she got her doctor to put her out for her whole pregnancy. I couldn't afford that. Good thing I had my baby before I came to Ford."

There's a brief scuffle, more women's laughter. "Sound familiar?" Fran asks me. "Why didn't you write a petition?" I tease her. "I tried," she says. "But these people are so scared for their jobs nowadays . . . there's so many plants closing—there's always a waiting list of people who want to transfer down here. That weighs on people's minds."

She pauses to light a cigarette, exhales noisily. "In Buffalo I had a supervisor tell me, 'The work is so hard here. Can't you find an easier job?' I asked him if I didn't do my job, if he'd ever heard me complain. He said, 'No, but this is so hard on you.' I said, 'As long as I'm doing my job, don't you worry about me.' "

"That sounds kind of familiar, too," I say.

"Exactly," Fran replies. "See what I mean? Same old shit we had to put up with twenty years ago."

·   ·   ·

In 1991, when I joined the progressive business group where I've found most of my consulting clients and many of my favorite friends, I was one of twenty or thirty women in an organization of three hundred. Membership was limited to "principals of the corporation," so, like many of the other women in the group, I squeezed in through a loophole: the CEO of the company where I toiled as a lowly editor designated me his representative.

Silly me: just because the mission of the group was to make business responsive to the needs of people and planet; just because it was a huggy, kissy group full of sixties activists; just because I figured I had at least as much in common with these guys—with their big hearts, long hair, and radical dreams—as I'd had with the men on the line at Ford, I assumed that sexism wouldn't be a problem in the group, or in our relationships. I was dispossessed of my naïveté within hours of arriving at my first conference.

"How come so few women?" I asked Jason, a founder and board member. "I know. It's a bummer," he said. "We just can't find very many female CEOs."

"How come no women on the panel?" I whispered to the woman sitting next to me, the only other woman in the overcrowded workshop called Wonderfully Wacky Ways of Watching the World. Facing us were five white men, each a well-known spiritual, business, or environmental guru. "Good question," she whispered back. "This is what they call the genius panel. They have one at every conference. I haven't seen a woman on one yet." When the panelists were finished speaking, she raised her hand. "Where's the Gaia energy in this discussion?" she asked. "Where are the voices of women?" The men on the dais and the men in the audience shifted in their seats, looked at each other, looked at us, looked away. Finally the moderator said, "You're right. There should be women speakers, and there should be more women in the room. Maybe you could help us find some for next year's panel."

I don't know what motivated me more—militant feminism or backsliding individualism—the year I decided to crash the traditional end-of-conference basketball game. No one had ever acknowledged that the game was for the "good new boys" only, but no woman had ever played in it before, either. In the privacy of my hotel room, I selected my outfit carefully. I wanted to look athletic yet nonthreatening; determined yet fun-loving. I chose a tie-dyed Ben & Jerry's T-shirt (to reinforce my loyalty to the group, while concealing unsightly bulges) and Lycra bike shorts (black, to minimize unconcealable unsightly bulges). I pulled my hair into a ponytail and strode out to the gym. I pulled open the court door. I stepped inside. The men looked up. They took in my outfit and my stance; realized that I was there to play, not cheer.

For a moment we regarded each other across the gym. Then my friend Craig bounded over and hugged me. "You can be on our team," he said. They—we—started playing. It quickly became clear that I didn't really know how to play. They—we—fell into a teasing banter as they ran circles around me. Elbows and knees, hands and hair were flying. This game was faster than an assembly line—and there was no one to thread my cotter pins for me, no one to help me catch up. I was on my own. Incompetent, humiliated, I capitulated. I couldn't play like a guy, so I played like a girl. I realized that my presence on the court was acceptable to them because I was playing like a girl. I wished I could be like the white guy in *White Men Can't Jump* and blow all their assumptions away. I wished I'd never thought of crashing this stupid game. I felt angry at them, ashamed of myself. After the game I slunk off to lick my wounds.

At the plenary session that night, the executive director announced the winner of the annual MVP award. Then he called me to the stage and said that a special award had been created just for me. In front of three hundred people he pronounced me MCP—"Most Courageous Player." I made nervous jokes into the microphone—"I'm sure this is just a coinci-dence, but I always thought MCP stood for male chauvinist pig." He kissed my cheek. I kissed his, right where I'd scratched him bloody during the game, when I was trying to steal the ball. I smiled and accepted my trophy: an official NBA basketball. The crowd whooped and applauded. I felt sick with shame. I was still playing like a girl.

After the ceremony my friend Sarah, the only female VP of a national chain of health food stores, took me aside. "I know you were trying to do a good thing," she said, "but that award was totally patronizing and sexist."

"I know," I said.

"It just reinforced the fact that women aren't welcome in that basket-ball game. You shouldn't have accepted it," she said.

"I know," I said again, miserably. "But I didn't know what else to do."

Over the years more women started joining the organization. Slowly we began to connect with each other. At the semiannual conferences small groups of us would go for long walks together, away from the genius panels and high-powered hallway networking and the all-male basketball games, and talk the way the Ford women talked in the locker room, the way women who are strangers one moment, intimates the next, do: about the CEOs who'd hit on us; the Mommy track that had derailed us; the loneliness of being the only woman VP, the only woman director. We also talked—effectively, apparently—about what we could do to recruit more women and make the organization more woman-friendly. Seven or eight conferences and much consciousness raising later, the organization has looser membership criteria, more women members, more women on the board, and more women on the panels (except for the still-sacrosanct "genius panel," which we women refer to as White Wonks Whacking Off While Watching the World Watch Them).

At most conferences now, time is set aside for the Women's Circle. There twenty or thirty CEOs and MBA students and nonprofit executive directors sit together in a meeting room, crying and raging. Strategizing in the last one I attended, Shanti spoke bitterly about her inability to get the financing she needed to expand her clothing company. "The SBA, the bank where I've done business for twenty years, the venture capitalists, even the guys in this group—none of them will help me. I know if I were a man it would be different." Ruth told us, through tears, that her daughter was in the hospital, beaten nearly to death by an ex-boyfriend who'd been stalking her for months. Caroline, whose company leads mountain treks for women, said she felt demeaned by the male CEOs in the group. "They don't take me or my company seriously. It's not about sales—mine are higher than a lot of theirs. It's just because my work is for women."

Twenty-year-old Margo, who comes to conferences with her CEO father, talked about what happened to her at work the week before. "A co-worker told me I had a nice butt," she said. The other women shook their heads. "I thought: I could call the guy an asshole, but I don't really need him for an enemy. Reporting him for sexual harassment won't work. I could tell the company to offer sensitivity training. I could quit.

"Or," she said, "I could suck down his rude remark along with everything else I've had to swallow since I went to work at that bank. I took a deep breath, smiled, and said, 'Thanks.' "

There was a muffled collective gasp. Then, being careful not to criticize Margo's response, the women gently started offering alternatives. As I listened to their suggestions, I was reminded, of course, of my interlude with the general foreman twenty years ago. *At least I had my co-workers and a union—plus a paint gun—to back me up,* I thought. *But what do white-collar women like Margo have to protect them now?*

There was a knock on the meeting room door. A man—a man I'd known and loved and worked with, off and on, for the past five years—stuck his head into the room. "Time to get everyone back together," he said. Twenty sets of eyes turned toward him. He looked at the wads of used Kleenex on the floor. At the women with swollen eyes. At the women leaning into each other's arms. A sigh—spontaneous, sympathetic, sweet—escaped from his lips. "Or maybe you guys need a little more time," he said.

BOYS AND GIRLS TOGETHER

"It's nine o'clock. Let's get started," says LaShondra. The tense buzz in the room quiets. A man pops the last of a bran muffin into his mouth. A woman reaches into her backpack, pulls out a packet of Kleenex, sets it on the floor beside her chair. "In case anyone doesn't know me, I'm LaShondra, executive director of the Pacific Center for Sexual Minorities," she says. She touches the arm of the handsome man sitting next to her. "And this is Teddy Jackson. Teddy does diversity training. He's donating his time to help me facilitate this meeting."

Normally—but not today—the Pacific Center Speaker's Bureau is a loving, affectionate group. At our regular Wednesday night meetings, while the other rooms in the center's three-story Victorian fill with gay teen rap groups and HIV support groups and Suicide Hotline training sessions, bureau members snuggle together on the threadbare couches, eat cookies someone brought to share, rub each other's shoulders, fill each other in on the new developments in their lives—the way gay men and lesbians working together for our mutual betterment tend to do. Then Leticia, the director, calls the meeting to order and we get down to business: talking about the speaking gigs we do, in male-female pairs or on panels, at the schools, workplaces, churches, hospitals, and jails that invite us to come and answer the questions their students and staffs and inmates have about lesbian, gay, bi, transsexual, and transgender sexuality—putting ourselves out there as Real Live Gay People, countering homophobic stereotypes and in the process, we hope, homophobia.

This morning, though, there's no snuggling, no gossiping, no laughing. The mood in the room is tense. And no wonder. There are fifty-five members of the speaker's bureau: thirty men, twenty-five women. But there are twelve people here: three men, nine women. The turnout itself makes the problem we're here to address—a problem I haven't experienced in this group, although I've certainly dealt with it in nearly every other mixed-gender setting in my life—seem even worse.

"I called this workshop to deal with sexism on the bureau," says Leticia. "The issue came to a head at last month's meeting, when one of the men said he didn't think the expression 'It's a man's world' is true anymore. He said he thinks women have it easier than men nowadays. The women felt his comment was a symptom of a bigger problem on the bureau. Since our whole purpose is to go out and talk to people about gender oppression, I figured we'd better get it straightened out. So I asked LaShondra and Teddy to come and help us do that."

"To start," says Teddy, "I'd like to ask each of you to say what you learned in your families about gender. Let's go around the circle."

"My parents put all their hopes and college money into my brothers," Susan says. "The message was, boys have futures. Girls aren't worth the investment." "From the day I was born, my father was down on me 'cause I wasn't enough of a *guy*," says David. "The only way to get his approval was to act like someone I'm not." "My mom was single and poor and stronger than any man I've ever met. She taught me to be a woman warrior," Lakresha says.

"Well, I guess I've already said enough on *that* subject," says Kevin, whose "man's world" comment at the last meeting sparked this one. "I don't want to get in any more trouble than I'm already in." He grins, looking around the room. No one returns his smile. Lisa, who's sitting next to him, says, "I'll pass. I don't feel safe enough right now to talk about anything personal." Maureen, next to her, says, "Same here."

"All right, then," Teddy says. "We'll break up into two groups. The men in Room B with me, the women in here with LaShondra. The women will talk about what you want from the men on the bureau as your allies. The men will talk about how we can be better allies to the women. We'll get back together at eleven."

David, Ron, and Teddy get up and walk toward the door. Kevin doesn't move. "Wait a minute," he says. "How come we're only talking about the men being allies for the women? That seems pretty imbalanced—pretty sexist, as a matter of fact. What about the women being allies for us? Aren't we all in this together?"

"Jesus Christ," Lakresha mutters. David glares at Kevin from across the room. *I kind of agree with the guy,* I think. *It* does *seem unfair.* "Kevin," Teddy says, "if I asked the white folks in this room to talk about how you-all could be allies for me as a black man, would you think I was being racist?" Kevin shrugs. "C'mon. We'll talk about it in our group," Teddy says. Kevin gets up, frowning, and follows him out of the room.

LaShondra pulls her chair over to where the rest of the women are sitting. We move close to each other to form a small, tight circle. "Do we need to take a minute?" LaShondra asks. "It might take more than that. Damn, I'm pissed," Lakresha says. "Why are there only three men here?" says Lisa. "We get up early on a Saturday morning to come to a workshop on sexism, and where are the guys?" "Like the straight girls say—men just don't get it," says Karen. "Even gay men."

The door opens, and Susan comes in, shaking her head. She sits down heavily, puts her face in her hands. "What's up?" asks LaShondra. "I was on my way to the bathroom," Susan says. "I ran into Kevin in the hall. He asked me for a hug. I'm totally furious at him, for obvious reasons. But I gave him a hug anyway. I can't believe I did that! It was that old knee-jerk 'I'm the woman, you're the man, so I'll take care of you' stuff." Susan starts to cry. "I hate it when I fall into that trap. It reminds me of what happened with my father when I was a kid. It makes me feel so . . . weak." Karen puts her arm around Susan's shoulders.

"This whole thing is so upsetting," Maureen says. "I've been doing speaking gigs with Kevin for years. I felt close to him. I trusted him. Now I can't stand to look at him. Every time I feel safe with a man, something like this happens." She starts crying, too. "I know I'm hypersensitive these days. I just got my first construction job. I'm the only woman on the site. I get hassled by the guys I work with all day every day. But I don't expect to have to deal with that kind of crap here. These guys are supposed to be our *brothers.*"

Lisa picks up the packet of Kleenex and hands it to Maureen. It gets passed from woman to woman around the circle. The women who aren't crying are comforting the ones who are. LaShondra watches, her face a somber, dignified mask, as if she's presiding over a sacred ceremony. I glance around the circle. Everyone else seems to be caught up in the intensity of the moment. But I feel distant, separate. I feel like I'm observing the ritual of an unfamiliar tribe. Maybe, I tell myself, it's because I'm a late-blooming bisexual, not a lifelong lesbian. Maybe it's because I never went through separatism in the seventies, when these women were living, working, marching, and loving in a world apart from men. Maybe it's because I've never been to a twelve-step meeting or a group therapy session. Suddenly I realize I'm not just feeling distant. I'm feeling angry. *They're acting like a bunch of victims. They're supposed to be feminist activists, and they're supporting each other in being victims.*

"Can I say something?" I ask. LaShondra waves in my direction. "I understand why everyone's so upset about Kevin's attitude. But what I don't understand is—why are we reacting this way? Kevin's just one man! Why are we giving him so much power?"

All the women look at me. I feel like a cad. *I feel like Kevin.* But I can't stop now. It's my feminist duty to say this. "I mean—where's *our* power in this situation?"

Leticia breaks the silence. "It's not just Kevin. I've heard complaints about other men on the bureau, too. The point of this workshop was to educate *all* the men, to make sure we're not putting out a sexist message when we do speaking gigs. That's why this turnout's so discouraging." I nod, feeling a bit foolish. "Are we ready to move on, then?" LaShondra asks. There's a bit of nose-wiping; a few wadded-up Kleenexes are tossed into the garbage can in the corner. "Okay. Let's talk about what kind of support you need from the men to make the speaker's bureau more effective."

An hour later there's a knock on the door. Teddy, Kevin, David, and Ron come back into the room. We rearrange our chairs and form a big circle again. This time the women are on one side, the men on the other. I notice that Kevin looks angrier than he did before. "The women will speak first," Teddy says. "Please say what the problems have been, and what you'd like the men to do differently. After each woman speaks, the men will say what they've heard, what they've learned, and what they're going to do to be better allies in the future."

It feels like they're being forced to do penance, I think. Is this diversity training? Or adversity training? Can we make the men understand women's pain by subjecting them to the kind of devaluation that causes it?

I think back to the mid-sixties, before feminism, before we knew that men and women working together for change meant that men and women, mostly men, had to change in order for us to work together. I remember all those meetings—antiwar coalitions, legal defense strategy sessions, underground newspaper conferences—when the men ran the show and the women kept the show running. In those days of innocent fervor, no one questioned that it was men who spoke into the microphones and women who rented the meeting halls; men who wrote the position papers and women who cranked the mimeograph machines; men who got famous for being arrested at People's Park and being on trial in Chicago, and men who got famous for defending them in court. There was no female Abbie Hoffman, no female William Kunstler. There would have been no one to cook the vats of brown rice and breast-feed the babies and beg the bourgeois liberals for bail money if the women didn't do it. And so we did. Until the decade turned and feminism burst into flames.

And that, I guess, is what got us here today.

"I'll start," Lakresha says. "A lot of times on speaking gigs, people ask really upsetting questions about my facial hair. They wanna know why I have it, why I don't get rid of it, if all lesbians have it or just African-American lesbians. The men I do gigs with never say anything to help me out."

"I heard you say you want support when you get asked about facial hair," David intones. *That's a good boy,* I think sarcastically. "I'd like to give you that support," David continues. "But I need help figuring out what to say." Lakresha rolls her eyes. I understand her frustration. *Use your brain, man. Have you ever heard of the beauty myth? Or wasn't that on the boys' reading list?* "Anyone else?" Teddy says.

"It shouldn't always be the woman's job to explain the connection between homophobia and sexism," Lisa says. "Last week when we spoke at a junior high, some of the kids started vamping on effeminate gay men. They were saying, Why would any guy want to be like a *woman?* as if being a woman was the worst thing anyone could possibly be. The man I was doing the gig with just spouted the party line: he said some men want to swish and dish just like some women do, and there's nothing wrong with that. He didn't respond to the anti-woman point at all. It felt like he didn't understand sexism any better than a bunch of thirteen-year-olds."

"I hear what you're saying," Ron says. "That was one idea we came up with in our small group: that men should bring up the issue of women's oppression, not wait for the women to do it."

"That would help," Lisa says. "Plus it would set a good example for the people we're speaking to."

"If I'd been there, I would've said it's better to be a woman anyway," Kevin says. "What's so great about being a man? I grew up knowing someday I might have to go to war. Women never have to worry about that."

"Kevin—we all know you think women are better off than men," Teddy says. "I'm not sure why you keep bringing it up. Are you trying to be provocative?"

"Just stating my point of view," Kevin says. "This group's supposed to be about tolerance. Is there any tolerance for a different point of view?"

"The Angry White Male comes to the Gay and Lesbian Speaker's Bureau," Lakresha mutters. *It's not that simple,* I think. *Sometimes white males have reason to be angry.* We have this conversation around our family dinner table pretty regularly—whenever my own white male feminist sons feel gender prejudice being aimed at them. Just last night Peter told us, angrily, about what happened yesterday in history class with his teacher, the head of the Berkeley High women's studies department. "We were talking about the International Women's Day assembly," Peter said. "Everyone had a different opinion. Things got kinda rowdy. Ms. Groves said, 'Everyone calm down. There's too much testosterone in this classroom.' That was totally anti-male. She never would have said 'There's too much estrogen in this classroom.' And it wasn't even fair—the girls were being loud, too."

And just last week, when I discovered a molding mountain of wet towels on Jesse's bedroom floor, I muttered at him that he was acting like a male chauvinist pig. Jesse accused *me* of being sexist. "What the hell does being too lazy to bring some towels downstairs have to do with being male?" he cried, his adolescent voice breaking and a look of betrayal on his newly shaved face.

It's not just the men who need to change, I think. Women need to stop giving hugs we don't want to give. We need to look men in the eye—at least men like Kevin, who may threaten our sense of progress but don't threaten our physical safety—and say what we have to say, not just retreat for comfort to a circle of crying women. We need to stop attributing everything evil in the world to testosterone, and stop using *male* as a pejorative adjective. We should know better than to shrug off an otherwise right-thinking man who's feeling discriminated against because of his gender—even if we think he's wrong, even if that makes him seem like the enemy. And we need to be willing to give up the goodies we get from gender inequality, too.

In the meetings I sit in a few times a year at Berkeley High, the usual gender dynamic is turned upside down, as it was in all the parent meetings at each of the kids' schools all the years before. Women vastly outnumber men. The fathers are the newcomers: disempowered interlopers, divested of authority by the age-old, entrenched power of *mother* and by their own gender's history—changing now, but slowly—of parental abstention. Here the men speak hesitantly, almost apologetically, as if they have to earn the right to be heard, the right to be there at all—*as if they were women,* newly admitted to the board room or the basketball court. And the mothers speak confidently, with great authority, because—still, for the most part—we're the ones who volunteer to work the school switchboard and make the brownies for the bake sales, the ones who call our kids' teachers and meet with our kids' counselors, the ones who ask the thousand questions required to elicit one piece of information about what and how our kids are doing at school each day.

Despite the trendy pop-psych analyses of men and women, Mars and Venus, dissonant interactive styles, and how cutting-edge communication skills might allow the genders to understand each other—I don't think it's style differences, or misunderstanding, or individual psychology, but *the distribution of power* that keeps men and women at war. And it's a redistribution of power in the world that will evoke a redistribution of power in our psyches and our relationships: as many female CEOs as male; as many male parents as female. The gender gap will narrow; the battle between the sexes will wind down when women know the anguish of laying off a hundred employees and the security of financial self-sufficiency; when men know the exhaustion of a long infant night and the soul-softening miracle of deep emotional connection.

And while we're working to bring about those external changes—arguing and laughing, talking and crying in our speaker's bureaus and PTAs, in our bedrooms and at our family dinner tables—we need to work to bring about the internal changes, too. We need to reach across the gender gulch, give up the familiar, comfortable notions of who we are and what our worth is and where it comes from and who can give it to us or take it away. While the lesson plan is being rewritten, we need to behave, somehow, as if the slate has already been wiped clean.

"You know, I used to feel the way Kevin feels," Ron says into the tense silence in the meeting room. "I thought women were blaming men for everything. I felt like, *I* never hurt any woman, so why should women treat me with such distrust?

"Two years ago I blew up at my closest woman friend about it. We got out of a class late one night. Sarah wanted to walk the long way around the parking lot; she said it was too dangerous to walk through the parked cars. I started yelling at her that she was acting like a victim, that women want all this power and respect but they keep acting like men are monsters with complete power over women. She walked away from me. We haven't spoken since.

"About a year later I went to Spain," Ron goes on. "I was walking alone one night and I found myself in a dark alley with this big burly guy yelling '*maricon*' at me. I was *terrified*. It made me think about what happened with Sarah. I realized that the way I felt in that alley in a foreign country—and I'm male, and six foot one—is how women feel a lot of the time in their own neighborhoods."

Ron faces Kevin. "Maybe you should spend some time with women. Get to know what their lives are like. There's this myth that gay men are more sensitive to women's issues than straight men are, because we deal with homophobia. But I'm not so sure. Straight men are educated by their wives' and daughters' experiences. Unless we have women friends, gay men can get pretty removed."

Kevin starts to say something. Teddy interrupts him. "It's almost noon, folks. Time to get some closure. Let's take a five-minute break. Then we'll get back together and talk about what we've learned."

As people file out of the meeting room, clustering in the hall and waiting on line for the one unisex bathroom, Kevin makes a beeline for Teddy. "I still don't see why women got most of the time today," Kevin says. "It just proves my original point: it's not a man's world at all." "And if that were true—which I don't believe it is," Teddy says evenly, "do you have a problem with that?" "I want women and men to be equal," Kevin says. "I don't want it to be a man's world *or* a woman's world. I want it to be everyone's world. I just want women to understand that it's hard to be a man, too."

A few weeks later I go to a speaking gig at an Oakland private school with Jerry, a man I've never met before. When we arrive, the teacher tells us she called in the speaker's bureau because one of her students recently became suicidal. "It got around school that her moms are lesbians. The kids were tormenting her," she tells us as she walks us to her classroom. "I'm so glad you guys could come. We need to do some education around here, and fast." I write the Pacific Center switchboard number on the blackboard and tell everyone to write it down, so the kids in the room who need it won't stick out. Jerry and I take our seats facing twelve bored-looking ninth-graders.

"Hi. I'm Meredith. I have two sons who go to Berkeley High, and I'm bisexual," I begin. When I finish my two-minute bio, Jerry starts reciting his. Listening, I feel a tug of disappointment: *Oh: he's one of* those *guys.* Some of the men I've done gigs with are self-contained, attuned to their audiences, clearly in service to the cause. Others seem to be on the bureau mostly because they like having captive audiences listening to them. Jerry fits into the latter category. ". . . And then finally I came out at age thirty," Jerry says, six minutes later. "A clear case of arrested development." *Clueless,* I think. *He's talking to a ninth-grade social studies class, not a psychology convention. Doesn't he know that to these kids, Arrested Development is a hip-hop group?* ". . . So, feel free to ask anything you want to know," Jerry concludes. "Remember: there are no stupid questions."

"This is for Meredith," says a girl from the back of the classroom.

"How do you know which bathroom to use?" "Which bathroom to use?" I repeat, dumbfounded. "Men's or women's?" she asks.

"For both of you—how did your parents react when you told them you were gay?" asks a girl in sagging jeans and Oakland Raiders sweatshirt.

"Jerry: how can you stand to do it with a *guy*?"

"Meredith: do your kids know you're gay?"

"Do you consider yourselves normal?"

"For Jerry," says a boy wearing a Megadeth T-shirt. "When you go to the gym, what's it like to take showers with other guys? Do you ever want to just grab them?"

"There's a social contract in our culture that prohibits us from imposing our urges on other people," Jerry answers. "Gay people obey that contract, just as straight people do."

A warning bell goes off in my head. We're not supposed to argue with a fellow speaker in front of an audience, but I can't let this go by. I'm sitting here looking at eight teenage girls, one or two of whom, statistics indicate, may have already been molested by someone who violated that contract. "I think what Jerry means is, people aren't *supposed* to impose their urges on other people," I say. "But as females we know it happens all the time—on the street with strangers, on dates, in our own homes." Out of the corner of my eye, I see the teacher nodding vigorously.

Jerry frowns. "Well, of course not everyone abides by the rules. But for the most part people don't just walk up to people and grab at each other," he says. "Men have done that to me several times in my life," I say. "I'm sure it's happened to some of the girls in this room, too."

The teacher is nodding again. "I'm glad you brought that up, Meredith," she says. "A lot of people think gay people go around hitting on everyone they see. But the fact is, most sexual offenders are heterosexual men." "That's true. Any other questions?" I ask, eager to change the subject.

I'm seething as Jerry and I walk through the parking lot. *He's not the enemy,* I tell myself. *We're on the same side.* "I was really taken aback by what you said in there," I tell him. "It made me feel like you don't have much understanding of women's reality."

"I was uncomfortable with what *you* said," he retorts. "You made it sound as though females are the only victims of sexual assault. I was raped once, by an ex-lover. It was horrible. I still haven't recovered." I stare at

Jerry, flooded with conflicting emotions. "I'm sorry," I murmur. "I was date-raped, too. I know how bad it feels." Jerry bobs his head curtly, his jaw rigid. I look at him—eight inches taller, seventy-five pounds heavier, and far more muscular than I am—and wonder: Was he overpowered by someone bigger and stronger? How *does* a man rape another man, anyway? And then suddenly my compassion and my curiosity are replaced by anger. How could he have been raped, and then say what he said to those kids? "You must know the statistics, Jerry. Men get raped, too, but it happens a lot more often to girls and women. Not just rape. All kinds of sexual abuse."

Jerry shrugs. "Sure, sure. But we shouldn't go out on speaking gigs perpetuating the myth that it only happens to women." I gape at him, speechless. Jerry gets into his car. I get into mine. We drive off in opposite directions. I go home and pace the floor, feeling the need to *do* something about this.

Now I understand why the women at the workshop were so upset, I think. *Now I understand the feeling that there's just no getting through.* I ask myself the question I asked them: *Where's* my *power in this situation?* I consider my options. I could call Jerry and try to talk to him some more. I could call another woman on the bureau for support.

I dial the Pacific Center. "I just came back from the gig with Jerry," I tell Leticia. "I'm really upset. I don't want to talk about Jerry behind his back, but I have to tell you—he said the most sexist things! I tried to talk to him about it afterward, but I don't think I made a dent."

"Well, there's good news and bad news on that front," Leticia says. "Ron and David came to see me the day after the workshop. They said they want to help organize another one. I told them I'd check with the women, see if they're willing to go through all that again. But that made me feel like at least it was worth doing the first one, even if we only reached two men."

"Two?" I say. "What about Kevin?"

Leticia sighs. "That's the bad news. Kevin came to see me, too. He brought me an article he'd clipped out of the paper. He said it proved that women kill their husbands more often than husbands kill their wives."

"What'd you say to him?" I ask.

"I told him his attitude discourages me from working with men," she answers.

WHEN I WANT A MAN

Ann and I are station-surfing on the car radio, headed north to the cabin for our annual Christmas-week escape. As if escape is possible: the airwaves are polluted with holiday schmaltz. A heavy-metal version of "Jingle Bells"—*not*. Country-western "Silent Night"—*no thank you*. A rap rendition of "Good King Wenceslas"—*I don't think so*. Just outside Ukiah I'm struck by a sudden thought. "What's the date today?"

"December twentieth," Ann says. "Why?"

"Tomorrow's my twentieth wedding anniversary," I say.

Ann glances at me, then quickly looks away.

Damn! How could I have been so insensitive—again? Ann and I have a wedding anniversary, too. But *our* twentieth won't be till April 23, 2014. Do I still consider my *real* wedding to be the legal one, the one that married me to a *man,* to my *husband*? "With Richard," I add.

Ann nods. "Did you and Rich get married on the solstice on purpose?" she asks. Ann and I chose *our* wedding day—the tenth anniversary of our first date—nine years in advance. "Huh," I say, relieved to have been forgiven so readily, this time anyway. "Richard and I didn't know from solstice. We got married before December thirty-first so we could save a few hundred bucks by filing a joint tax return. I chose the twenty-first 'cause I figured it would be easy to remember—same date as my birthday."

"How romantic," Ann says.

"Yeah," I say. "Well, it wasn't really romance I was after when I married Richard."

"What was it?" Ann asks, although we've talked about this many times before. And maybe because it's my twentieth wedding anniversary, or maybe because this question—*What is it you want, Meredith?*—has been such a flash point between Ann and me lately, I think about it now, really think about it, before I answer.

What was it I wanted when I married Richard?

The boyfriend before Richard was eleven years older than I was, working-class, world-wise, and competent. Danny and I had been running in the same underground-newspaper circles for years, but I fell in love with him one day in 1971, right after we rear-ended a Toyota in downtown Berkeley. Danny was driving, an old Citroën he'd borrowed from his friend Rob. I took one look at the Citroën's bashed-in fender and panicked. Danny and I had no money, no insurance; neither, I was sure, did Rob. Calmly, as if he'd planned the whole thing, Danny told the other driver that if he handed over fifty bucks in cash, Danny wouldn't file an insurance claim against him. *But it was our fault!* I thought. Incredibly, the guy handed over the cash and drove away. Danny reached down, pulled the dent out of the fender, drove us to Rob's house, and gave him the money. "Thanks for the use of the car," Danny said, never mentioning the accident, because he didn't have to. He'd fixed it. Just like that.

I looked back at the Citroën as Danny and I walked away. It was as if the accident had never happened. I was moonstruck. His woman for life— or I could have been, if I hadn't started pressing Danny for more talk, more commitment, a baby. If Danny hadn't started edging away from me, creeping into our bed late at night, as silent, self-righteous, and self-contained as he was the day he undid the damage to Rob's car—the day I'd crawled breathlessly under his wing. I wanted someone who could fix things, take care of things, the way Danny could—but someone who wouldn't break me into little pieces in the process. Someone trusty, stable, solid. After two tumultuous years with Danny, I found Richard. I grabbed him and held on tight.

Richard was six feet, four inches tall. He had to bend way down to kiss me. Our hugs were awkward, gangly, more space than embrace. But Richard came home to me every night. When I lay down with him in the dark, the length, the heft, the bulk of him made me feel encompassed, protected, safe. When we walked down the street together, I lost all fear of muggers, creeps, and rapists. Nothing bad could get through him to me.

Richard could fix cars, build furniture, install tile, pilot a plane. He knew how interest rates were determined and what made earthquakes happen and who was going to win the next election and why. I was twenty-two; Richard was twenty-five when we moved into our first apartment together. He unpacked two grocery bags full of T-shirts and jeans, three boxes of books by Lenin, Mao, Marcuse, and Fanon, a couple of scarred Teflon frying pans, and several crates of used Volkswagen parts. When we had somewhere to go—a United Farmworkers' picket line, an October League cell meeting, his mom's house in Redwood City, or his favorite barbecue joint way out in East Oakland, where the line spilled onto the street and we were the only white folks on it—Richard would fold himself into the driver's seat of his '65 Volkswagen Bug, his knees grazing his chin. I sat in the passenger seat. If the car wouldn't go, or wouldn't go fast enough, or quietly enough, or if he decided it might be nice to have a sun roof, or a tape deck, or firmer seats, he'd spend a few hours in the garage swapping this part for that. Then off we'd go with the wind in our hair, a Jimmy Cliff tape booming from the speakers, spare parts and a toolbox in the trunk in case anything went wrong. I bought an old Bug too, so I'd never have to take my car to a repair shop again.

My husband loved me loyally if not passionately. Apart from his occasional outbursts of rage (maybe five times in ten years he scared me, punching the wall, slamming a door so hard the mirror broke, screeching off in his car), he was steady and sure. After all that painful passion with Danny, Richard was just what I was looking for: the oldest son of a widowed-young mother, well trained in taking charge, toughing through, swallowing feelings, keeping the family going. Throughout the thirty-six hours of my first labor, he kept meticulous charts and notes: "Up to pee, 4:46 A.M. Contractions two minutes apart, 6:14–9:44 A.M. Nembutal 12:15 P.M." When at last Richard cradled newborn Peter in his arms, his first words to his son were, "No motorcycles, young man." In 1982, to stave off my increasing restlessness, I took a trip to New Mexico. I came back from visiting my old haunts and old boyfriends to find our family room transformed into a study for me. Richard had built elegant cedar bookshelves and folding cedar doors and refurbished an old oak desk, to encourage me to stay home and write. One year later, when our despairing marriage counselor prescribed a more romantic home environment, Richard ripped out the back wall of our bedroom, replaced it with an immense bay window, and custom-fitted a waterbed into it so we could sleep with our heads in the garden—an often-expressed fantasy of mine.

Still my husband and I couldn't sleep together. Night after night he snored on the living room couch while I lay alone, sleepless in the bedroom of my dreams. Day after day we blamed each other for the widening chasm between us—between how we'd expected our life to be and how it was. His mother died; the October League splintered; we both lost our jobs; we had no friends, two babies in diapers, and half as much money as we needed. After ten years of marriage, I was bored and depressed, lonely and disconnected. "The thing that draws most couples together to begin with," our counselor told us, "is often the thing that drives them apart in the end." How could I have ever believed that feeling safe would be enough to make me happy? I could *hire* someone to build me a bookshelf or renovate my bedroom! I wanted what money couldn't buy, what no big, strong, capable, rational guy like Richard could give me: intimacy, excitement, hot sex, pillow talk till dawn. The delicious stuff I read about in lesbian novels.

What was it I wanted when I married Richard?

Whatever it was, I wanted something different ten years later, when I went off looking for Ann.

"More than anything," I tell her finally, "I guess when I married Rich, I wanted to feel taken care of. Safe."

I check the gas gauge, then glance at Ann. Just as I feared, she's looking at me, her lips pinched. "Not loved, not in love—just *safe*," she says.

It was just a month ago, the last time we came to the cabin together, that I had the outburst we've been talking and arguing about ever since. We were driving—*I was driving, because it's* my *car we take when we go to the cabin, because my car is newer, because I'm the one who has more money*—up the dirt road, treacherously rutted by last winter's rains. Suddenly there was the sharp clang of rock hitting metal, the sickening crunch of metal crumpling from the impact. I inched the car forward, felt the rock fall away, heard the unmistakable sound of *something wrong with my car.*

"I want a *husband!*" I yelled, before my brain could warn my mouth to shut the hell up. Once I'd started, it was like driving up that steep, narrow road: I couldn't stop. "A husband with a brand-new four-wheel-drive truck! A husband who'd know what's wrong and how to fix it when something like this happens. *So someone else would be in charge and it wouldn't all be on me!*"

Even as my anger crashed over me, a solid bit of information floated up to my consciousness. I knew exactly what was wrong with my car: a rock had punched a hole in the muffler. And I knew exactly how much it was going to cost to fix it: two hundred dollars. A lot of money, but no more than I had in my checking account. Even as I plunged into feeling helpless and dependent, I knew I wasn't quite as helpless or dependent as I felt. I'd spent six months apprenticing in a VW repair shop in the sixties— installing exhaust systems, as a matter of fact—and four years building trucks on the Ford assembly line. There were plenty of potential husbands out there who knew less about cars than I did. Plenty of potential husbands who had less money in their checking accounts than I did. But all those *facts* had nothing to do with what I wanted so desperately right then—*what I wanted when I married Richard.*

"We *always* take my car when we come up here!" I shouted above the muffler's roar. "It's always *me* who has to pay when this damn road tears it up. Why do *I* have to be the one with the better car—the grown-up, the provider? I want someone to take care of *me!*"

Ann said nothing. Nothing about our early years together, when *she* was the one who earned more money, the one who bought Disneyland vacations for Peter and Jesse and expensive presents for me when my income barely covered thrift-store clothing and groceries. Nothing about our first year in the cabin, when *she* bought a '68 Volkswagen bus so we could transport endless loads of furniture and firewood, when *she* was the one who drove and *she* was the one who paid for car repairs. Nothing about the fact that she would still be the driver if *I* hadn't decided, once the cabin was furnished and I'd started making good money, that it was time to buy a cushier car. A new car, five years ago; a car with a hole in its third muffler, now.

I pulled into our driveway and parked a few yards from the cabin. I turned off the engine but left the headlights on, the way we always do when we unpack the car in the dark. The muffler's clamor and my own were silenced. The only sounds in the black moonless night were the soft whir of winter breeze through the fir boughs, and the clicking of the car's catalytic converter.

I glanced at Ann. Her jaw was rigid. I leaned back in my seat, stared through the windshield at our beloved cabin, illuminated in the head-lights' glare. I remembered how it looked when we bought it six years ago. From the outside it seemed to be leaning in several directions at once. The front porch, the storage shed, the deck railings were rotting, falling away from the house. Half of the windows had cardboard taped over them where the panes were cracked or missing. Inside there were tin can lids nailed over some but not all of the holes in the wood plank floor; cinder blocks propping up the useless sink; rust holes in the stovepipe; copper gas lines and plastic water pipes dangling from the wall.

From the moment we first crossed its rickety threshold, we adored our disheveled cabin in the woods. We adored it because it was what we could afford and we adored it for what it could become—*if only*, I secretly thought, *we had a handy husband.* Barring that option, we had to find the next best thing: a plumber/carpenter/glazier/roofer/handy person or per-sons who would work for cheap, without power tools, on weekends only, when Ann and I could be there to supervise and to learn. We didn't know any local tradespeople—or any local people, period. So we put the word out among our Bay area lesbian carpenter friends, offering fifteen dollars an hour plus a free stay in our country house to anyone who could help make it habitable.

A couple of weekends later, we found ourselves in the company of two competent dykes. One was a plumber; tall, blond, and lean; the other was a carpenter; short, black, and stocky. Both women were businesslike, mus-cular, and tireless; both of them, impossibly, were called C.J. When they arrived, Ann and I tried to guess whether they were lovers or just partners; after spending a weekend with them, we still couldn't tell. While their dogs chased deer up and down the mountain, short C.J. taught Ann and me to cut glass and putty windows; tall C.J. joined pipes and installed faucets. Short C.J. took a handsaw to a sheet of plywood and cut out a countertop. Tall C.J. single-handedly shoved the cast-iron tub into place. At night they ate heaping plates of spaghetti, tucked their hounds and their tools into their truck, and slept together passionlessly on our queen-sized sofa bed. When we paid them their $300 each on Sunday night, the cabin had running water, a stove to cook on, floors safe to walk on.

Remembering that first industrious weekend and all the industri-ous weekends since, it occurred to me, as I sat in the dark in the car with my rage cooling and Ann still seething beside me, that it was a *man*—a man who made his living as a carpenter—and his wife who had lived in our cabin for the five years before we bought it. A *man* who had taken silver duct tape to the windows and the pipes rather than repair them; a *man* who had nailed orange juice lids to the floor instead of replacing the broken boards. A man with a pickup truck and bulging muscles and all the "manly" skills I'd just finished screaming at my girlfriend for not having.

And then it was women—the C.J.'s and Ann and I to begin with; Ann and I with a little help from our friends ever since—who scrubbed and fixed and nursed our cabin back to health. Ann who trudged off into the woods with her hatchet and her chain saw, day after day, year after year, clearing ever-widening views and chopping endless cords of firewood. I who insulated the pipes so they stopped freezing every winter. Ann who built the notched-log wall around the well. I who built the table we pull our chairs up to when we eat on the deck in the summer.

And yet—when that rock hit my car, it knocked unconscious the part of me that remembered all of that. In that moment I forgot all that Ann and I have done, all that each of us separately and both of us together have proved we're capable of doing. I forgot all the reasons to want what I have. What I wanted in that moment was to be rescued. I wanted someone with more money and more strength and more know-how to swoop in, fix my car, and keep me from harm forevermore. *I wanted a man.*

It happens all the time.

When we go on vacation in a small town in Mexico, or a small town in America. When I go shopping for a new car. When the hot water heater springs a leak. When I hear gunshots outside my bedroom window. When the toilet paper holder comes loose from the wall because I screwed it in where I wanted it, not where there were studs in the wall to hold it—*I want a man.*

When my mother hurts my feelings or I find a lump in my breast or my therapist tells me she's moving away or my best friend isn't, anymore—when my heart needs holding—I want Ann. I want what I have. I want a woman.

But still . . . when I take BART alone late at night; when a chunk of plaster falls from the ceiling; when one of the kids is late coming home and someone has to go looking in scary places—*I want a man.*

The first man I turned to was not physically competent. It's possible that my father was capable of changing a light bulb, but I never saw him do it. My mother, not my father, oiled the drawers when they stuck, set up the hi-fi, refinished the armoire. Hired workmen fixed the car, installed the washing machine, painted the kitchen. Both of my parents skittered constantly on the thin ice of chronic fear; neither of them could soothe or contain their own needs and anxieties, let alone mine. But in this one way, at least, I felt safe in my family: my father provided abundance.

Even when my mother's mouth was pinched with anger for days or weeks at a time; even when my father raged and threatened; even when my brother and I huddled together for warmth in the arctic zone of our family—there was always this one thing to count on: more than enough money in my father's wallet to buy what we needed; more than enough money in my father's wallet to fix what broke. Sometimes I would stand in the chill of the open refrigerator, soothing myself into a trance, gazing at the glossy contents of its overstocked shelves. How could anything be as awful as it seemed, when there was so much food in the house? My mother was the one, of course, who shopped and cooked and baked; the one who clipped supermarket coupons and collected S&H green stamps and kept the cookie jar full and the lamb stew simmering on the stove. But there wasn't a quart of milk in the fridge, a can of Campbell's soup in the cupboard, a bloodstained package of T-bones in the freezer that my father had not paid for.

Somehow I knew this, and somehow, early on, I absorbed what the culture had to say about it. My father was the essential member of the family: the provider, the man in charge. My mother was his implementer, his enforcer, his household staff. I picked sullenly at the balanced meals my mother shopped for and cooked and put on the table three hundred nights a year. I squealed with delight when my father came home with greasy deli bags full of thick corned beef sandwiches—two for each of us, more than we could possibly eat—and gift-wrapped boxes of English toffee. My father dressed in tailored suits, left the house every morning in a cloud of aftershave, went to breakfast meetings at the Plaza and lunches at Delmonico's, came home to find his shirts dry-cleaned, his boxer shorts ironed, and his favorite dinners on the table. My mother made beds, washed clothes, bought food, cooked it, and bought some more. What my father did paid for our Upper East Side apartment, my riding lessons, my brother's private school, the Bendel's cocktail dresses my mother wore to his business parties. What my mother did was undone almost as soon as she did it. What my father did made him important in our family and in the world. What my mother did made her trapped and bitter.

I can't remember a time when I didn't know that men were more valued than women; a time when I didn't know the best thing to be was a man. Thirty years before anyone thought of encouraging little girls to become the men they wanted to marry, I resolved to marry the man I wished I could become. And I did that—starting at sixteen, when I ran away from my parents to live with Paul; and ending at thirty-two, when I ran away from Richard to find a woman. I got what I wanted with Ann: for ten years now I've had my intimacy, my hot sex, my pillow talk till dawn. I've been abundantly loved and known and held; the emptiness of a thousand corned beef sandwiches filled at last.

But still . . . there are times when feminism and reason abandon me; when I lose all hope of finding what I need within myself and start thrashing around looking for it anywhere else; when I yearn for the reassurance of what first reassured me. Times, too, when those fossilized longings are reinforced in the present. Just last week Phoebe called while Ann and I were attempting to lug Ann's new desk up two steep flights of stairs. I answered the phone, panting. "Why are you doing that yourselves," Phoebe asked, "when you have two strong young men there to help you?" We didn't, actually—Peter and Jesse were at Richard's that night—but later I wondered: Would Phoebe have advised us to enlist the help of our two strong young daughters?

Times, even now, when I call what I want "a man."

I wonder if I'm alone in this.

I think of Doris and Mildred, two fifty-five-year-old women I know. For fifteen years they have lived their isolated, closeted lesbian lives on a mountainside in the Sierras: built their own two-story house; installed their own water and solar energy systems; and pulled more than one snowbound city slicker out of the ditch with their four-wheel-drive truck. Does Doris, does Mildred lie in bed at night, secretly wanting a man?

I think of my feminist heterosexual friends: would self-doubting, wealthy Julie; would social worker Leslie admit to being swayed in her choice, even a bit, by wanting what I want when I want a man? Julie's boyfriend Brent did the research and the negotiating when she bought a new car, marks his calendar so he knows when it's time to change the oil, and changes it for her. Leslie's engineer husband Ray earns $100,000 a year—so Leslie can work part-time, and the two of them can take vacations in Bali and Costa Rica every year.

Even among the long-married lesbian couples I know—women who came of age before women's liberation, Stonewall, or lesbian chic—I see familiar dichotomies, and I wonder: is the whole sexual population divided into those who want to be taken care of, and those who want someone to take care of? Arlene is a nurse: emotional, domestic, artistic; her lover Dor is an electrician: pragmatic, even-tempered, capable. Laree is the mother of six grown kids, a high-profile activist who flies around sparking feminist fires; her lover Sue keeps their bills paid, their toaster in good repair, and Laree's feet on the ground. Lynne cooks and decorates and goes to therapy; her partner LaVonne waxes both of their cars, assembles the patio furniture, is uncomfortable discussing feelings.

Is it the balanced yin-yang, the inevitable polarity of coupledom—or the tyranny of archaic gender roles—that made these women choose their lovers and their husbands? Did Julie, did Leslie seek out an attractive opposite, a "better half," an exotic "other"? Or were they looking for what I'm yearning for when I want a man: a spouse who takes care of them in ways they grew up believing they couldn't take care of themselves?

And what are men looking for when they want a woman? Does the longing to be *made to feel whole* transcend gender and sexual orientation? Did Richard's helplessness in the kitchen make him as dependent on me as my helplessness in the garage made me on him? Did Richard's need for an emoter propel him toward me as forcefully as my need for a fix-it man propelled me toward him? Does the search for *what's missing* inevitably triumph over self-sufficiency—or is finding that mirroring partner what makes self-sufficiency possible?

I turn off the highway, checking the mountaintops for snow. My gut clutches: what if we have to put chains on in the dark? "You know," Ann says as we turn onto our dirt road, "I've been thinking: we really *could* use a truck."

I swerve to the right to avoid a jackrabbit, then swerve back to keep us out of the ditch. A rock hits the underside of the car; I hold my breath for a moment but hear no evidence of metal tearing.

"Not four-wheel drive, necessarily," she says. "But something with better clearance off the ground. And more room for hauling kids and firewood."

For once in my life my brain is actually controlling my mouth, which mercifully remains closed.

"I told you I've been planning to cut back on therapy," she says. "If I do, I could afford to make payments. On a new truck. Want to shop around next weekend?"

"Sounds great," I choke out. I feel grateful, and ashamed. Delighted, and guilty. *She really does want to take care of me. How could I have been such a jerk? Longing for a woman when I'm with a man. Longing for a man when I'm with a woman . . .*

Ann puts her hand on my thigh.

"I can't do the kinds of things Rich did for you, Mer," she says. "I'll probably never make as much money as your father did—maybe not even as much as you do. But I do love you. I do want to make you feel safe however I can."

"You do so much," I say. "With the cabin, with the kids, with me. . . ."

"It's not enough," Ann says sadly.

"It is," I say.

I pull into our driveway, turn off the engine, leave the headlights on. Ann and I sit quietly for a moment, looking at our cabin. "The porch— you were right," I say. Ann nods. "It looks fine now," she says. We both thought the new porch looked strange when Scott first built it a few months ago. I wanted to complain, ask him to fix it. Ann said we should wait and see; that it would blend in better with the house when the boards had time to age.

"The way I feel when I say I want a man—that's my problem, not yours," I say. "What you do for me—it's more than enough. More than I'd dreamed of."

I take Ann's hand. "I mean it," I say. And I do. At least in this moment, I do.

Pain and Power

"The suffering and courage and humor and rage and intelligence and endurance that spilled out from the pages that came in from different women! The facts we came up against, the statistics! The history, the insights into our own lives that dawned on us! I couldn't believe—still can't— how angry I could become, from deep down and way back, something like a five-thousand-year- buried anger."

From the introduction to

Sisterhood Is Powerful

I'm talking to Jeannie, a twenty-eight-year-old friend, about my new boss, a thirty-one-year-old woman. I'm raving about how much progress women have made in my lifetime. Just one generation ago, there were no female CEOs, newscasters, truck drivers, senators! I was suspended for wearing pants to high school! Parents saved their college money for their sons! Women unthinkingly took their husbands' last names!

Jeannie is silent. I notice that she's staring at me numbly. She shakes her head. "My father molested me when I was little. I've been in therapy since I was a teenager," she says. "I've been on Prozac for two years. I'll probably be dealing with depression all my life.

"Then there's the anxiety. I spend half my paycheck on rent so I can live in a safe neighborhood, but it's still not safe to walk down my own street at night. I drive around with my car doors locked. I won't get into an elevator with a man I don't know." Jeannie looks at me intently.

"Sure, I can get a better job than my mother could," she says. "But I live in constant pain and fear. She didn't." Jeannie pauses. Then she asks me, "How can you call that progress?"

What we had in mind, when my friends and I threw away our bras, examined each other's cervices in free clinics, and picketed beauty pageants wearing hot dog necklaces around our necks and baloney slices glued to our breasts, was power. We had that in common with our less flamboyant sisters: some of us noisily filed class action suits; some of us quietly started wearing power suits. Some of us joined WITCH; some of us joined our union's women's committee. Some of us stopped shaving our legs; a lot of us started telling secrets. But however we expressed them, our goals were the same: we wanted the world to widen to women. We wanted more respect, higher wages, better marriages than our mothers', bigger lives than any generation of women had ever known.

We've won, or are slowly winning, much of what we've fought for. We earn more money than our mothers did, at jobs they never dreamed of doing. We are less likely than our mothers were to stay in unhappy or abusive marriages; to be pressured into having children. We have reason to encourage our daughters to dream even bigger dreams.

But for all this expansion, in many ways the world seems to have closed in on us. Women who once led marches now lead incest survivors' groups. Women who once fought to prove they could do "men's jobs" now fight to keep the affirmative action door ajar. Our goals seem to have shrunk from the ideals of empowerment and equality to the bare bones of safety and survival. The task of a modern mother of daughters is grim. As therapist and author Judith Herman says, a mother must "protect her daughter from male exploitation, teaching her to avoid molestation, rape, incest, prostitution, and physical assault." But how can a mother protect her daughter; how can a woman protect herself from bulimia and breast cancer, depression and suicide?

For girls, for mothers, for women like Jeannie—and there are many women like Jeannie—the experience of being a woman today is very much an experience of recovery from what came before, and coping, with diminished resources, with the dangers of life today. . . .

THE DAMAGE DONE

The last time Ann and I passed through Petaluma, on the way home from our cabin a month ago, Polly Klaas was still missing. In every shop window from Ukiah to Oakland, on every gas station wall, on the sides of the huge semis that roared past us on the freeway, on every vertical surface everywhere, was plastered the "Stranger Abduction" poster: a police artist's sketch of the bearded, fat-lipped kidnapper beside a photo of Polly's smiling twelve-year-old face—a face that so resembled my niece Josie's that Josie was occasionally stared at and questioned by strangers on the street during the two months that Polly was missing.

Throughout that time my sons and I had repeated and heated discussions about Polly. They felt that worse things happened every day to poor kids, ghetto kids, than whatever had happened to Polly, and that no one cared, no one even knew. "Just because she's white and rich and pretty," thirteen-year-old Jesse said angrily a few days ago, when Polly's kidnapper was arrested, "everyone's so worried about Polly. I don't *care* about Polly. I don't want to hear another *word* about Polly." I was shocked into silence by his response: how had he become so callous, so hardheartedly politically correct? Had Jesse's life as I'd defined it—ironically, in hopes of instilling compassion born of everyday diversity training—instead robbed the compassion from his soul as stealthily as Polly was robbed from her bedroom?

Richard reassured me that our sons' responses in fact demonstrated compassion—for the less mediagenic but no less deserving multitudes of children who are abused in this country every day. Ann's therapist reassured her that Jesse's reaction to the kidnapping was not uncommon among children his age: unmanageable terror rendered manageable by anger. I remained unreassured; neither terror nor embittered anger was a state of being I'd envisioned for my children.

While Polly was missing, the Petaluma Auto Mall on Highway 101 replaced its usual electronic billboard message—"Lowest Prices in Town/ Special Deals on 4 X 4s"—with a plea to "Help Find Polly/Call the Polly Klaas Foundation/1-800-587-4357." Driving past it now, on our way to the cabin for a long Christmas getaway, I see that the auto mall billboard is back to normal. "Holiday Sale On Today/Best Deals of the Year!" The sign is back to normal because Polly is now known to be dead: murdered—and raped, I feel certain, although this has not yet been confirmed—by the fat-lipped bearded man who snatched her from her home while her mother slept a few feet away.

I do not discuss the sign or my feelings about it—*as if it never happened; back to selling cars now that Polly's dead*—with Ann. Ann and I have been fighting constantly throughout the past month, so that now I drive past the auto mall billboard with my chest aching for Polly, but my love for Ann locked in cold storage in a dark chamber of my heart. . . . *And throw away the key. She knows I need . . . If she would just . . . I know I'd feel . . .* Happily in love at Thanksgiving, Ann and I had promised ourselves a whole week at the cabin for Christmas. Now the much-anticipated time alone together seems fraught with danger. Every argument, when the thread that binds us is as frayed as it is now, could be our last. *From whom would either of us have learned to love the other?* Breakfast this morning was tense; packing the car was tense; driving north through Berkeley, San Rafael, Petaluma is tense. I make little deals with myself: If I pass that pickup truck, we'll have a good week. If that truck passes me, we'll break up.

December has always been the worst month for me: the time of year when children are invited to think of things, hope for things, even ask for things they want and don't have. As a child, I knew how to ask for the appropriate presents: a curly-haired Shirley Temple doll, a P.F. Flyer sled, a Betsy Wetsy that cried real tears. But there were no words to ask for what I really wanted. *I'll learn to be good; then Mommy and Daddy will love me. My real parents will come for me soon. Someone will touch me, gently.*

One December, just before Christmas, I trotted behind my parents along Fifth Avenue, downtown from Washington Heights for the day like sightseeing tourists. My mother in her prized Persian lamb coat, its steel-gray pelt whorled as tightly as my own black curls. My father in his scratchy navy blue overcoat. The two of them striding ahead of me through the throng of Christmas shoppers, their familiar heads bobbing above and then disappearing into the swirling sea of mink and wool. As I scurried to keep up, to keep my eyes fastened on my mother—who had disappeared from my reach in crowds like this before, requiring me to choke back tears and report myself "lost" at skating rinks and department stores—the most famous Christmas windows in the world passed by me in a glittery blur. F.A.O. Schwarz, Bonwit Teller, Tiffany's. Santas and elves, mangers and choirboys, pink-cheeked smiling families gathered 'round red-brick mantels hung with white-trimmed stockings. *For someone else, not for me.* When I fell too far behind, when my shaky bravado failed me and I cried out, "Wait for me!" my mother reached a leather-gloved hand impatiently back in my direction in a way that felt just close enough to keep me running, but not quite close enough to touch. At Rockefeller Plaza I leaned against the polished brass rail, its chill quickly penetrating the bulk of my "good" winter coat, burning my lips and tongue on steaming hot chocolate and watching the skaters circling endlessly beneath the towering tree. *Other families had Christmas trees like that at home—I just knew it—with lights and angels and candy canes and mountains of red-and-green presents, and parents who loved each other and their children.*

Not surprisingly, December has been hard, every year for nine years, between Ann and me. Ann's arms are soft and downy, like a mother's. Her love for me is encompassing and knowing, like a mother's. The resemblance seduces me. Each December I wait for her to beam at me while I open the mountain of red-and-green presents, to draw me close to her bosom, stroke my face adoringly, soothe me back through time and forevermore. *To come for me, at last.* But she isn't the good mother I long for. She isn't a mother at all—just an unloved daughter like me. And so each December, my hopes dashed once again, like my thirteen-year-old son I turn pain to anger; plunge like a mad bull into my wildest blood-boiling rages. And so each December Ann and I have our most damaging fights; retreat back, back, back into our deepest distances. This December has been no exception.

The legacy of unloved daughters, raised by unloved, unloving mothers. Newly in therapy several years ago, my mother shared with me a December memory from her own childhood. On the first night of Hanukah, her father, flush with the wealth he had quickly acquired and would just as quickly lose in the Depression, presented his wife with her first fur coat. The candles were still burning a few evenings later when he flew into one of his rages, the fits of temper that usually ended with him beating his wife, or his two daughters, or all three of them. But this time my mother's father—a truly evil man, at whose funeral people celebrated not his life but his death—instead commanded his wife to put on her new mink coat, which he then ripped, while his terrified daughters watched, into pieces with his bare hands.

The legacy of daughters unprotected by their mothers. Polly's mother, Eve, is a woman much like myself: my age, with two children, an ex-husband, a second marriage. One daughter alive, now, one daughter dead. What could Eve have done to protect Polly? My therapist, my spiritual teacher, my Buddhist texts would tell me that grief is grief, loss loss, heartbreak heartbreak: Eve's, Polly's, my mother's, my mother's mother's, Ann's, mine—the kidnapper's, even. But to lose a daughter twelve years old to a monster of a man . . .

Unloved child, grow up! I chastise myself. I take my right hand off the steering wheel and rest it on Ann's left thigh. Still she stares ahead, steeped in the bitterness we have brewed these past weeks. I summon the courage to leave my hand on her thigh, nonetheless, fight the feeling that I am running to catch up to someone who does not want to be caught. *This is now.* This *woman* does *love me.*

Just south of Cloverdale I speak into the silence in the car. "Somewhere right around here," I say, "is the spot where they found Polly Klaas. I wonder if there's a marker or anything."

A moment later I see a group of people off to the left, standing together in the shadow of an abandoned sawmill, their backs to the freeway and their heads bowed. "That must be it," I say. Ann turns her head and watches as we drive by. "It looks like they're having a memorial service. Do you want to stop?" I ask her. Ann shrugs but says nothing, so I keep driving, glancing again and again into the rearview mirror until the town appears before us and the gathering disappears behind.

Cloverdale is the halfway point between home and the cabin, our favorite place to stop if we stop at all—at the Owl Café when the kids are with us, for buttermilk pancakes and hash browns; or at the Corner Deli when it's just the two of us, for car-food to go: cranberry Calistogas and microwaved lasagna. Driving home in Fourth of July traffic when it's a hundred degrees in the car and it takes forty minutes to drive the two miles of freeway that run from one end of Cloverdale to the other, we line up at the Hi-Fi Drive-In behind men with lobster-red shoulders and speedboats hitched to their four-by-fours for chocolate-dipped cones and root beer freezes and a cup of ice water for our panting dog, Joe. Ann and I are afraid of these men, of what they might say or do if they should realize that we are lovers, lesbians, *dykes,* and so, on line with our sons at the Hi-Fi, we are careful not to touch or look at each other too intimately.

Still—unlike Oakland, where Ann and I hold hands on the street but never leave our house without setting the burglar alarm—Cloverdale is a safe town, a town in which there is almost no crime, and so whenever we stop in Cloverdale, I get great pleasure from leaving the car unlocked. Ann always locks her door, always warns me, "Even in a town like Cloverdale, you never know . . ." but she pretends not to notice when I don't lock mine. Our plan for the future, if Ann and I are still together in five years when the kids leave home, is to move to the country near a small town: "Like Petaluma or Cloverdale," we always say. Or used to say, until Richard Allen Davis crept into Polly's bedroom in Petaluma and then drove her, dead or dying, up Highway 101 and dumped her in a field outside Cloverdale.

I stop the car in front of the bank in the middle of town. Ann looks at me questioningly. "I feel pulled to go back there," I say finally. "If they're having some kind of service for Polly, I'd like to be there. It just seems so incredible that it would be happening now, right when we're driving by. Do you want to go?"

I feel guilty for presenting Ann with this decision. It's a conflict I grapple with often in this relationship: Do I protect her (or imagine I'm

protecting her) from painful feelings she might have, by missing an opportunity to confront painful feelings of mine? Do I bring home a video I
really want to see, even though I know (or imagine) it might trigger her
most distressing memories? Forgo demands of mine because they replicate
demands that were inflicted on her by others? *Wounded daughters of
wounded mothers, running to catch up. And never reaching each other.* Something in me wants to go to the memorial, wants to feel whatever being
there might cause or allow me to feel. While the whole world was crying
about Polly these past few weeks, I was arguing with my kids, with Ann,
juggling my December dramas. Maybe I just need a good cry of my own
right now.

But for Ann, I know (or imagine), this seemingly minor decision is
more loaded. Throughout her childhood, beginning when she was much
younger than Polly, Ann was physically and sexually abused. The discovery, three weeks ago, of Polly's white tights in a Santa Rosa field beside an
unwrapped condom, the arrest and confession of convicted rapist Richard
Allen Davis, and most especially the discovery of Polly's decomposing
corpse a few feet from the freeway just south of our favorite town,
Cloverdale—all of this had to have been more than difficult for Ann. And
now I am asking her to stand with me and a bunch of strangers on the
piece of ground where Polly's body was found—to expose herself to the
scene of the crime.

Finally Ann murmurs, "Okay." I hesitate for a moment, then decide
to take her at her word, to trust her to protect herself. *(From me? From the
memories? How often and how easily I confuse myself with the perpetrators of
her wounds: as often and as easily as I confuse her with the perpetrators of
mine.)* I do a U-turn and drive back to the place where the people are
gathered. I'm relieved to see that they're still there: we haven't missed the
service. I pull off the freeway, onto a frontage road lined with cars. I park,
and turn to Ann. "Sure you're okay with this?" I ask. *Is my attention to her
feelings a diversion from—or an entree to—my own? Have I even considered
whether I'm okay with this?* Ann nods, and we get out of the car.

Spread out along the muddy edge of the wooded field in front of us is
a homemade, spontaneous shrine to Polly Klaas: several decorated Christmas trees, maybe fifty dead and dying potted poinsettias, a glass crèche
filled with dozens of candles, most burned down to blackened nubs, a few
still flickering faintly. In the center of the shrine is a tall wooden cross with

a photo of Polly tacked to it and these words written in white paint: "For a short while an angel rested here." Someone has laid two thick pine planks across the mud, a narrow boardwalk that traverses the length of the shrine. As Ann and I walk out onto it, I am reminded of the morning in 1987 when we walked hand-in-hand at sunrise onto the Capitol Mall in Washington D.C. and watched as the AIDS Quilt was unfurled for the first time, panel after panel after panel, before thousands of witnesses standing together in shared silent grief. The feeling is the same here: long expanses of quiet stitched together by sobs, whispers, and the slow shuffling of feet.

A rough-hewn cabinet has been built or placed at the edge of the woods; its shelves are crowded with teddy bears of all shapes and sizes. One, the kind you'd find in a tourist shop, has a red heart on its chest imprinted with the words, "Bear Hugs From Petaluma." Pinned and taped to the Christmas trees and to the teddy bears and to the wooden cross, and lying on the ground between them, are dozens of photos of Polly—that same photo that was on the poster, the one that never fails to make my heart lurch: *Josie!*—wrapped in plastic for protection from the December rains, affixed with lavender ribbons and notes written in the wobbly innocent slant of children's handwriting. "We still love you Polly." "Polly you're still in our hearts." One letter, written on three-hole binder paper and enclosed in a plastic Safeway bag, begins, "My mom says when a kid is taken from her bedroom it's like a war. And I agree with her. . . ."

I see now that this is not the organized memorial service I thought it was, but a steady stream of people coming and going. A wrinkled, white-haired old man parks his gun rack–toting pickup truck, helps a little girl out of the passenger seat, takes her hand, leads her wordlessly onto the wooden boardwalk. A heavy-set woman arrives with two adolescent boys and a younger girl, all dressed in worn, ragged clothing; while the children gawk openmouthed at the photos, the Christmas trees, the candles, their mother lovingly tucks a spanking-new teddy bear dressed like Santa Claus into the cabinet beside the others. Ann bends to read the children's letters. I stoop to touch a well-worn basketball lying among the trinkets. A snapshot comes to mind: *Josie posing with the other girls for her basketball team photograph, her long, bare legs as muscular and vulnerable as a colt's; her beaming triumphant smile so much like Polly's.* Around us people keep coming: parking their cars, leading children to the shrine, silently examining the mementos other people have left there, leaving mementos of their own. And going: the children wide-eyed, the men grim, the women, many of them, crying.

Ann comes up next to me. "Ready to go?" she whispers. Her face is white and pinched, like a virgin canvas stretched too tightly across a frame. I nod and we walk slowly back to the car. Every time I swallow, I feel how close my tears are. There are gallons of tears, an ancient unshed flood of tears in me. I hear the cynical words of my sons, of their father: "I bet Polly Klaas would've been thrilled," Richard told me a few days ago, "if she'd known that Joan Baez and the governor of California would show up at her funeral." *Is his response born of fear? Of anger? Of compassion?*

I think of the other children, the hundreds of thousands of American children whose childhoods have been aborted as cruelly as Polly's was. The African-American boys my children have grown up with, many of whom, statistics predict, will be dead or in jail long before they're men. The one in six American children between the ages of ten and seventeen who has seen or knows someone who has been shot—and the other five out of six, for whom it's just a matter of time. And the girls—the girls Polly's age and younger, whose bedrooms and bodies are broken into not by fat-lipped bearded strangers, not once in a lifetime, but every week or every night, by their fathers and their stepfathers.

I think of Ann as a five-year-old girl with big blue eyes and freckles and blond braids down her back and no one to protect her. I start the car and glance back one last time. A young woman in blue jeans is walking two small blond girls to the shrine. The three of them stop in front of the cross; the woman drops to her knees, wraps one arm around each of the girls' shoulders. She whispers intently to them, looking first into the eyes of one, then into the eyes of the other. She points emphatically to the cross, to the basketball, to the photos, then draws the girls in close to her again. The girls stare back at her, their eyes dark circles in their thin pale faces.

Seeing the woman whispering to the little girls is like a match tossed onto the pyre of my grief. My tears explode at last. "What can she be telling them?" I cry. "What can she possibly teach them that would keep what happened to Polly from happening to them? *'Don't have slumber parties'? 'Don't let a strange man carry your best friend from her bedroom, even if he's holding a knife to her throat'? 'Don't feel safe, ever—because you're female, and you never will be'?"*

I remember the night last summer when my thirteen- and fourteen-year-old sons took Josie—Josie with her blossoming fifteen-year-old body and her sparkling smile and her trusting nature—for a walk after dark in our Oakland neighborhood. The three of them seemed suddenly to be late in coming back, so Ann and I jumped into the car and drove through the blackened streets, looking for them and not finding them anywhere. I remember how shocked I was to realize that I was more worried about my niece than I was about my own two sons, how horrified I was by the pictures that kept playing in my head of what some man or some group of men might make of Josie's long young legs in the denim miniskirt she'd been wearing when I saw her last. How in that moment of panic, when it seemed that Josie and my sons had simply vanished, and my very eyeballs ached with the need to see them safe, the bitter words burst from my lips: "Thank God I didn't have daughters."

Is this what it's come to? Such diminished hopes as these? *Mothers of daughters: hoping for nothing horrible to happen. Mothers of sons: grateful their children might be spared the horrible things that happen to daughters.*

In the open letter she wrote after the arrest of Richard Allen Davis, Polly's mother Eve asked an anguished public, incredibly, to "open our hearts to forgiveness and healing"; to "focus on the changes we can and must effect." To "grieve together for our hope lost, for our faith betrayed."

Ann and I are crying together now, reaching across the abyss for the first time in weeks. "I feel like I know . . ." Ann says, gesturing toward the shrine, toward the place where Polly's body was left to rot. "I know," I say. This time she takes my hand when I offer it.

"I'm sorry we've been fighting," Ann says to me. "I know December is hard for you. I wish I could do better, make you feel more loved somehow."

"I'm sorry," I say to her. *I want the cycle to end: right here, right now.* "About projecting all my old stuff, all my neediness onto you. And mostly—about what happened to you when you were little. If I could undo it somehow, I would."

"I know you would," Ann says, looking at me deeply. "Thank you." She strokes my face softly for a moment, and then I start the car and we move on together.

What Am I Doing Here?

I've never been to the town of Napa before, never had a reason to come here before. Where I live, fifty miles away in Oakland, the word *Napa* is mostly used as shorthand for Napa State Hospital, as in "Keep acting crazy, and you'll end up in Napa." "Napa" is where people—people who can't afford better, that is—are sent when the fragile threads that hold them together, that hold us all together, fray or snap or otherwise come undone.

Approaching the outskirts of Napa now, I drive past the hospital, with its steel-grated windows and menacing warning signs and incongruously lush green rolling lawns. I wonder who lives behind those steel-grated windows and why, and what secrets they took in there with them. I wonder about the people who loved them and the people who hurt them, the people who might be waiting for them to walk out of there, all bound back together again, and the people who are hoping they never will.

I drive on past the Volvo and SAAB dealerships and turn left into the center of town. I feel, suddenly, that I've stumbled onto a stage set of contemporary Americana: small-town America as it once was or never really was, America as we still wish it would, somehow, turn out to be.

Tastefully restored old redbrick buildings surround a picturesque plaza shaded by thick-trunked willows. On Main Street, women my age with artfully streaked hair stroll along chatting and window-shopping, waving back at people who wave at them. Handsome young men sit at sidewalk tables outside an espresso bar, greeting friends and sipping their morning cappuccinos. Shopkeepers sweep their sidewalks. It's 9:10 on a Wednesday morning. The children of Napa, of course, are in school.

Parking near the courthouse, I notice that the heads of all the parking meters have been sawed off their posts: free parking in Napa, all day, every day. I wonder what caused the town to change its mind about the meters—if a mall has gone in somewhere close enough to threaten the town's businesses, or if the local citizens raised a fuss about paying to park while they do their errands and drink their coffee.

I pull open the heavy wooden doors of the courthouse and approach a Sonoma County sheriff in the lobby. "Excuse me—I'm looking for the trial of—" "Second floor," he interrupts me, nodding toward the stairs. I guess I'm not the first stranger to come to this town, to this courthouse, looking for this trial. Upstairs there's a throng of people milling around: men in suits and ties talking intently to each other; children of varying ages; reporters whose bulging shoulder bags and narrow notepads reveal their intentions. Everyone stares at me as I edge through the crowd toward the courtroom.

Why?

Because I'm not a regular at this trial?

Because they want to know what I'm doing here?

Because they want to know which side of this war I'm on?

The courtroom is small, intimate, old-fashioned, with a worn oak floor and forty or fifty wooden fold-down seats, divided into two sections by a narrow aisle. It feels like the kind of room in which a kindly but strict judge might knit his brow and administer a stern warning, along with a few weekends of community service, to some mildly errant teenager whose parents play bridge with the judge on Saturday nights. But no, that's not the kind of case that's being tried in this courtroom. Not the kind of case at all.

I'm still standing in the doorway deciding where to sit when the crowd from the hall pours past me into the courtroom. The reporters head unhesitatingly for the right-hand section of seats, bending to plug their computers and cameras into the outlets on the wall; and so do the men in suits; and the children, who sit beside the men. All of the women and a couple of casually dressed men go directly to the left-hand section.

I sit in the second row on the left, behind a group of highly coifed women wearing linen and tweed and good leather pumps. I sit there because it appears to me the two sides of this courtroom reflect the two sides in this trial. And there are only two sides in this trial. I sit with the women because I sense danger on the other side of the courtroom, danger in those tight-lipped men with the well-behaved children at their sides.

Why would anyone bring a child to this trial?

What are they doing here?

What am I doing here?

I want to sit with the people on my side, the people who are here to support Holly Ramona, the twenty-four-year-old woman who has accused her father of sexually abusing her throughout her childhood and adolescence. This trial is her father's answer to Holly's accusations: Gary Ramona is suing his daughter's therapists for eight million dollars for having implanted in her "impressionable" psyche "false memories" of molestation. These false accusations, he claims, have cost him his relationships with his wife and his three daughters, all of whom believe that he molested Holly, as well as his $500,000-a-year job as vice-president of a local winery.

As "proof" that her father abused her, Holly can only offer: her memories, which she says she repressed for several years, then recalled in a series of flashbacks; her history of depression and bulimia; her mysteriously torn hymen; and her aversion to sex. Holly, in fact, has testified that at age twenty-four she has never dated, has yet to be kissed—by a man of her own age, she hastened to add.

As "proof" that he never abused his daughter, Gary offers only his denial, and his daughter's lack of evidence.

Next to me sits a friendly-looking man in his sixties—*but how do I know which side he's on?*—with a yellow legal pad resting on his knee. "Have you been coming here a lot?" I ask him. He nods. "Every day for six weeks. I'm retired. Jack's my name." He extends his hand. *He must think I'm on his side.* Hesitantly I accept his handshake. I don't know how to ask him what I really want to know. *What are you doing here? Are you the enemy, or do you believe Holly?* "I think what that man has done to his daughter is sick beyond belief," Jack says. "Don't you?"

I nod, relieved. "Who are all these people?" I ask. Jack gestures at the attractive, well-dressed woman directly in front of me. "Holly's mom, Stephanie Ramona," he whispers. He points to the older woman next to her. "That's Holly's grandma. A real sweetheart. The others are Stephanie's friends. Those people at the table are the defendants: Holly's therapists, who treated her for bulimia and depression, and her psychiatrist, who took care of her when she was hospitalized."

Jack looks at the men in the seats across the aisle. "Those are the fathers," he says. I look at him questioningly. *The fathers?* "They're from the Sacramento chapter of that False Memory Syndrome Foundation," Jack explains. "There's a busload of them here every day, and every day they bring kids with them. They'll tell their stories to anyone who'll listen. But their stories are all the same. They say their daughters ruined their lives the way Holly's trying to ruin her father's. And that guy"—Jack points across the courtroom—"that's the sleazeball. Gary Ramona."

I stare at that man, that *father,* in his perfectly tailored green suit, his thinning brown hair neatly arranged on his head, his black leather oxford shoes shining. He is leaning back in his chair at the plaintiff's table, a big grin on his face. He looks confident and powerful. The judge bangs the gavel; the men and women of the jury file into the courtroom. Gary Ramona jumps to his feet, stands at attention with his hands clasped behind his back, smiling and peering into the eyes of each juror as they pass him. "He does that every single time the jury comes in or goes out," whispers Jack. "It's creepy, huh?"

Why do I believe what so many others deny; what the people in this courtroom have been assembled to confirm or disprove: that Holly Ramona was raped by her father?

There was a time when I wouldn't have believed Holly. When no one, probably not even her mother, would have believed Holly. A time, not so long ago, before there were social service agencies and hotlines and laws to protect and treat children and adults who have been sexually abused; before first-graders were taught the difference between good and bad touch; before we knew or acknowledged what some parents—fathers, mostly—were capable of doing to their children—daughters, mostly. A time when I would have looked at Holly's impeccably dressed, highly paid, highly respected father, this proverbial pillar of his picture-perfect, affluent community, and disbelieved that such a man could rape his daughter. That any father could rape his daughter.

And then there was a time, a long period of time that hasn't quite come to an end, when I believed that any father could rape his daughter. When every father looked like a rapist to me, every daughter a victim or potential victim, every child in need of protection from her father, her stepfather, her grandfather, the janitor at her elementary school. When new statistics seemed to indicate that any woman who hadn't found sexual abuse of some kind in her past had simply not done her work yet. When most of my women friends were in therapy with one or more of the multitude of therapists who had started identifying themselves as incest specialists—many of them as incest survivors—examining their psyches for memories, their childhoods for clues, themselves for symptoms of forgotten sexual abuse. When my lover was waking next to me, night after night, sweating and shaking from nightmares of sexual abuse. When all the women's bookstores added new sections called Incest, or Sexual Abuse; and as fast as they could build them, their shelves overflowed with heart-wrenching personal accounts, feminist analyses, and self-help handbooks for incest survivors; and bulletin boards and telephone poles everywhere were papered with flyers announcing support groups for incest survivors, partners of incest survivors, lesbian incest survivors, bulimic incest survivors. . . .

It was during that time that I started to wonder whether my father had molested me.

Why?

Because I was as suggestible as Holly's father says she is—convinced, not by my therapists but by the incest-focused culture that surrounded me, that what had happened, what was still happening, to so many other little girls might have happened to me?

Yes—in part.

Because after five years of editing books about incest, writing magazine articles about incest, interviewing dozens of therapists and victims and perpetrators of incest, and ultimately speaking on TV and radio shows as a journalist-expert on incest, I'd finally decided to take the advice I'd been given by many of the therapists and survivors I'd interviewed—to examine this mysterious obsession I had with the subject of incest?

Yes—in part.

But it was nothing so cerebral, so external that first made me wonder if there was something I might not remember or understand about what had—or had not—happened between my father and me. That question slapped me in the face one night in 1983, long before I'd read *Kiss Daddy Goodnight* or *The Courage to Heal*. I was on assignment for *The San Jose Mercury-News*, researching my first feature story on incest. I'd been sitting in on family therapy sessions at a local sexual abuse treatment center, watching through a one-way mirror as a mother and her four molested daughters struggled to repair their torn relationships. Now I was sitting in a circle of convicted incest perpetrators—including the father of those four young girls—in a court-ordered group therapy session. Midway through the session I suddenly stopped taking notes, laid down my journalistic defenses, and noticed where I was.

What am I doing here? I asked myself.

I looked around at the men—fathers, grandfathers, uncles who had raped and fondled and ejaculated into the mouths and vaginas and anuses of their daughters and granddaughters and nephews. Men who were African-American and Caucasian and Mexican and Filipino. Who had automotive grease under their fingernails and high-powered Silicon Valley jobs. Whose victims had been two and seven and sixteen years old. Who sat in their uncomfortable chairs and forthrightly admitted and vehemently denied and sobbed as they recounted in nauseating detail the abuse they had inflicted on the bodies of the children who loved them.

A middle-aged white man in a three-piece suit was saying that he'd become insanely jealous when his fifteen-year-old daughter—his favorite daughter, the one he'd been molesting since she was an infant—started dating "other men." He'd strangled, nearly to death, the boy she was seeing. As the man spoke, I heard my father's voice throughout my teenage years, forbidding me to see each of my boyfriends, until finally I ran away from home at age sixteen and went to live with Paul.

Instantly the old feeling of betrayal felt as raw as freshly ripped flesh.

Until I hit puberty and my brother was old enough to throw a baseball, my father was my favorite, and I was his. From the time I could talk, we did *everything* together—things he liked to do, things my mother never wanted to do with him, things that soon became indistinguishable from what I liked to do. We played catch for hours in Bennett Park. Flew off to Louisville, just the two of us, to see the Kentucky Derby. Got up at six on weekend mornings and went out looking for adventure. My father made me hamburgers for breakfast; when my mother's back was turned, he dumped the milk she'd poured for me down the sink, winking at me over her shoulder. Along with everything else we shared, my father and I had this in common: We didn't like doing things with my mother. She didn't like baseball or going to the track. She didn't understand us. We understood each other.

Then I turned thirteen. I had budding breasts, blood between my legs, pulsing urges. I wanted to do things my father didn't want to do. I wanted to do things my father didn't want me to do—with my friends, and with "other men." I didn't want to sneak out of the house with my father on Saturday mornings anymore, to drive down to Canal Street for bagels and kippered salmon, or drive around looking for an open newsstand that sold the racing form. I wanted to spend my Saturdays with my best friend, staring enviously at the beatniks in Greenwich Village, or making out with my boyfriend in Central Park.

Suddenly my hero—the one who'd conspired with me against my oatmeal-for-breakfast, four-glasses-of-milk-a-day mother—became my worst enemy. Now I wasn't my father's favorite. I was his prisoner. He forbade me to see my boyfriend and my friends, to go to the Village, to talk on the phone; then he forbade me to go out at all because he'd caught me talking on the phone. It was war between my father and me: our apartment shook with door-slamming, threat-screaming battles that escalated as I grew more enraged, more defiant, more separate. My stay-at-home mother was enlisted as my father's occupying army—enforcing, in his absence, the restrictions he commanded. My brother was taken hostage, cowering in silence as the missiles flew around him.

Twenty years later I sat in that therapy group in San Jose, and I looked at the face of the incest perpetrator in the three-piece suit, and I thought of my father the night my boyfriend Paul defied his edict and came to the door of our apartment, determined to rescue me from the one who had once been my rescuer. I saw my father's hands grabbing Paul's shoulders; saw him shaking the boy I loved, yelling at him, threatening him, while I stood there screaming at my father to stop, stop, stop. . . .

When the man in the three-piece suit stopped speaking, the therapist who was leading the group said, It's common for fathers who have sexually abused their daughters, physically or emotionally, to explode when their daughters begin to direct their sexual attentions elsewhere. I opened my reporter's notebook, and I wrote down what the therapist said. And then the group was over, and the men went back to jail, and I tucked my tape recorder and my notebook into my briefcase and got into my Volvo to drive home to my husband and my sleeping baby sons. But when I got there, when I climbed into bed with my husband, I started sobbing and shaking, and I couldn't stop. My mortified husband, who had never, in ten years of marriage, seen me crying that way, kept asking me what was wrong. But the only words I had that night were: "It's about my father. It's about my father."

All I knew was that I couldn't sleep with a man that night, not even my mostly gentle husband; that I couldn't imagine sleeping with a man ever again. And so I went off to sleep on the couch, where I didn't sleep but cried until morning. And later, when people asked me why Richard and I had gotten a divorce, why I'd become a lesbian, I would tell the more reasonable story, but I always thought, with a strange combination of utter confusion and complete clarity, of that night as the Pandora's box that held the real answer.

Maybe I didn't want the real answer. Maybe there was no real answer. Maybe it was just too tempting to put the question away, to keep it locked in the box. My father lived in another country; I hardly ever saw him or talked to him. I was going through a divorce, learning to cope with single motherhood. I had plenty to deal with in the present, and little motivation to probe the past. In therapy I was focused on my divorce, on my own grief and my children's. But then I started having disturbing dreams. Once a month; then, once a week.

Dream: *I tell a psychiatrist that my father molested me. Immediately I am suffused with happiness because I finally told someone.*

Dream: *I accuse my father of molesting me. He cries and admits it.*

Dream: *I'm sitting in an incest treatment center, surrounded by molested children. Suddenly I realize: I'm here because their pain is my pain. I'm here because what happened to them happened to me.*

I didn't know what the dreams meant. I knew they didn't prove anything. I wrote them in my journal. I put them in the box.

Soon after Richard and I separated, I fell in love with a woman who told me a secret on our first date: that she had been molested throughout her childhood. Ann's memories, Ann's abuse were so much clearer, so much realer to me than my own shadowy suspicions. It was so much easier to empathize with her—as a wounded child, as a bravely struggling adult—than to empathize with myself, with my unhappy but unlabel-able childhood. Now I had a girlchild to champion, a victim to avenge. Now, when the therapists and survivors I interviewed asked why I was so interested in sexual abuse, I had a ready answer. A reasonable answer. An answer that turned the mirror away from me. When I sat in sessions with pedophiles, I no longer wondered what I was doing there. I was there for Ann—for all the girls and women like Ann. I was going to make sure that what had happened to Ann would never happen to anyone, ever again. Maybe my reaction to other people's sexual abuse was like my reaction to the Vietnam War, I thought. In 1967 I used to lie awake at night crying about the napalmed babies, the way I was lying awake obsessing about incest now. I had dreams in those years, too—I was the baby, the GI, the mother of the baby, the baby's burning skin. The grief fueled my anger; my anger sent me out into the streets, determined to end that abominable war. Was incest another war I was grieving about, enraged about, determined to end?

In 1986 my father moved to San Francisco. For a year we had sporadic, uneasy contact: tense lunches, mostly spent arguing about our relationship. He thought I should "get over the past, already." I thought he should understand why I couldn't. The dreams started up again.

Dream: *I'm telling a therapist, "The problem with seeing my father is, I can never remember if we're still being sexual or if it's stopped."*

Dream: *I'm running through Central Park. There's a sign on a tree that says "Only children who were sexually molested are permitted to run in the park." I know that means me, so I keep running.*

Dream: *I'm lying in a crib with my father. I'm pressing myself against the side rails to keep him from touching me.*

Then my father called to uninvite Ann to a family Christmas dinner because, he said, he didn't consider Ann "family." He and I spent a few days fighting on the phone—furiously, cruelly, the way we used to fight when I was thirteen. Angry letters were exchanged. Finally I realized I didn't have to do this anymore. I told him, calmly, that I needed a break, that I'd call him when I was ready to talk.

Little did I know what kind of break I was about to have. I spent the next month in bed, crying, staring at the ceiling, willing sleep to offer me even an hour of relief. I couldn't work, couldn't drive, couldn't sleep, cooked dinner for my children each night in a swollen-eyed daze. I wasn't having a problem with incest dreams anymore: I wasn't having dreams at all. A psychiatrist prescribed Halcion and therapy. I started sleeping four hours a night, waking in a panic the instant the drug left my bloodstream. All I could do in my therapist's office was cry. The only words I had were "It's about my father. It's about my father."

Eventually the magnetic pull of the present tugged me back from the past, and the jagged edges of my psyche began to mend. I cut back on the pills, went back to work, laughed with my children again, made love with Ann again. When I was feeling stronger, when I'd come to trust her a bit, I told my therapist that I wanted to start working on sexual abuse. Not for Ann, not for all the hurt little girls of the world—for me, this time. And I wanted to work on it until I found out for sure whether or not my father had molested me. My therapist warned me that, barring a confession from my father (if in fact, she added carefully, there was a confession to be made), my truth—my *feelings* about what had happened in my family— might be all I'd ever know. Learning to believe myself, she said, might help me more than any "answer" would.

But I was a journalist, an investigator by nature and by profession. I was determined to uncover the facts. I went through my journal, put Post-its on the pages where I'd written my incest dreams. (Soon my journal was awash in little yellow flags.) It was so hard to imagine my father molesting me that for a while I considered the possibility of another perpetrator: my mother's violent father, with whom I'd been left alone as a toddler? An uncle? A stranger?

I'd given a copy of *The Courage to Heal* to Ann, and another copy to my best friend Wendy. For my birthday Wendy gave a copy to me. Soon that book, too, had Post-its protruding from its pages, marking lists of symptoms that matched mine, family descriptions and childhood stories that reminded me of my own.

I made a list of indicators that I *hadn't* been molested: no clear memories, shaky physical evidence, and mostly—the voice in my head that kept insisting my father simply could not have done that to me. Then I made a list of indicators that I *had:* the classic incest dynamic in my family (favored daughter pitted against mother by father). The sexual clutch I felt whenever I was with my father, or even thought of him. The mysterious, often undiagnosed illnesses that had persisted throughout my childhood. The unexplained vaginal infection when I was ten. The torn hymen the gynecologist discovered during my first pelvic exam at age twelve. ("Have you ever fallen off a horse?" he asked, his head between my shaking legs.) The intense identification I had with the girls at the incest treatment centers. My compulsion to attend incest workshops, read incest books, choose sexual abuse survivors for my friends and my lover. And—the dreams. Was I still being drawn to the most grievous wrongs, the most wounded victims? Or was I drawn to them because they moved wounds in me?

By 1988 my relationship with my father had been reduced to an exchange of Hallmark cards on birthdays, and news reports passed in both directions by my brother. Peter was complaining that he wanted to see his grandfather, who gave his cousins expensive presents and took them on fun outings. My brother, my sister-in-law, my ex-husband, even my mother offered to take my kids to see my father. I didn't know how to explain why I couldn't let them go. I still hadn't spoken the word *incest* to anyone besides Ann, Wendy, and my therapist. Finally I took my brother out to dinner and said it to him. I shook as I watched him choking on his salmon, struggling to swallow his disbelief. He'd read my articles; he knew what not to say. The next day he and Roberta called to offer me their support and love. They didn't say whether they believed that my father had molested me or not. I didn't ask. Soon after that I made a date to talk to my mother.

Ann went with me to my mother's apartment. The three of us sat down at her dining room table. For a frozen moment I wondered, *What am I doing here?* Then I took a deep breath and clutched Ann's hand, and I told my mother that I was about to say something no mother wants to hear, something I couldn't prove, something that nonetheless was causing me great pain. I told her that I wasn't looking to blame her, that I wanted her to help me find the truth. I said that although I had no specific memories of being physically molested, that I *felt* my father had molested me.

My mother burst into sobs. I wished I was behind a one-way mirror again, watching someone else's mother receive this news. But this was my mother this time. My mother's reactions ricocheted wildly. For the next two hours, she careened from tearful apologies to categorical denial to rage: at my father, at herself, at me. She remembered how "sickened" she'd felt when I was two years old and my father told her angrily that I looked "too sexy" in my bathing suit. She spoke bitterly of how "you and your father ganged up against me." She told me she'd assumed my vaginal infection and my torn hymen came from "sticking your dirty fingers into your vagina," and she stared at me skeptically when I told her that self-penetration hadn't been a habit of mine when I was ten. She pulled me into her lap, stroked my cheek as I'd always yearned for her to do, crying, "How could I have let this happen to my baby?" Two minutes later she said coldly that it was simply impossible: my father couldn't have molested me. "He didn't even like sex with *me*," she said.

I was roused from a sleepless night by a phone call early the next morning. "I'm glad you told me about your . . . feelings, Meredith," my mother said in measured, distant tones. "And I'm really sorry you've been in such pain. But now that you've gotten this off your chest, can't we put the past behind us?" Later that day Roberta called to ask if I thought her kids were safe with my father—they often spent the night at his apartment. My mother's iciness, Roberta's question pushed me right back down into the sinkhole of disbelief: *my father,* molesting spunky ten-year-old Josie or Buddha-faced little Nicholas? My mother was right. It was simply impossible.

I came out of these conversations with all the uncertainty I'd felt before, and a hundred times the guilt. I'd been neither believed nor disbelieved; I'd gotten neither confirmation nor denial. And now my accusation—my *question*—about my father was spreading like an indelible stain across my family: my children deprived of a relationship with their only living grandfather; my brother and sister-in-law surreptitiously examining their children for signs that they'd been molested; my nine-year-old son's tears when I told him, finally, that I didn't want him to spend time with his grandfather, at least until he was older, because I thought my father might have hurt me when I was little. My deepening estrangement from— my utter loss of—both of my parents.

And all for what?

Back into the box went my incest question. This time it stayed put for a while. No more incest dreams, no sleepless nights, no crippling depression. I stopped writing incest articles and editing incest books; I got a regular job doing regular things with regular people. Ann and I went to a couples counselor, in part because I'd become increasingly impatient with her recovery process. I switched from verbal therapy to Rosen body work, and there, in silence, stripped of the self-defense weapon—words—I'd honed in combat with my father, I started learning to recognize the difference between someone else's ideas, feelings, and needs and my own. I began to turn inside for answers, to stop relying on my father—or on his voice in my head—to tell me what and whom to love, hate, want, reject, be.

My father called me one day in 1989—oddly enough, on the very day that Ann and I decided to move in together. The sound of his voice made my edges start to curl; I said it was too painful for me to talk to him. Because I felt guilty about the accusations I'd made? Or because I wasn't ready to confront my perpetrator? The next year my kids were eleven and twelve—old enough to take public transportation to San Francisco, old enough to protect themselves. I told them they could see their grandfather whenever they wanted to. Richard had my father and his wife, Anny, over for dinner once; my father and Anny took my kids out for dim sum one Sunday; my father took my kids and my brother's to a baseball game. And then my father stopped calling my kids or trying to see them. On their birthdays he sent a check, folded neatly inside a Hallmark card.

In the winter of 1994, the box started rattling again. Roberta told me my father and his wife were thinking of taking her fourteen-year-old son Nicholas to Europe for a month. "Do you think it's safe for him to go?" Roberta asked me. A tidal wave of remorse crashed over me. What a mess

I'd left behind when I decided to stop dealing with incest. It wasn't just me who'd been left bouncing around between conflicting realities. "Did anyone ever tell my father what . . . what I . . ." I mumbled. After a long silence Roberta said, "Sort of. A few years ago Josie told Anny what you'd told Peter: that your dad had abused you, maybe sexually, so you didn't want your kids to be around him. Sorry, Mer—I know you didn't want any of us to talk to him about what you said—about what happened to you."

What happened to me? Roberta didn't know what happened to me. My therapist didn't know what happened to me. I didn't know what happened to me. There was only one person who knew what had or hadn't happened to me, and I wasn't speaking to him.

I was forty-two years old, and I still didn't know what happened to me. Once again I was in therapy, trying to figure it out. Once again my therapist suggested that I grapple with what I know, face the pain of what I know about what happened in my family, instead of setting out on a detective mission. She reminded me that I was doing this painful but seemingly unavoidable work not to lay blame or falsely accuse or escape responsibility, but to *feel better,* to understand my past and be a better, happier person in the present. She told me that suspicions of sexual abuse—whether proven, unprovable, or false—don't arise in healthy families, families in which boundaries have not been violated. She asked me what I would do if one of my children suspected that I'd abused him; when I told her I'd put myself in service to his process, even knowing it wasn't true, she pointed out how different that was from what my parents did in response to my suspicions. I listened impatiently, and I told her, again, that I wanted to know *what happened.*

In June 1995, ten years after I first cried all night about incest, my father had his first heart attack. My brother called me from the hospital; he said the doctors believed it was likely he'd have another, more serious one in the near future. A month later I sent my father a birthday card—the first one in eight years. He called and asked if I was ready to talk. I said I was. A week later we met. He opened the door, hugged me, said, "Hello, sweetheart." My insides melted, unclenched. And in that softening I felt the other side of all my questioning, all those accusations: the longing for my father to be . . . my dad. "Hi Dad," I said, hugging him back. His arms around me felt comforting, not threatening. Was this what I'd been waiting for all my life—no threats, no punishments, no bonding at my mother's expense—just *love*?

I felt certain in that moment that my father loved me, that he'd hurt me emotionally if not physically, that he'd never molested me. I feel certain of all of that still.

My certainty feels, on some level, like a betrayal. Of Ann's truth, of Holly's truth, of the truths of girls and women. Because twenty years after child sexual abuse was finally yanked out from under the rug of denial in America—twenty years after an act of Congress first mandated teachers and therapists to report suspected cases of child abuse, and first funded child abuse treatment programs—there is, in fact, a war being waged not between North and South, NLF and GI's, but between belief and disbelief. It is raging in the media and in the courts and in therapists' offices and in families, as it raged, for eight years, in mine.

The very same newspapers and magazines that once published my articles, and others, about the prevalence and devastation of incest; the very same talk shows that once lauded the courage of incest survivors and their therapists, now bristle with outraged "exposés" of families being torn apart by "false claims of sexual abuse." A father accused by his daughter of molestation, and his partner, an advocate of pedophilia, have invented a "syndrome" and named an organization after it: the False Memory Syndrome Foundation. The FMSF defends fathers like Gary Ramona against their daughters' accusations, and brings charges against therapists for "implanting false memories." The feminist-led movement to stop sexual brutality in families—once recognized as life-saving—is now being mocked, discredited, compared to the Salem witch hunts. Every accused father is portrayed as an innocent victim, burned at the stake by his misguided, suggestible daughter and her manipulative, greedy therapist.

In my morning newspaper, a column by the ever-liberal, normally pro-feminist Jon Carroll, called "Are You Nuts, Or Just in Denial?": "In the vast world of pop-psych repressed-memory handbooks, almost anything can be a sign of childhood sexual abuse. . . . You may have one or more of these symptoms, and yet you sincerely believe that you were not abused as a child. Clearly, you are in denial. Next week: breathing, a key sign of incest."

And also, in my morning newspaper: daily reports on the trial, initiated by Gary Ramona, against the therapists who treated his daughter when she was hospitalized, twice, in an institution not unlike Napa State Hospital. A trial in which blown-up renderings of Holly Ramona's ripped hymen and accounts of Holly Ramona's inability to eat mayonnaise, yogurt, or whole bananas are pitted against expert testimony that it is physiologically impossible for a human being to forget, and then later remember, half a lifetime of forced oral sex and rape. A trial in which therapists are being sued—successfully, it turned out—for affirming what they believed to be their patient's reality, and a mother is discredited for believing her daughter.

A trial I am drawn to, a trial I put down my work for and drive an hour to the town of Napa in order to attend.

Why?

Because I want to know: Is it possible for "the truth" to be neither black nor white but gray? Is it possible that "the truth" lies unexplored, buried in the vast realm between "memory" and "feeling," between "real" and "imagined"?

Yes, in part—but I didn't think a trial would answer these questions.

Because my lover was sexually abused? Because our culture is disbelieving women and children again, and therefore my lover is having more trouble than ever, these days, believing herself and being believed? Because, despite my wavering ability to ward off the onslaught and provide the steady support she deserves, I still want to be my lover's hero; still want to slay the dragons of disbelief for her?

Yes, in part. Even as I worry that my own questioning might add fuel to their misogynist fire.

Because I am outraged by the False Memory Syndrome Foundation, by the backlash against women and children that has spawned and fosters that organization and its philosophy? Because I am terrified about the damage that will be done—to my lover, to me, to the untold abused children who need to be believed in order to be healed—if this poison should be allowed to reinfiltrate our culture's bloodstream?

Yes, in part.

Because there was a time when I could easily imagine my own father joining that organization, dragging me and my therapists into court, putting me on the witness stand and having his lawyer ask me . . .

What actually happened to you?

Is your father the guilty one, or are you?
What are you doing here?

During the morning break in the trial, I step into the hallway to get a drink of water. A young boy steps away from the fountain, trips, and nearly falls. "Careful, son," calls one of the men from the False Memory Syndrome Foundation. "You'll get hurt. Then the next thing we know, you'll be having flashbacks and recovered memories!" The boy turns to face the man, his face miming shock and horror. "Oh!" he exclaims dramatically. "I'm having a flashback!" The boy and the men who have witnessed his performance break into laughter. I slink back into the courtroom.

During the afternoon break I'm sitting in my seat taking notes on my Powerbook, writing down some things I learned from a defense witness about recovered memory, things I want to share with Ann when I get home tonight. A shadow falls across my screen. I look up into the grinning face of Gary Ramona.

"Is that a Macintosh?" he asks, his smile widening. I am suddenly aware of the V-necked blouse I'm wearing, of the view it affords Gary Ramona as he stares down at me from his standing position. I sit up straight, throw my shoulders back, glare up at him, and nod curtly. "Is that the mouse?" he asks, reaching out to touch the computer in my lap. I yank it away from him, move as far from him in my seat as I can. I close my computer, put it on the seat next to mine. "Are you a reporter?" he asks. "Here for a newspaper? A TV station? A magazine?"

I shake my head and stand up to face Gary Ramona. I'm surprised to realize that I'm taller than he is.

"It's none of your business what I'm doing here," I say.

BREAST CANCER ACTION

On my desk there's a wicker basket. In the wicker basket, along with bills to be paid, receipts for things I've bought and might still return, and the shopping list for the cabin, there are three unfilled prescriptions. One is dated two months ago: the yeast infection I ended up treating with vinegar instead. One is from a year ago, when an eye exam proved what the blurry type swimming on the page had already made clear: I needed reading glasses. "You're forty-two. Right on schedule," the gray-haired ophthalmologist smiled; but I disagreed and never filled it. The third prescription is six months old. That one's for a mammogram.

On the prescription form, beneath the column of boxes where my doctor, Janet, checked "Mammogram," there's a line labeled "Indication for Exam." There Janet wrote "Fibrocystic" and, in medical code I learned to decipher many mammograms and one lumpectomy ago, "Fhx Breast CA." *Family history, breast cancer.* Every year when I read my mammogram prescription, I wonder about the purpose of the shorthand. Is it to spare Janet a few milliseconds of scribbling time? Or to spare me the lurch I feel every time I read it?

Janet wrote the prescription automatically when I went in for my physical last January, as each of my doctors has done every January for the past eight years. My "Fhx Breast CA"—my mother's premenopausal bout with breast cancer in 1977—convinced my first doctor that age thirty-six was none too soon to start me on a regimen of annual mammograms. "This will be your baseline," she explained. "All the others will be compared to this one." In that moment I saw my future spread out before me in a growing stack of X-rays in manila folders: one a year, every year, for the rest of my life. Going for that first mammogram felt routine, not so scary. It seems incredible now, but only eight years ago I didn't know anyone besides my mother who'd had breast cancer. Then the technician came back after the first round of X-rays and told me she needed to take a few more. "Did I move? Are they blurry?" I croaked hopefully. "Just a little shadow the radiologist wants another look at," she answered, and then added, "Nothing to worry about, really."

As it turned out, there *was* nothing for me to worry about, that time. But what there is to worry about every January has become more worrisome each year—especially now that more and more friends my age, and younger, are being diagnosed; and most especially since January 1991, when my best friend Wendy had a mastectomy and my doctor found a lump in my breast. This winter, as my checkup appointment approached and the familiar anxiety buildup began, another feeling—*resistance*—grew around it, like kudzu engulfing a tree. *Do I really need to go through this?* The controversy about mammograms for women under fifty was taking up front-page space in the newspapers and endless hours on talk radio. Nothing I'd read or heard had convinced me that I didn't need an annual mammogram, but I hadn't been convinced that I did need one, either. A few days before my appointment with Janet, I pulled out my breast cancer file and reread the articles and brochures I'd stuffed into it.

The National Women's Health Network says mammograms are unnecessary and inaccurate for women under fifty—they miss real tumors and identify false ones; and the accumulated radiation from all those mammograms might even *cause* cancer, later. *Mother Jones* says overuse of mammograms is a plot by General Electric and DuPont to sell mammography machines and X-ray film. The American Cancer Society and the AMA say the new machines emit only low-level radiation; even in women my age, mammograms find malignancies that manual breast exams can't.

Also in the file: from the Women's Cancer Resource Center two blocks from my house, flyers advertising Toxic Links meetings, grief groups, support groups for African-American women with cancer and lesbians with cancer, and a petition demanding that the American Cancer Society "confront corporate polluters." A brochure for the Women and Cancer Walk for Our Lives that happened in Golden Gate Park two months ago. I meant to go but didn't—somehow the date passed me by.

From *The Boston Globe,* September 1994: Ellen Goodman's column about the discovery of the "breast cancer gene." "Only 5 percent [of breast cancers] are caused by the newly discovered gene. It will take a year or two before there is a way to test for it. So this is what we have been waiting for. Now we wait for the cure." From the *San Francisco Chronicle,* July 1995: "New Study Finds No Breast Cancer Risk From Estrogen Therapy." "Less than a month after researchers reported that taking estrogen may increase the risk of breast cancer, a new study indicates that there is no such danger."

Eat organic broccoli, breast-feed your babies, demonstrate for a cure, the consumer advocates and feminists say. *Check your breasts once a month, have a mammogram every year,* the medical establishment says. Politically I have no trouble choosing between the *Mother Jones* perspective and the AMA's. But medically—which do I want to trust my life to? I've always believed that taking care of myself means facing the risk head-on: a breast exam with Janet every three months, a mammogram every January. Now I wonder if taking care of myself means doing exactly the opposite: taking a break from the annual dose of radiation, and the daily dose of fear.

"I'm thinking of going longer between mammograms this time," I tell Janet at the end of my exam, as she hands me the prescription. She looks up from the notes she's making in my chart. I just know what she's thinking. "This cancer-phobe who insists on having her breasts checked even when she comes in with the flu, the one who holds her breath through six or seven breast exams every year and gets deliriously chatty as soon as they're over—this woman wants to put off her mammogram?" "For how long?" Janet asks.

"I was thinking maybe eighteen months," I answer. "I hate to expose myself to all that radiation—especially if there's no good reason to do it. Mammograms aren't that accurate for women my age, are they?" Janet shakes her head. "The radiation is minimal," she says. "But you're right—breast tissue is denser in women under fifty, so there's a higher rate of false positives and false negatives.

"Also—mammograms don't seem to improve mortality in women

your age," she says. "There's a new study that compared the survival rates of women who had routine mammography throughout their forties to women who didn't. It found no significant difference."

I take a deep breath, struggle to make sense of this new bad news. "You mean even if a mammogram finds a tumor early, it's just as likely to kill me as a tumor I don't find till it's big enough to feel as a lump?" Janet nods. "I guess you have to weigh the peace of mind you'd get from putting off your mammogram against the peace of mind you'd get from having one," she says. I stare at the Berkeley Women's Health Collective poster on the wall behind her head. Janet glances at her watch, then back at me.

"Meredith . . . ," she says gently. "I know your mother's history makes you nervous. I know the statistics are really scary. I can't tell you how frustrating it is for me as a doctor—and a feminist—to watch this disease eating up so many women's lives. But as bad as the statistics are, as bad as this epidemic is—you still only have a one in six chance of getting breast cancer. There's a five in six chance you *won't*. It's still a matter of *if*, not when. Maybe it would help you to try and see it that way." She stands up, hands me the bill. "I know there's a lot of confusing information out there," she says. "Why don't you get another opinion? Call Barry Gardner. Breast surgery is all he does these days. He's always up on the latest research."

"Good idea," I say. "Thanks." Janet nods and pulls the door closed behind her. I sit on the edge of the examining table with the prescription and the bill in my hand. Janet is right: for years I've been feeling victimized—at times, nearly immobilized—by a disease I don't yet have. I've come to see breast cancer as the parentheses around the sentence of my life, the inevitable unhappy ending to my story, however happily I might try to write it.

I wasn't the only one who was responding to the epidemic this way: Since her aunt died of breast cancer five years ago, my friend Zoe fights the thought, *Why bother? I'm going to die of breast cancer anyway* every time she fights a career crisis or depression. Rochelle, who has her breasts examined by her doctor as compulsively as I do, says her breast cancer anxiety would slam the brakes on her life if she let it. "The more successful I get," she told me, "the more scared of breast cancer I get. It's as if breast cancer is the punishment I deserve for breaking the rules, being a woman who gets what she wants. It makes me want to hide, become invisible, so breast cancer won't know where to find me."

Other friends have the opposite reaction to the same fear. "My mother used to talk to me as though I was doomed because she had premenopausal breast cancer," Meg said. "That really pissed me off. I thought, 'I'll be damned if I'll assume I'm gonna die.' But I'm so determined not to dwell on it that I actually missed my last couple of mammograms. The whole thing's too scary to think about—so I don't." And when Wendy discovered a lump in each of her breasts, five years after her first bout with cancer, she put off her exams and then her biopsy, shoved her fear away, managed to believe that it wouldn't be bad, not this time, not her, not again—until the moment she awoke to the surgeon standing somberly beside her hospital bed.

I want to take care of myself, I thought, as I shrugged off the thin cotton gown. *I want to love my body, not fear it.* I looked down at my small but still-healthy breasts, ran a finger across one nipple, then the other. I shivered with pleasure, then dread. I pulled on my jeans and T-shirt, and left Janet's office. *And the more I learn, the less I know about how to do that.*

I went home and put the prescription on my desk—not in the wicker basket, where I might forget about it for a while. I looked at it every day for a week and then I called Barry Gardner. His number was still in my Rolodex, where I'd written it four years ago, when he removed the lump from my right breast. Barry didn't remember me, of course—all those women, all those breasts, all those lumps—but I sure did remember him. The last thing I'd said to him, after he'd pronounced my lump benign, was, "Hope I never talk to you again."

Barry's nurse put me through to him right away. "Up to age fifty, every eighteen months is fine," he said. "Even with a family history of breast cancer?" I asked him. "How many relatives, and which ones?" "Just my mother," I said, thinking of the women I know with grandmothers and aunts and sisters who have died—and of the women like Meg's mother, who have their breasts amputated preventatively because so many women in their families have died. "Every eighteen months is fine, then. No problem," he repeated, in the oddly jovial tone I'd found so comforting four years ago.

"You're in good hands, now, Meredith," Barry said the day he examined my breasts for the first time, his big, clean-scrubbed hand, in fact, nearly covering both of mine. "No matter what this is, we'll handle it together. You'll be okay, one way or the other. I'll see to that." *What a weird job he has,* I thought that day. Trying to convince half the women he sees not to let breast cancer fear rule their lives; breaking the news to the other half that breast cancer is threatening theirs. Empowering women by wresting their lives back from cancer's grip; infantilizing women by giving them this big competent Daddy to turn their worries over to.

"Great," I said. "I guess I'll put it off for a while, then. Thanks, Barry." But when I put the phone down, I didn't feel great. I felt alone and scared. All the years I'd spent in the Berkeley Women's Health Collective, passing out plastic speculums and marching for legalized abortion, fighting for women's right to control our own bodies—and now I had to admit I wanted someone else to control mine. I wanted Barry to distill all the conflicting study results and confusing expert opinions and *just tell me what to do.* I wanted him to give me a prescription for breast cancer prevention, to take away my fear the way he'd taken away my lump.

Admitting what I wanted from Barry didn't make me stop wanting it, but it didn't make it possible either. So I summoned my politics up from the swamp of my fear and gave myself the same advice I'd given all the patients at the Women's Free Clinic twenty years ago: make your own decisions, take charge of your own care. I opened my date book to July 15, wrote "Get mammogram" in red ink, and dropped the prescription into the wicker basket on my desk.

For the next six months I ignored the prescription, but I couldn't ignore the raging of the epidemic. Reading a conference brochure, I learned that Joanne, whose son is Peter's age, now lists herself as a therapist, author, and breast cancer survivor. From a mutual friend I learned that Regina—fellow member, twenty years ago, of the Berkeley Women's Health Collective, fellow Berkeley High mom now; passionate vegetarian and nurse practitioner—had just finished chemo and radiation. My mother called to tell me that her best friend had died, leaving behind a daughter my age. "Are you getting your mammograms? Are you checking your breasts?" my mother asked, her worry humming through the wire. And of course there was Wendy, whose breast cancer history was following her into the future—first, robbing her body's ability to birth a baby; now, making her an undesirable candidate to adopt one.

And I couldn't ignore the invitation to a benefit for Breast Cancer Action, an advocacy group based in San Francisco, that appeared in my mailbox: "In solidarity with breast cancer survivors . . . In honor of the women we've lost . . . In order to expose the link between environmental pollutants and breast cancer—Sponsored by *Mother Jones* and featuring Bella Abzug," so I paid my $75 and took my two breasts and went. I stood in the sculpture garden of a trendy San Francisco gallery, chatting with wealthy donors and one-breasted activists, dipping baby zucchinis into nonfat hummus, sipping nitrite-free California wine from a paper cup and listening to Bella Abzug—herself recovering from a recent mastectomy—telling us things that I, for one, didn't want to know. That breast cancer now kills 46,000 American women a year—one woman every eleven minutes; more than one in four of the women who get it. That in the last thirty years, the breast cancer rate has doubled in the United States and quadrupled among women my age in Northern California—"The breast cancer capital," according to the World Health Organization, "of the world."

"Thirty-one years ago," Bella barked, her hand smacking the lectern in time with her words, "the WHO acknowledged that eighty percent of cancers come from human-made carcinogens. But to this day the cancer industry is still focused on the small percentage of breast cancers that come from known risk factors, like the five percent that are inherited and the twenty percent or so that come from high-fat diets, having kids late or not at all, things like that. They've barely begun to address the causes of the other seventy-five percent—the cancers that come from the pesticides we spray on our lawns and the bleach we use to scour our sinks."

Wait a minute, I thought. *The* five percent *that are inherited?* All the worrying I've done because my mother had breast cancer; all the times I've reassured myself that I had my kids young, stopped eating meat, grow my own broccoli—all that adds up to *twenty-five percent* of what will cause me to get or prevent me from getting breast cancer? *So the good news is, I'm not at much greater risk than other women because my mother had breast cancer. And the bad news is, I'm not at much greater risk than other women because my mother had breast cancer.* We're *all* at risk, whether we get mammograms once a year, once a decade, or ever; whether we check our breasts once a month, once a year, or ever. We're at risk because we were born with breasts and we eat and clean our houses and breathe. How could I not have known this? And how can I take charge of my own breast health when seventy-five percent of it is outside my control?

"Pollution is profitable. Prevention isn't," Bella said. "So the cancer industry tells women to eat less fat and have mammograms every year, but they don't tell Dow to stop producing poisonous chemicals. We've got to change that—now! We've got to convince the government to fund prevention research—to keep women from getting breast cancer, instead of slashing, poisoning, and burning us once we've got it. We need a people's movement that's prepared to act.

"Will you join me?" Bella hollered. "YES!" the crowd answered. "Good. Get to it, then. Write your legislators. Write a check," Bella said. She pulled the broad-brimmed hat off her head, handed it to a woman wearing a Breast Cancer Action button, and sat down heavily, mopping her glistening forehead. As the hat circulated through the crowd, people pulled wallets from their pockets and checkbooks from their purses. I dropped a dollar into the hat and drove home alone, more disturbed than inspired. *Another battle I don't have the time or energy or money to fight.*

A few days after the benefit I showed up for my volunteer stint at Berkeley High, where my co-volunteer Sally and I spend every other Tuesday morning handing out hall passes to visitors and rebuffing kids' pleas to use the office phone. "What's new?" I asked Sally, after we'd locked our bags in the principal's closet. She gave me a long look. "I assumed you'd heard," she said. "I found out last week—I have breast cancer."

"Oh, Sally," I said. I leaned toward her. She pulled away. "I'm lucky," she said. "My doctor says my tumor is the most treatable type, the best kind to have." "That's good," I said, following her lead. "My mother died of breast cancer when she was forty-eight—two years older than I am now," Sally went on. "So I've been having mammograms every year since I turned forty. That's how I found my tumor." The familiar panic clutched at my throat. *I'll get a mammogram tomorrow.* I fought it back down. *I've got to get off this roller coaster. I've got to find a better way to deal with this disease.* "It was so small and deep, my doctor says if I hadn't had the mammogram, I wouldn't have been able to feel it until it was much bigger."

I remembered what Janet had said: *"Mammograms don't improve mortality in women your age."* And I remembered the interview I'd heard when I was listening to NPR in the car the other day: Dr. Susan Love, the breast cancer expert whose book I clung to in the days before my biopsy. "The notion of early detection is really wishful thinking," she said. "We wish it would work, but it doesn't. We've sold this idea that cancer goes from a grain of sand to a pea to a grapefruit, and if you find it when it's a grain of sand, you're in good shape. But in some women it starts out as a grapefruit; it was never a grain of sand.

"It's not evil for women to do breast self-exams. And every woman over fifty should be getting a mammogram every year or two—I wouldn't start before forty. But we should be putting our money into finding a method of early detection that really works: a blood test or something like that."

"It's good you found it early," I told Sally, feeling like I was parroting outdated propaganda. The breast self-exam, early-detection-can-save-your-life posters were still plastered everywhere—in BART stations, the women's bathrooms in gay bars, the women's locker room at the Y. But now their promise seemed hollow, their optimism cruel. *We really are working without a net.* "Is there anything I can do to help?" I asked. "Depending on how the treatments go, I might have to miss a few Tuesdays," Sally said. "Can you handle this job alone if I don't show up?"

Of course I could, I said, but as it turned out, I never had to. Sally scheduled her treatments for Tuesday afternoons so she could put in her time at Berkeley High and have time to recover in between. And then school was out, so Sally and I didn't see each other anymore, and then it was July and time for me to make my decision, again.

That's where I sit right now: at my desk, with my date book opened to the red-lettered command—"Get mammogram!" Trying to find a way to live without breast cancer, and live with the breast cancer epidemic, again. I try to visualize myself doing what some part of me still believes is the right thing to do, the self-protective thing to do: riding my bike down Broadway to the Imaging Center, where the high-risk women like me must go, offering one breast and then the other to be clamped between the jaws of the machine. I think back to the day last year when I did that. It was January 5, exactly one year after the mammogram before. After the first set of X-rays, the tech came back into the room and said the films showed "a new calcification" in the left breast and a "thickening" in the right. "The calcification doesn't look like cancer," she said evenly. "And the thickening in the right breast might just be the scar tissue from your biopsy." She led me back to the machine, lifted my right breast onto the cold metal shelf, clamped it tightly, told me not to breathe. I heard the whir and click of the machine. "Okay," she said, and came out from behind it.

"Do you ever feel like you're on the front lines of a war?" I blurted as she reached for my left breast. *What a melodramatic thing to say,* I scolded myself, but she answered without hesitation. "That's exactly how I feel," she said. "I've been doing mammograms for twelve years. Every year we diagnose more malignancies. Every year the women come in here more afraid. And who can blame them? It *is* like a war—and we're losing it." She took her position behind the machine, told me not to breathe, then said "Okay" again. "The radiologist will be in to talk to you soon," she said. "Try not to worry. I really think you're okay."

I was okay, and I savored the real or imagined security of the postmammogram moment—until I got home and listened to the message on my machine. "Sorry to tell you this way," a stranger's voice said. "But Deborah Weinstein died yesterday."

Deborah. Deborah and Ann and I had spent a blissful weekend at a Zen retreat just last summer, after her third recurrence, lolling naked beside the waterfall, her one breast and our four breasts browning in the mountain sun. I'd always known Deborah was likely to die, but in that moment all I knew was how much I didn't want her to. I sat and cried for Deborah, for her five-year-old daughter, for the tragedy of this epidemic. I wanted to wail the names of all the friends and heroines whose voices I have relied upon and cannot hear anymore, and the names of all the faceless, one-breasted women whose voices never will be heard. But I didn't wail. I called Ann at work and told her that my mammogram was okay. And then I told her that Deborah was dead.

Later that night we were lying in bed, numb and sleepless, watching Mary Tyler Moore reruns when a news break interrupted the laugh track. The announcer said that President Clinton's mother, Virginia Clinton

Kelley, had just died of breast cancer. "I wish they'd find a cure for this fucking disease already!" I cried. And then Ann and I cried together.

Now it's a year and a half later, and there's still no cure, and a cure isn't all I'm wishing for. Not just a cure but prevention. Not just early detection but prevention. Not just broccoli and breast-feeding, but the kind of mass movement that can force the "cancer industry," as the Breast Cancer Action brochure says, to change its loyalties and its priorities. And for me, right now: *a better way to deal with this disease.* I stare at the prescription in my hand, trying to decide who to call. The high-risk clinic for a mammogram appointment? Janet for a manual exam appointment? Barry, or Wendy, or my therapist, for advice? I dig through my breast cancer file and find the number for Breast Cancer Action. Its founder, Nancy Evans, answers the phone.

"My mother had premenopausal breast cancer," I tell her. "I'm forty-three. I'm trying to decide when to have my next mammogram, and I don't know who or what to believe. Do you have any suggestions?" "We do recommend annual mammograms for women over fifty," Nancy says. "The jury's still out on mammography for women your age, but with a family history the majority opinion still favors mammography every year or two. Mostly we advise women to be as well informed as possible. Read Susan Love's book and as much of the literature as you can. Get doctors' opinions. And definitely—talk to other women in your situation."

"I'm a feminist," I say. "I believe in making my own health care decisions. I don't want to be in denial, and I don't want to go on feeling powerless about this disease. But I don't want to spend my whole life in medical libraries or doctors' offices either."

"It's tough," Nancy agrees. "I was a medical writer when I was diagnosed, so I had access to the latest research. I was lucky; so many women don't even have access to basic medical care. Still, knowing what I know now, I'm not sure I made the best decisions. My tumor was discovered through mammography when I was fifty-two. You could say I'm a mammography success story—the tumor was small, with no lymph node involvement. On the other hand, it's possible that my previous twelve years of annual mammograms contributed to the growth of my tumor. Knowing what I know now, I'm not sure I would have had the mammograms during my forties. But you can't go back."

"I'm trying to face the reality without being overwhelmed by the fear," I say. "Breast cancer terror is an epidemic of its own," Nancy says. "All the media attention has been good in some ways—it's informed women and policy makers and helped get resources focused on the problem. But it's also raised the anxiety level. Women with family histories are getting their breasts cut off. Other women are falling into the voodoo syndrome: if you read about it or think about it, you'll get it. That's dangerous, too.

"It's a crapshoot either way," she says. "Maybe you'll get a mammogram when you're forty-three and find a tumor early. Maybe you'll get too many mammograms and you'll end up with a tumor you might not otherwise have had. The best thing you can do is improve your general health: exercise, eat well, find ways to relieve stress. By doing that, you'll reduce your risk factors for breast cancer as well as heart disease, and other diseases that affect women as we age."

Nancy was silent for a moment. "The bottom line is, there just aren't any sure things in life."

I guess that's the one sure thing in life, I think as I thank Nancy for her time and hang up the phone. *And I guess* that's *what I need to find a better way to deal with.* It strikes me that breast cancer is much like the other risks and fears known to women: running our fingers over our breasts in the shower, getting into a car with a man on a first date, walking down a city street at night—we take chances. And what choice do we have? Either we let fear narrow the perimeters of our lives—perimeters we spent the last twenty-five years fighting to expand—or we face the danger, protect ourselves as much as possible, and then *go on.* Go on and live—as well, as long, as fearlessly, and as powerfully as we can.

Last time I walked around the corner to the Women's Cancer Resource Center to browse through their research files, I copied down a quote by Jackie Winnow, a lesbian writer I knew who died of breast cancer in 1989. "We have to stop being nice girls and start fighting as though our lives depended on it. Because they do." That day I also picked up the latest newsletter of WomenCARE, the nonprofit support agency Wendy co-founded after her mastectomy. On page one was a speech Wendy gave at a fundraising event, a speech I didn't even know she'd given. "Some New Age psychologies would have us believe cancer is a gift," she wrote. "Personally, I think cancer sucks. But I do believe that how we cherish and stand up for ourselves and each other is the gift. As the mineworkers' organizer, Mother Jones, said, 'Pray for the dead and fight like hell for the living!' "

Fight like hell for the living. What would it mean to do that? I still long for the comfort of believing that there's a "right" choice to be made and a reward to be reaped from making it. I still lean toward the familiar roller-coaster ride of fear and relief, relief and fear—but I know now that living with this epidemic means one is as delusional as the other. I don't want to careen around and around, up and down anymore. I want to go forward, as steadily as I can.

I call the clinic and make an appointment to have a mammogram in two weeks. Then I call the Women's Cancer Resource Center and make an appointment to come by and talk about what I can do to help. And then I put the mammogram prescription back into the wicker basket and go back to work.

HUNGRY

I'm strapped to a cold metal table. Flat on my back. My bones ache everywhere they meet the metal—hips, spine, shoulder blades, skull. My innards are bursting with the fluid that has been pumped into me, the barium that appears now on the monitor just above my head as a white river running through the convoluted gray labyrinth of my intestines. A moment ago my mind was still too occupied with the outcome of this procedure to focus on what was happening to my body. Now I can focus on nothing else.

"Turning now," the lab tech announces. The table groans and tips me upside down, heels over head, barium and blood rushing to my brain. "Don't breathe," she says, stepping behind her machinery. I hear the whir and then the click of the X-ray machine. "Turning again," she says. Now I am upright but still strapped to the table, like an insect specimen pinned to a board. "I-need-to-go-to-the—" I spit through clenched teeth. "That's just the barium," the tech says flatly, her eyes on the monitor, hands on the controls. "We'll get you to the bathroom in just a few minutes. Hold your breath now." Whir and click; the table levels again. The tech unfastens the restraints at my ankles. I spring up, poised to leap off the table. She puts her hand against my shoulder. "Lie on your right side, please," she commands me. "Just a few more pictures."

I want to scream at the tech; at the pathologist who waits, watching through the cloudy window, to read my X-rays; at the doctor who sent me here, who surely could have recommended a more humane lab than this one, a table with some padding maybe, a tech with a little compassion. *It's no one's fault but your own,* I reprimand myself. No one would have strapped me to this table if I myself had not complained: first to Ann; then to Barbara, my acupuncturist; and then, when months of acupuncture and conscious breathing and massage and positive visualization had failed to cure me, to my doctor; and finally, at her insistence, to the gastroenterologist, Dr. Rand. I wasn't bruised or limping; there was no lump or lesion, no visible evidence that for the past year my stomach has been hurting nearly all the time. That I've been waking every morning with a knot of pain below my breastbone; that I can tell time by the location of that pain as it works its way down to my abdomen by night. That I often find drops of bright red blood in the toilet.

But once the words were spoken, the symptoms named, there was no choice but to proceed, to surrender my body to the whirring machine of Western medicine. No choice, that is, other than to go on living with the pain—and the fear. "First we'll rule out the, um, most serious possibilities," Dr. Rand told me at my first visit two weeks ago. He'd glanced at my chart, listened without question or comment to my list of symptoms, cursorily palpated my midsection, then led me back to his office where he faced me across his vast, cluttered desk. "Then, after that, we'll—" "What are—what *is* the most serious possibility?" I interrupted him. "There's no family history, and you're young, so it's very unlikely—" he said. *Young?* I thought. *I haven't been young for twenty years.* Then I remembered what I'd learned from all the books I'd been reading: for this disease, yes, young. Most people get it when they're in their fifties or older. "Colon cancer," he said, glancing at his watch, then standing to usher me out of his office. "That would be the first thing we'd want to rule out."

It certainly would be. Which is why I was willing to undergo the ordeal that "ruling it out" entails: a two-day fast (as yet unbroken), which induced not only the predictable ravenous hunger but also: inexplicable tears, a pleasant, spacey high, pounding headaches, and sudden rushes of rage. Then, at six this morning, a self-administered enema; followed by a visit to Dr. Rand, who silently explored my emptied insides with a lighted probe; and finally a trip to the lab across the street for a barium enema.

Which Dr. Rand had said might cause me "some slight discomfort"—an understatement so colossal that it destroyed his credibility as a sensate human being. Whatever the results of this awful test, I tell myself as the X-rays and the minutes click by, I am going to have to find myself another specialist.

"All finished," the tech says, releasing me. Dizzy, doubled over with cramps, I stumble to the bathroom, where I sit shivering and expelling air and barium for the next twenty minutes. As the pain subsides, I focus again on the reason for it: the diagnosis. I find Ann in the waiting room, where I'd left her. She jumps up, puts her arms around me. "Was it awful?" she asks. I'd seen my face—the color of barium—in the bathroom mirror, so I don't bother answering. "Let's go find the radiologist," I say. Ann nods; she knows my plan. When I left Dr. Rand this morning, he said he'd call me in a day or two, after he'd had a chance to read and analyze the lab report. *A day or two? Doesn't this guy get it at all?* "I don't want to wait that long for the results," I said. "I'll just stay at the lab after the test and talk to the radiologist myself." Dr. Rand frowned and shook his head. "They'll only release the results to me. You'll just have to be patient." I knew there was no point in arguing with him. I'd just have to use the same rude, effective strategy I used three years ago after my breast lump was mammogrammed, then sonogrammed, at this same lab: ask politely to see the radiologist, then refuse to leave the premises, if necessary, until my request is granted. I find it's easier the second time around: I know which door the radiologist hides behind.

"I'd like to see my X-rays," I say firmly when she answers my knock. She mutters a few words of protest but steps aside as Ann and I walk past her into the room. I see a series of X-rays with my name on them clipped to the light box. "The results are inconclusive," the radiologist says. She points to some dark splotches on the film. "These don't look like tumors, but they could be polyps. Or fecal matter. Did you fast and purge the way you were supposed to? This isn't a clean study. You'll need to take the test again."

Take the test again? No way. This is the one outcome I'd not imagined: neither bad news nor good. I notice, though, that my body, which doesn't lie, has relaxed with relief. Even as my mind races to cover every angle, spewing out questions, barely waiting for the radiologist's answers, a calm, certain message comes up from inside. *I don't have colon cancer. I have to work on this problem some other way.*

A few days later I carry my X-rays and chart to a new gastroenterologist. I want a second opinion, a white-jacketed confirmation that it's safe for me to stop the search for a medical solution. Dr. Wylie greets me warmly, tells his secretary to hold his calls. He spends an hour taking my history, reading every lab test and note in my chart, asking me detailed, sympathetic questions. He confirms that there is no tumor on my colon. He says the splotches on the X-rays are unlikely to be polyps. He agrees it's not necessary for me to take another barium enema. Already, I feel better.

Dr. Wylie is quite certain that I have irritable bowel syndrome, for which the cure is neither drugs nor surgery but what he refers to as "lifestyle adjustments." He asks about my sleep patterns, stress factors, exercise routine. Nothing suspect there: I sleep well most nights; feel good about my life; work out three times a week.

Then he asks me about my diet.

"Healthy," I say. "Very healthy."

"And by 'healthy,' you mean . . ." he prompts me.

"Vegetarian," I say, a trifle smugly. "I mean, I do eat sweets—too often, I guess. But I eat lots of whole grains, vegetables, fruit—you know, healthy."

Dr. Wylie gazes at me through his bifocals. The chronic pain in my belly dissolves into queasiness—a familiar signal that my mind thinks I'm telling the truth but my body knows better. Suddenly I imagine that this kind man can see through my facile self-assessment the way the X-rays bored through my bones. That he knows the truth, my secrets: How I feel about food. How I feel about my body. How I eat. And just how "healthy" that really is.

"I, um, don't always eat breakfast," I murmur.

Dr. Wylie gazes at me steadily.

"Well, never. I never eat breakfast."

He nods knowingly.

"Actually I usually eat one meal a day. Lunch or dinner, depending on what—what's happening that day." *Depending on what the scale says in the morning when I step onto it, holding my breath and waiting to see what kind of day I deserve to have.*

One twenty-three: *You've been good; you can have a little fun today. Go ahead, celebrate—pick up that pint of Chocolate Fudge Brownie.* One twenty-five: *You just wouldn't listen when I told you to put that ice cream away last night. Now look what you've done.* One twenty-seven: *Bad, bad, bad. You're out of control completely! And you've got that business lunch today. No dinner for you tonight—unless you want to weigh one twenty-eight tomorrow. And who knows how much the day after that!*

"Breakfast is the most—" Dr. Wylie begins.

"I know, I know," I interrupt him. "The most important meal of the day."

"If you know that," he says, "I wonder why you never eat it."

Because I want to weigh less tomorrow than I did today.

I remember exactly when I stopped eating breakfast. It was the summer of 1982, when I decided to change my life. I was thirty-one. I hadn't had a baby for two years, but I still weighed 135, twenty pounds more than my prepregnancy weight. Every time I looked in the mirror, I saw myself as I'd been when I was nine months pregnant with Peter: *one hundred and eighty-five pounds.* I saw my eyes, chin, cheekbones sunken into the bloated balloon of my face. The dimpled, loose flesh hanging from my thighs and upper arms. The rolling mountain range of my postpartum stomach. The unforgiving face of the scale, which reported dispassionately upon my return from the hospital that even after delivering a seven-pound baby and consuming nothing more caloric than ice chips, Jell-O, and bouillon all that postsurgical week, I still had fifty-three pounds to lose. *Fifty-three pounds!*

"Eating for two" (or in my case, for twenty-two) had given me the excuse I needed to relax my vigilance, indulge my long-suppressed hunger, surrender at last to my demon lover: food. And what a price I'd paid. My mother's warning had finally come true. "Your father was skinny, like you, when he was a kid," my mother used to tell me. "Then when he was twenty, he got fat, practically overnight. And you have your father's body." Now that haunting image—my once-trim self trapped forever in my father's fat body—was staring back at me. *See what happens when you let yourself have what you want?*

It wasn't just the twenty pounds (and gaining) that made me decide to change my life. I hated living in San Jose, hated my Silicon Valley job, my marriage, my size-fourteen jeans, my inertia. Every morning I tried to come up with one thing I could look forward to that day; food was almost always it. A corporate lunch with co-workers at that all-you-can-eat Chinese buffet. The butter cream–frosted birthday cake we'd ordered for a secretary's birthday. The coffee ice cream in the freezer; the jar of hot fudge sauce in the fridge.

After four years of marriage counseling, our therapist prescribed a weekend apart. I spent it at my friend Leslie's apartment in San Francisco. Leslie gave me the secret recipe for her newly svelte body: three or four cups of fresh-ground decaf for "breakfast." A cup of low-fat cottage cheese with unsweetened applesauce to make it through to dinner. And dinner— I was tired of cooking those meat/starch/iceberg lettuce meals that Richard loved, the meals his mother (and mine) had served every night of our childhoods at precisely six o'clock. This, at least, I could do something about. I stopped buying roasts and chops, started buying fish and pasta. Stopped slathering butter on everything; stopped dragging Richard out for overpriced, overcooked restaurant meals every Saturday night; stopped settling down with Richard when the kids were finally asleep with a half-gallon of ice cream and two spoons.

Stopped settling down with Richard altogether. It was as if by setting my own food on the table, I had set my own discontented, newly determined self there, too. Without the consuming daily distraction of food to soften my jagged edges, without the smooth gloss of fat to coat my tongue, I could no longer deny that what I wanted more of was neither steak nor hot fudge. In November 1982 I quit my job and started writing for magazines. In March 1983 Richard and I separated. I fell in love with Ann, moved to Oakland; made a life I loved in Oakland—a life with plenty to look forward to besides food. Reached all those goals, and this one too: I was down to a hundred fifteen pounds. And one meal a day. People said I looked great, asked what my secret was. A few friends—all of them women, obviously just jealous—asked worriedly if I was eating enough. "Are you sure you're not getting too thin?" *Too thin!* "You're so skinny, your ribs are showing." *Skinny!* I ate it up.

And now, after ten years of watching my baseline weight creep up to

118, then 122, then 125—fighting every pound, depriving myself of more and more, longing to recapture "the old me" I continue to think of as "the real me," the 115-pound me—something is eating *me* up.

"I needed to lose a lot of weight after I had my kids," I tell Dr. Wylie. "I guess I got into some bad habits I haven't quite broken."

He nods. "This diet you've been on could certainly explain your symptoms," he says. *Diet? I don't go on diets—I'm a feminist! I know better! I just eat . . . lightly.*

"Having little or no food in your system for most of the day, then eating one big meal," he continues, "can really foul up the digestive process. I think if you start eating three healthy meals a day"—he peers at me intently—"three *full* meals a day—you'll feel better."

Three meals a day? I can barely stay at 125 on one meal a day!

For the past ten years, I have unthinkingly, unhesitatingly chosen being thin over being healthy. Now this doctor and my own body are telling me I need to make the opposite choice. To end this punishing relationship with food, this denial of my own hearty appetites. To actually live what my feminist principles and common sense dictate: to eat when I'm hungry, stop when I'm full, indulge the occasional craving, give my body and mind the fuel and the faith they need to do what they were designed to do. I contemplate this possibility now with longing, and terror. *Three meals a day. Not walking around hungry. Watching the numbers on the scale go up, and up, and up . . .*

"Are you worried about gaining weight?" Dr. Wylie asks. *Busted!* This is my double shame: not only am I in daily violation of feminism, obsessed with my weight, hatefully critical of my body, in slavish submission to the beauty myth—but I'm not even overweight enough to justify it. If I weighed 185 now, as I did fifteen years ago, Dr. Wylie would understand my fixation. He'd sympathize, suggest a weight loss program. He'd help me. But Dr. Wylie looks at me and sees an average woman, a fit woman, maybe even a thin woman. How can Dr. Wylie, how can anyone look at my five-foot-six, 125-pound body and understand the sinking of my heart, the roar of recrimination that fills my head on those dark mornings when the scale reads 126? Only I know how much better I'd look, how much better I'd feel, how much better I'd *be* if I just weighed ten pounds less.

How can I explain that my need to keep my hard-won title—Size Eight—is every bit as powerful as my craving was to earn it?

"Meredith?" he prods me. Then, gently, "I'm sure you know how dangerous it is to starve yourself. And how prevalent eating disorders are among women in this country. . . ."

"Of course I do!" I snap.

Of course I do.

I am a student of eating disorders, an eager reader of every magazine article on the subject, every news story, research study, and novel. I watch all those made-for-TV movies, every documentary and talk show, even the occasional after-school teenage special—publicly writhing with feminist outrage; privately hoping to pick up a useful weight-loss pointer or two.

I have two friends who tell me horror stories about their battles with bulimia as teenagers. Liza, who's thirty-five now, eats as heartily as any woman I know; if she's still worrying about her weight, she keeps it to herself. Stephanie, who's my age, still panics every time she gains half a pound.

But it's the stories my niece Josie tells me that chill me to the bone. Josie describes what goes on every day in the lunchroom of her expensive, exclusive girls' prep school: the girls who never eat, the girls who drink half a diet Coke for lunch every day, then run to the bathroom to vomit. Josie says that she and her friends, "the ones who don't have eating disorders," as they distinguish themselves, keep looking for ways to help their class-mates "without ratting on them."

"Sometimes we try showing them we care," Josie says. "We ask them if that's all they're having and offer them some of our food. Some days we try ignoring them, 'cause you never know—they might just be doing it to get attention. But nothing helps. They won't eat no matter what we do." Josie's friends, the girls who eat, constitute a minority group at their school. Last year more than half of her classmates were diagnosed with eating disorders. Nine out of thirty of them were hospitalized.

I've worried, too, about whether Josie truly has been spared—if she really is a "girl who eats," if she really is as different from her anorexic and bulimic classmates as those of us who love her might hope. Rail-thin, an exotic beauty, Josie worked as a model when she was twelve: posing in

bikinis and jeans for Macy's newspaper ads; smiling and biting into chocolate bars on Hershey's commercials. Josie's dream of becoming an actress
seemed to be coming true: she went out on local casting calls, performed
on an educational cable TV show. Then Josie hit fifteen and the phone
stopped ringing. Her agent told her that it happened to everyone, that
she'd reached "the awkward age," that she could start modeling again as
an adult when she was seventeen or eighteen.

Now, while she waits for "adulthood," while she tries to keep her
classmates from starving themselves to death, Josie bends herself double to
check for "flab" around her twenty-two-inch waist, and twists her head
around to peer disapprovingly at the backs of her lean, sinewy thighs. We
go to a restaurant for lunch; I order only a small salad myself because I
know I can count on her leftovers—because, like my teenage niece, I
wouldn't consider eating a whole sandwich for lunch. *Not unless I'm not
having dinner.*

Even the politically active, politically correct young feminists Peter
hangs out with—the Berkeley High public school girls whose mothers
threw away their bras and whose fathers fought the pigs at People's Park;
the girls who shun fashion, gender roles, and all things traditional—are
not immune. Lazing at the swimming hole near our cabin with Peter and
his friends one August afternoon, I wondered aloud, in a rare moment of
sleepy, sun-baked candor, what it would be like to eat, just eat, and not
worry about my weight for once.

"God, that sounds good," said Alexis, who is fifteen, lovely, curvy,
and far from fat. "I'm totally stressed out about my body. So are all my
friends. So's my mom, and she's *skinny.* I don't know a single girl or
woman who isn't obsessed with losing weight. It's the media's fault. All
those skinny models. I mean, just think about what the word *model* means!
We're all supposed to model ourselves on that image. And we do! It pisses
me off, the power they have to make us hate ourselves 'cause we don't look
like Cindy Crawford."

"But people like you and your friends, and your mom—and me—we
don't usually swallow media bullshit," I said. "Why do you think we
accept it when it comes to our bodies?"

"Because it's such a big secret," Alexis answered. "I only admit how
hung up I am about my weight to my best friends. My mom only admits
it to me. It's easy to keep it secret—everyone's so into health foods and

exercise these days, how do you know who's trying to be healthy for real, and who's just trying to get skinny? It's hard to fight back against something you're too embarrassed to talk about."

"Don't you think it's partly male attitudes?" Peter asked. "How can women stop trying to look like Cindy Crawford as long as guys are still trained to want them to look like that?"

"Partly," Alexis said. "But it's up to females to change it. We have to start loving our bodies and rejecting the brainwashing. But I don't know how we'll ever get strong enough to do that."

Am I strong enough to do that?

"What I'd like for you to do, Meredith," Dr. Wylie says now, "is to try eating three meals a day for a month. Then come see me, and we'll talk about how you're doing." He extends his hand across the desk. "Is it a deal?"

Only a month. Even if I gained, say, five pounds, I could always do a fast and lose at least three. . . .

"Deal," I say.

I head for home, determined to keep my end of the deal, determined to find an end to this pain. I stop at the health food store, buy cereal and bread for breakfast, hummus and pita bread for lunch *(lunch!),* fruit smoothies *(160 calories per eight-ounce serving, but no fat or sugar)* for in between. Jesse eyes the Kashi and Brown Rice Crispies I've added to the family cereal collection with suspicion, accuses me of trying to sneak healthy cereals into his diet as I've done, to no avail, in the past. "Relax," I tell him. "Those are for me." He looks unconvinced. I realize that Jesse has no reason to believe I might eat breakfast, that my sons have almost never seen me eat breakfast. When I make Sunday waffles, they know not to set a place for me at the table. I cook, don't eat. At dinnertime every night they ask if I'll be eating; when the answer is no—as it is about half the time—I don't need to explain. "Had a big lunch, Mom?" Peter says knowingly.

It occurs to me that if I were the mother of daughters—pain or no pain, colon cancer or no colon cancer—I would have had to deal with this obsession a lot sooner. I regret the message about women and self-acceptance and standards of beauty that my behavior conveys to my sons—who fret at times about their zits and their hair and their muscles and even their weight, although seemingly without suffering that peculiarly female anguish. But I simply could not have allowed myself to convey that message to daughters. I would have had to learn to live without the scale, without the weighing and measuring, the deprivation and self-condemnation. *Or would I have learned, instead, to hide how I feel and what I do about it?*

I start eating.

Week One.   The first thing I notice is how often I get hungry. How many times each day I've been lying to my body to keep myself from eating. *I do get hungry before noon. I do get hungry for dinner—even if I have had lunch.*

How harsh, how unloving was the lie—"You're not hungry, you're just bored," my mother used to say, and decades later I joined in the chorus: *It's not even ten o'clock yet; drink some decaf, and get your mind off your stomach.* How sweet and soothing is the cool hand laid now against my own fevered brow, this kindness of giving my body the nourishment it needs. *If you're hungry, I'll feed you.* This promise alone ungirds me. My belly softens; my breath deepens. The barricades are coming down, the barricades I erected against my own hunger, my own unkindness, my own need for kindness. . . .

Day Four.   *127!* I panic; eat nothing until dinner.

Day Five.   I force myself to eat; wonder if maybe a three-day fast would help cleanse my system.

Day Six.   *125.* Breathing again. *(124 would be better.)*

Week Two.   I realize how much more time and energy I have now that I don't begin each day planning my food intake for the next twelve hours, and end each day cataloging my failures. And how freeing it is, how simple and satisfying it is, to eat what I want when I want it.

Week Three.   My stomach only hurts first thing in the morning. After I've eaten breakfast, it hardly hurts at all. There's no blood in the toilet anymore. I call Dr. Wylie and move my follow-up appointment back a month. I want to continue this experiment awhile longer.

Week Four.   I absorb the information that although I'm no longer being chased around by my hunger; although I seem to have doubled my food intake (but maybe that's just perception; now that I'm not starving half the time, I'm not bingeing as often)—my weight seems to have stabilized at 125.

The bigger changes take longer to notice. But I do notice them. I'm not walking around waiting for someone to feed me anymore. I'm feeding myself. It's becoming easier—enjoyable, even—to spend time alone. My needs are turned more inward, less outward. I'm not walking around envying people who *just eat:* the commuters on BART chewing mouthfuls of muffins; friends eating pastries together at sidewalk cafés; my co-workers pulling hefty sandwiches and plastic-wrapped cookies out of grease-stained deli bags; my own children, scarfing pizzas and sundaes and chips *without weighing and measuring and planning and regretting. Just eating.* I begin to imagine that someday I might just eat, too.

I'm not walking around feeling deprived all the time. I'm not waiting for someone to give me a treat to reward me for my deprivations. I don't feel entitled to eat a scone because I didn't have dinner last night; I feel entitled to eat a scone because I want one, and eating one won't hurt me. *I'm contemplating the possibility that giving myself what I want won't hurt me.*

Believing my hunger changes everything. I stop assuming that what I want is wrong, too much, bad, inappropriate. I stop needing other people to blame for not getting it. I stop waiting for the great breast to descend from the heavens; I begin to consider forgiving my parents.

Week Five.   Ann points out that I haven't been complaining about my stomach lately. *128, but for once I accept the "excuse" that my period is due.*

Week Seven.   My old friend Leslie calls; we agree to meet for dinner. We haven't seen each other for years, haven't been close since we helped each other through our divorces a decade ago. I watch through the restaurant window as she walks down the street. My mouth falls open.

She's an emaciated version of the Leslie I used to know. The Leslie who taught me to drink decaf for breakfast instead of eating toast. I wonder if she has AIDS or cancer; if that's why she called me.

We hug each other; I feel I could snap her in two. "Are you okay?" I ask. She nods once, hard. "Fine," she says emphatically. "You're so thin. Have you been . . ." Leslie interrupts me. "Everyone's always telling me I'm too skinny," she says. "I'm not worried about it, okay? Now let's talk about something else."

I order what I want: spanikopita and dolmas—even though I had lunch today. Leslie orders spinach salad. I eat pita bread and butter while we wait. She drinks water. We talk about our relationships, our careers. The food comes. I eat with gusto. Leslie pushes spinach around on her plate. We talk about my children, her painting. I try not to notice that she hasn't eaten a bite. I try not to feel like a gluttonous pig for eating when she isn't. We talk about our mutual friends. Leslie asks if I want to taste her salad; I nod and she shoves her plate in front of me. I stab a mushroom with my fork, set it down again. "Aren't you hungry at all?" I ask. Leslie shakes her head and signals for the check. "I had a big lunch," she says.

Week Eight.   I cancel my follow-up appointment with Dr. Wylie. "Reason?" asks the receptionist. "I'm fine now," I say.

Fine? Well, better. Definitely better.

THE DAMAGE, UNDONE

One night four years ago, Ann came home from her first karate class wearing a stiff white canvas *gi,* an immaculate white cotton belt knotted around her waist. I thought she looked cute, all her softness hidden inside that big brittle package, like a little girl in Easter Sunday crinolines. But then the next thing I knew, my lover was climbing out of bed at dawn for morning karate workouts, leaving the house before dinner for karate classes three nights a week, spending occasional Saturdays and weekends at karate tests and karate promotions and karate camps. Martial arts magazines proliferated in our mailbox. Martial arts books appeared in my bed. An endlessly repeating message floated across Ann's computer screen: "Practice. Practice. Practice." As if she needed reminding. My days began and ended to the sound of Ann's karate shoes shuffling up and down, up and down our driveway as she practiced her animal form *katas:* tiger, deer, crane, snake.

Ann had always been afraid of snakes. But now, early in the morning or late at night, I could peek out our bathroom window and watch Ann on the driveway, lower lip gripped between her teeth, frowning with concentration: learning the snake, becoming the snake, coiling and uncoiling her body with all the measured power of the snake.

Every few months she'd pound another nail into her bedroom wall, hang up another belt, until finally the wall was a rainbow of knotted cotton: white, yellow, blue, green, purple, brown. I picked her up at the airport when she came home from her black belt test in New Mexico; Peter and Jesse were preparing the house for her triumphant homecoming. Ann walked in and saw that the kids had hung every black leather belt we owned from the ceiling. "Congratulations!" they yelled, hugging her. She ducked her head shyly; uncomfortable, as always, with being the focus of other people's attention. Before karate, it had even been difficult—a violation of her childhood training—for her to be the focus of her own. Hanging in the doorway was a gigantic "Go Ann!" sign, with a yin-yang for the O. Jesse presented Ann with the welcome-home drawing he'd made for her. It was "Young Grasshopper"—Ann's head, complete with wire-rim glasses and androgynous haircut, on a grasshopper's body, with a black belt tied around its waist. Below the picture Jesse had inscribed his benediction: "You have succeeded as a young grasshopper in the grassy fields of life. Who knows how far you will hop ahead. You will now be a homosexual co-mother with two teenage sons living in the worst ghetto in the world. Look out, Geraldo, she also has a black belt!!! All is well in your future, if only you cut down on those god awful puns. Love, Jesse, your son."

I was proud of Ann, amazed by her determination, awed by all she had accomplished. But as Ann's karate became more and more important to her, it became more and more of a problem for me. It wasn't a simple problem. I wanted Ann to get what she needed from karate. I saw that she was getting it. I could look out my bathroom window and watch her becoming stronger before my very eyes, more graceful, more contained, more . . . resolute. Less afraid. When we walked down the street together, she didn't keep her head down, her hands jammed into her pockets anymore. Being invisible or running away weren't her only options anymore. Knowing that, she seemed to believe there was less to run away from.

"I'm just a student," she would protest when the kids bragged to their friends about how "yoked" she was, or when I called her my bodyguard. But sparring in class every week with men twice her weight, teaching children half her size to plant themselves in balanced stances, had planted Ann more firmly on the planet. Her arms, her thighs, her calves were rock-hard, striated with muscles. Her feet were thickly callused. I called her my "iron girl." She came home from her workouts glowing with sweat and satisfaction. I didn't need to read the bumper sticker I saw plastered onto beat-up Toyotas and Hondas all over Berkeley—"Women Healing Through The Martial Arts"—to understand the effect karate was having on Ann.

I was her greatest fan. And I was her most insidious detractor. I whined at her constantly that she was gone too much. That her attention was turned too much of the time away from me, from the kids, from our home. Peter and Jesse were both flunking algebra, and they had to wait till ten o'clock at night for Ann's help with their homework. (They certainly couldn't turn to me; I'd never passed a math test in my life.) I was exiled to solitary weekends at the cabin when she went to karate camps in Santa Cruz or New Mexico. The household bills she was responsible for were paid late every month. We hadn't prepared a meal together, except at the cabin, in years.

I wanted Ann to heal. But mostly I wished that what she was healing from had never happened. I wanted her past to disappear. I wanted to wake up one morning beside a lover who'd had a perfect childhood. Every night when the kids and I sat down to dinner without her, every night when she rushed in from work, galloped upstairs to change, then dashed through the kitchen in her *gi,* kissing us all good-bye, running out the door with a yogurt and a banana in her hand, I was reminded of the damage that had been done to her. I didn't want to be reminded. I wanted her to feel powerful and safe and whole without having to do karate. I wanted our family to be her healing. I wanted her to sit with us at the dinner table. Even though she loved me, took care of me, gave me more in her bits of unscheduled time than anyone had given me in a lifetime; even though she had stuck it out with me through ten difficult years, penetrating my distancing armor and yielding so that I might penetrate hers, I couldn't quite believe that someone who'd been hurt as badly as Ann had could be there for me. Cooking alone, going to the cabin alone, correcting spelling words alone convinced me that she couldn't. I whined and complained, thrashed and threatened to make her prove me wrong.

I wanted her to do her damn karate. And I wanted her to stay home every night.

So it was with understandable trepidation that Ann approached me a few weeks before International Women's Day 1994 and asked if I was willing to spend one of our precious Friday date-nights at an all-woman martial arts demonstration. My hackles rose: *Karate—on* my *time? No way!* My desire to support my lover arose. *She's trying to share her life with me.* The opponents sparred. *I want to go to the movies on a Friday night, like a normal person! This means so much to her; it's time I showed a little interest.* "It's a celebration of International Women's Day," Ann said. "The theme of the program is power."

I rolled my eyes; I couldn't help myself. Ann averted hers; hoping, no doubt, to discourage me from launching into my well-worn spiel about feminists and martial arts and "power." I'd taken a karate class, too, back in 1972, when all the Berkeley sisters were voting to become lesbians and growing our armpit hair and forming all-woman *dojos.* I'd kicked and punched with the best of them in my own stiff white cotton *gi,* barking *"Aiya!"* and thrilling to the angry snap of my sleeve as my clenched fist flew through the air. All those determined young women—hippie chicks in communes one day, feminist separatists in wimmin's collectives the next—practicing our kicks and *katas* in junior college gyms and quickly converted storefronts, our imaginary common target the would-be rapist who might have the bad luck to try something on any of *us.*

And then my best friend Cheryl *was* raped, in the middle of the night, as she lay asleep in the basement bedroom of her group house. The stranger who broke into Cheryl's room and into her body did not know or care whether there was a yellow or even a black belt hanging on her wall, would not have been deterred by a lifetime's worth of carefully practiced kicks and punches. He only needed to hold the sharp icy edge of his knife to Cheryl's throat in the dark, and then he was able to breathe his foul breath into her mouth and take what he wanted from her body and disappear back into the night. Soon after that Cheryl checked herself into the hospital to have her tattoo of a red star—the symbol of her commitment to the revolutionary movement—surgically removed from her ankle.

In bitterness I quit karate. If I couldn't protect Cheryl—or myself, or any other woman—from a rapist, at least I could protect myself from false hope. It was futile to rage at the nameless, faceless man who had raped my best friend and still roamed the streets. My rage, turned inward, would serve me better than any kick or *kata.* I'd been a fool to believe in the power of my own punches. I'd made myself more vulnerable by imagining that I wasn't. Never again, I swore, would I be lulled into believing that women could keep themselves—that I could keep myself—safe. A year after I quit karate, I married a six-foot-four-inch, 220-pound man who walked by my side on dark streets and slept by my side at night.

Twenty years later I peek out the window at my five-foot-six-inch, 110-pound lover on our driveway. I watch her soft, downy arms becoming weapons; her long, lean legs whipping out lightning strikes. And it happens again: my longing to feel safe in the world roils in my gut like a hastily swallowed meal. Hope stirs—*Maybe she could . . . maybe I'm not . . . maybe she really could . . .* And then the anger rises. *She's wasting her time! As if she could really* do *something if someone attacked us.* It's harder, even, than giving up believing I could protect myself: swallowing the hope that Ann could protect me.

"I'll pay for the tickets," Ann coaxed me. "If you get bored, we can leave." "Okay," I said finally, mustering a reasonable imitation of the kind of supportive lover I wish I actually was.

We arrive at the Elks hall a half-hour early to find the seats sold out and the auditorium overflowing. People spill out into the lobby, onto the front steps, down the block. White women and Asian women and black women, butch dykes and femme girls, young women and old women in black *gis* and white *gis* and exotic warrior costumes intermingle with the hundreds of people, mostly women, who have come to watch them demonstrate "power." Ann suggests that we step outside to decide whether "we're" willing to buy standing-room-only tickets. She is, of course; but until she takes my emotional temperature, she won't know whether the evening might cost her more points than it's worth. On the sidewalk we run into Wendy's ex-boyfriend, a therapist who runs men's groups. His specialty is teaching his clients to find or create and then worship power objects. As usual, Mario talks enthusiastically about himself; when interrupted, he asks a single perfunctory question about Wendy—with whom he lived for three years and who has, since their breakup, been diagnosed first with breast cancer and then with premature menopause. His eyes glaze over by the time I'm two sentences into the answer. "Give her my best," he says, and walks away. "In a million years your best wouldn't be good enough," I mutter, wondering why it is that men like Mario are so drawn to feminist events, and to feminists. Maybe he's hoping to take one of these martial artists home, turn her into his next power object, I think sourly.

Suddenly I hear a series of small explosions in the distance. "Gunshots," Ann says, her voice tight with tension. The crowd around us falls silent. We're on the edge of a favorite neighborhood of West Berkeley's drug dealers. And right in the middle of about a hundred black belts. I might as well be surrounded by schoolchildren for all the protection they can offer in this moment. *So much for power.* Two more shots ring out, closer this time. No one moves. It feels like we're all holding our breath. The silence stretches, the way it does when an earthquake stops shaking, when everyone's hoping it's really over. People shake their heads, shrug their shoulders, resume their conversations. "Let's go get our tickets," I say. Ann and I walk into the auditorium, find places to sit on the floor in the space between the stage and the first row of seats.

The women from one martial arts school after another demonstrate their expertise in judo, tae kwon do, tai chi, kung fu, capoeira, aikido. They spar and leap and yell and fall; they joust with sticks, with fans, with sabers, with nun chucks. Their movements are graceful, deliberate, and sure; their bodies are different shapes, sizes, ages, and colors. But they are all strong, in their own ways, and supple. I watch the determined faces of these women and wonder who among them is here to undo the damage that was done to her, and what that damage might be; who among them is here to try to prevent damage yet undone; and who among them might have had the pleasure of choosing martial arts freely, joyfully—not to heal or to protect but to enjoy—as Peter took up surfing and Jesse devotes himself to art.

Right after intermission a group of children run onto the stage: girls and boys of varied ethnicities and ages. The girls are wearing black *gis;* the boys—the first males to appear on the stage tonight—are dressed like gangsters, with knit caps on their heads, bandannas tied around their faces, black satin jackets, sagging jeans. The girls saunter across the stage together, chatting and laughing. The boys follow close behind. "Hey, baby—what's your name?" a boy calls out. "You sure are fine, girl," says another. "You gonna gimme some of that good stuff?" asks a third.

I feel the familiar grip of fear in my gut: *a woman's fear, the fear of men, of what men want, of what men might do.* My cells remember every single terrifying time I've been threatened that way. The night in 1968 when I was mugged on the Lower East Side—not once but twice in fifteen minutes, the first time by three teenage boys pretending to have a gun; then again, three blocks away, by a tall, glowering man who really did have a knife. The sunny afternoon in 1981 when Wendy and I were chased down a Los Gatos street by a brand-new BMW convertible full of young men yelling "Dykes! Lezzies! We're gonna get you!" The times my husband's temper flared and I locked myself in the bathroom, afraid that the gentle man I'd married to keep me safe would act like a violent stranger, would use his six-foot-four-inch, 220-pound body against mine. The many nights two years ago that Ann and I spent cowering in our kitchen, dialing 911 and dreading the sound of breaking glass, as the man who called himself Ozzie came back again and again, pounding on our front door, yelling, "I know you girls are in there!" The times I've driven around the block before parking in front of my house because a strange man was lurking on the street. *The lifelong everyday woman's fear of men—fear of men we love and fear of men we don't know. The necessary, corrosive woman's fear of what men want, what men might do.*

But these girls don't do what I've done when I've been afraid. They don't run; don't look around frantically for help; don't scream and hope someone hears; don't ignore the threat, hoping that it will simply disappear. They don't act helpless. They whirl around to face their harassers, plant their hands on their hips and their feet shoulder-width apart on the floor, announce with every fiber of their beings that they-are-not-and-will-not-be-victims. "Leave us alone!" shouts a teenage African-American girl. "We don't want to talk to you. Back off, or else!" commands a young white girl. "NO! Get out of here!" yells a tiny Asian girl, who looks to be about six years old. The boys advance, more menacingly now. "C'mon, baby," says one, touching the oldest girl on her arm. "Don't be so cold," says another, grabbing the Asian girl and pulling her toward him.

"We warned you!" says a young black girl. She grabs the nearest boy, flings him over her head, stands grinning down at him with her foot on his chest. The Asian girl twists the arms of the teenage boy who's clutching her, flips him onto his back. The white girl plants herself nose-to-nose with the boy nearest to her; he turns and runs away. "Next time you think about messing with a young lady," she advises the boys pinned onto their backs on the floor, "think about this!" The girls release their captives.

"Now go home and learn some respect!" The boys scramble to their feet, scurry off the stage. The girls give each other high-fives, then turn to face the cheering audience. The boys return to the stage, take the girls' hands. Together they take their bows.

My eyes well with tears. Suddenly my ambivalence about "women healing through the martial arts" feels hollow, false-hearted. What if Ann had found karate, what if Ann had found her power not at thirty-six but when she was a little girl, when she needed it most? What if someone had wrapped me, when I was a little girl, in a stiff black *gi,* taught me to yell "No!" in my strongest, loudest voice, showed me that I had the power to throw teenage boys to the ground? What damage might not have been done? What might we have accomplished in the world; what contributions might we have made, if we hadn't been so consumed, all these years, with undoing it?

I know that nothing can shield these girls, or Ann, or me, from the life-threatening condition of being female. No kicks or punches, no yelling or facing down fear—nothing can stop a bullet in flight, a husband on a rampage, a rapist in the night. But I know too that the girls—and the boys—on this stage just cannot be as susceptible as Ann was, as I was, as our fathers and our brothers and our boyfriends were, to the woman-hating that misshaped every one of us. Will a girl who knows she can throw a teenage boy to the ground suffer her father's sexual abuse in silence, or grow up to marry a man who beats her? Will a boy who's been thrown to the ground by a little girl grow up to rape his daughter, or beat his wife?

Or—has help come too late for these powerful little girls in their stiff black *gis*? Was that tiny girl so fiercely shouting "NO!" practicing for her future, or re-enacting some horror from her past?

Soon after our evening at the martial arts demonstration, a year after she came home from New Mexico with her black belt, Ann tells me she's decided to cut back to one karate class a week. She says she wants to spend more time at home with the kids and me. On the nights she used to go to class, she'll work out on the driveway instead. So now we can all have dinner together almost every night, and if Peter needs help with his geometry or Jesse wants company while he's shooting hoops, she'll be there. *She'll be there.*

I burst into grateful tears. "I'm so happy," I say, clasping Ann to me. But even as the much-longed-for relief washes over me, my ambivalence—the guilt—comes seeping through. "But karate's so important to you," I say.

"What's important to me is to feel safe," Ann says quietly. "In the world, and in this family."

She doesn't need to say more. In ten years I've learned—although I can't always show that I know—what makes Ann feel safe. In ten years I've learned—although I can't always show that I know—what makes Ann feel unsafe; what makes her feel that what happened to her when she was a little girl will happen again; is happening again; that no one cares enough to keep it from happening again.

"I'll try harder to help you feel safe," I promise Ann, and myself. "Let's both try," she says. I nod, pull her to me. "We'll just have to practice," I say. "Practice, practice, practice."

Changing the Family, Changing the World

"The nuclear family unit is oppressive to women (and children, and men). The woman is forced into a totally dependent position, paying for her keep with an enormous amount of emotional and physical labor which is not even considered work. . . . When men think up alternatives (such as divorce or "just living together" or communal living) . . . they royally louse women up, so this time we must create the alternatives that we want, those we imagine to be in our self-interest."

FROM THE INTRODUCTION TO

Sisterhood Is Powerful

I'm having dinner with my friends Jake and Lily, and we're talking about their creatively constructed family. Before he met and married Lily, Jake conceived a child with Jane, a lesbian looking for a donor-father. Now Jane and her lover Amy live two blocks from Jake and Lily; nine-year-old Emma splits her time between the two houses. Jake, Lily, Jane, Amy, Emma, and Amy's son are the best of friends: they celebrate holidays and birthdays and take family vacations together. Free of the usual messy residue of divorce and the divisiveness of sexual jealousy, guided by their shared commitment to equality, their blended family is the most harmonious one I know.

As we pass around Jake's homemade pasta, I'm complimenting him on his parenting of Emma. "If more men were primary to their kids the way you are," I say, "it would change the world."

"Men will never be as close to their children as women are," Lily says. My mouth drops open. Is this my militant feminist friend talking?

"The baby grows in the woman's body," she goes on. "Nothing can surpass that bond. That's why it's a shame that feminism and the economy have forced women into the workplace. Women should be home with their kids when they're young."

Stunned, I turn to Jake. "But you're as close to Emma as Jane is, aren't you?" I ask. He chews a mouthful of salad. "Not quite," he says finally. "When Emma's here, Jane calls every night. She can't go a day without missing her." *Like me with my kids,* I think.

"And you?" I ask.

"When she's not here, I don't think about her that often," he answers.

.   .   .

"The Personal Is Political," the banners said, and when the second wave of feminism hit these shores, there was no institution so subject to scrutiny—personal and political—as the family. Who did the housework and to whose standards it was done; whether to be coupled or communal, living together or married; whose last name the baby (and the wife, if that dread word was used) would bear—each choice was magnified beneath the feminist lens and analyzed for signs of patriarchal infection. During the year (1969) it took to compile *Sisterhood Is Powerful,* Robin Morgan noted, that of the team who collectively produced it, "five personal relationships were severed, two couples were divorced, and one separated. . . ."

"The new family will rise," we vowed, "from the ashes of the old."

Like so many of the promises made by the mostly white women's liberationists, the solutions we envisioned—all-female communes, feminist collectives, matriarchal tribes—were not so compelling to the masses of women, or to women of color. Five of the seventy articles in *Sisterhood Is Powerful* were written by and for black and Chicana women. Their concerns were forced sterilization and genocide, not housework and bourgeois monogamy.

There is no doubt today that the old family, for better or for worse, has been charred to smoldering ash. Even the frantic fanning by political opportunists and nostalgic sentimentalists alike is unlikely to revive it. But what has arisen in its place—single motherhood, absentee fatherhood, and "alternative" families like Jake and Lily's and my own—is not exactly the glorious, liberated phoenix we once envisioned.

Even those who are raising their children within that quaint anomaly, the two-parent family, are scrambling to find the time, money, and energy to do the job well. And even those who enjoy the luxury of concern for more than their children's empty stomachs have had a rude awakening from the dream. Stubborn creatures that they are, our daughters refuse to play with trucks; our sons point the dolls we've given them at us and say "Bang! You're dead." Our teenage daughters wear makeup and miniskirts; our teenage sons sing along to rap songs about bitches and ho's. While once we vowed to raise dynamic, fearless baby women and sensitive new men, we now pray for our daughters' safe return from school each day and do whatever we can to try and save our sons. . . .

SCENES FROM A FEMINIST CHILDHOOD

When I was ten, I started a list called "Things I'll Never Do to My Kids." *Yell at them in front of their friends. Give them notes to take to their teachers in sealed envelopes. Take them to boring museums. Leave them with evil baby-sitters. Leave them at all.*

In the throes of adolescence, I vowed that when my kids were teen-agers—even if they were as wild as I was—I would never: *Call their friends' parents to check up on them. Examine their underwear to see if they're having sex. Restrict their phone privileges to weekends only. Punish them for getting bad grades, for smoking cigarettes, for smoking pot. Punish them at all.*

The sixties inspired new no-no's. Neither I, nor any member of the international youth tribe, would ever inflict these injustices upon our chil-dren: *Raise them in a nuclear family. Make them wear clothes. Feed them infant formula, Cocoa Puffs, cheeseburgers. Teach them to mindlessly obey the government, their teachers, their parents. Ask them what they're going to be when they grow up.*

I put the list aside for a while in the early seventies, when my sisters in the women's movement were leaving their boyfriends for each other, set-ting up feminist collectives, becoming plumbers and doctors, carpenters and writers—anything but mothers. "Free Child Care for All" was a plank in the women's liberation platform, but we didn't have much need for child care at our meetings. I knew only one woman who was a mother, and she was too busy with her kids to join our group. In that era a committed feminist's list of "Things I'll Never Do to My Kids" would have included just one item: "Have them."

I wasn't *that* committed. I still had a boyfriend; still dreamed of the day I'd be in the market for child care myself. I swore when that day came, I'd carry on the struggle for gender equality; somehow I'd have my feminism and my family, too. I started a new list: "Things I'll Do When I Have Kids." *Banish pink and blue; dress my kids in purple and turquoise. Encourage my sons to cry and my daughters to speak unapologetically. Share housework, income producing, and child care equally with my children's father. Teach my sons to sew and my daughters to fix cars. Model gender-irrelevant behavior at all times.*

Then it was 1980, and I was the mother of two infant boys. My list was pretty yellowed around the edges by then; already my husband and my sons and the real life we were living had proved to me that my vows weren't going to be so easy to keep. But I had to try—harder each day than the day before! After all, these were *men* I was raising! In a few years these innocent, smooth-skinned babies of mine would be part of the solution—or if I failed in my task, part of the problem. I just couldn't let that happen. And so I tried. Goddess knows, I tried. . . .

S N A P S H O T : 1 9 8 1

It's 6:15 A.M.—Peter's second-favorite time of day for meaningful conversation. (His first choice is anytime after bedtime.) As is his morning custom, Peter is wriggling around on my side of the waterbed while at my other side his father snores, deafened by the yellow foam earplugs he and I take turns wearing on our alternating "off-duty" nights. As is my morning custom, I'm trying to talk to Peter and sleep at the same time.

"Tomorrow's my birthday, Mommy," Peter says.

"I know, sweetie," I mumble. "You're gonna be three. A real big boy." *There—that should prove I'm awake and paying attention.*

"You're my best friend, Mommy. You can come to my birthday," my son tells me.

"Thank you, Peter," I say. "I accept your invitation."

"Mommy," Peter pushes on, "can I have a G.I. Joe for my birthday?"

"Now Peter," I say, manifesting more patience than I feel, "we've talked about this before. Remember? I told you—I don't want to give my money to the company that makes G.I. Joe. If people keep buying G.I. Joes for their little boys, little boys will keep growing up wanting to be soldiers because they think war is fun. You don't want little boys to go to war and kill people, or get killed themselves, do you?"

The escalating tension in Peter's thirty-five-pound body tells me that my lofty (if slightly oversimplified) feminist-pacifist principles are not going to get me out of this one so easily. I can feel it: Peter has a plan.

"Well—what if someone *gives* me a G.I. Joe for my birthday?" Peter asks. "Can I keep it?"

It's still dark outside; he's not yet three years old; and already this kid is conducting high-powered negotiations. "Umm . . . ," I stall.

"Can I, Mommy?" Peter presses me.

"Well, I guess I wouldn't make you give it back . . . ," I say.

"Yay!" Peter cries. He leaps out from under the covers, jumps on the bed a few times and then off it. A tidal wave rolls across the waterbed in his wake. "I can't wait to tell Salvatore!"

"Tell him what?" I ask sleepily.

"Salvatore asked me what I want for my birthday present. Now I can tell him to get me a G.I. Joe!"

"Peter!" I'm wide-awake now. "I didn't say you could—"

"Thanks, Mommy! I love you!" Peter says, and runs out of the room. I sit up, considering my options. I could chase Peter down the hall, fight this out with him yet again, explain yet again that I'm not trying to keep him from *owning* a G.I. Joe; I'm trying to convince him not to want a G.I. Joe. Or—I could concede this one battle just for today, maybe catch a few minutes of sleep instead. I fall back against the pillows. My eyes close. Ah, yes, that's nice. Tomorrow. *I'll come up with a better argument tomorrow.*

S n a p s h o t :   1 9 8 2

Richard is working swing shift at the machine shop, relegating me to single parenthood of our toddlers during the witching hours between nap-time and bedtime—hours I often spend driving around suburban San Jose with Peter and Jesse strapped into their car seats because I simply can't survive another minute in the lock-down isolation of our house: the juice they can't stop spilling, the fights they can't stop having, the demands they can't stop making.

One day I sit them down and tell them—calmly—that I need a break from the word *Mommy*. "Just for a few days," I tell them. "You can call me anything you want, as long as it's not Mommy." Eager to please, innocent to the ominous implications of my request, my sons make a game of granting it; naming me after their favorite cartoon character one day, an action figure or superheroine the next. And so later that week, when Peter wanders away from me at Safeway, and I am frantically wheeling Jesse through the aisles searching for him, I finally hear his tear-edged soprano calling to me from across the store: "Princess Leia! Princess Leia! Where are you, Princess Leia?" And then, his thin voice breaking: *"Where are you, Mommy?"*

S N A P S H O T :   1 9 8 3

I haven't quite worked up the nerve to actually have sex with a woman yet, but I can feel it coming at me like a speeding train. For that reason and others, I've decided to attend my first Gay Freedom Day Parade this year, and to bring my kids with me.

As it turns out, there's a big labor march going on in San Francisco earlier the same day. How convenient! Peter and Jesse and I start out on Market Street, where we fall in behind the banner of the UAW, the union I belonged to until the Ford plant closed two years ago. Lots of other people have brought their kids, some in strollers, some riding on their parents' shoulders, most of them looking as bored and tired as mine are after marching a few blocks and chanting a few chants. ("Two-four-six-eight/organize before it's too late!" "Hey, hey/ho, ho/Union busting's got to go!")

At the first sign of whining (the last thing I want to do is give the kids a negative impression of demonstrations), I herd us all onto a bus bound for Castro Street. I'm surprised to see that Peter, Jesse, and I seem to be the only people going from one parade to the other. Have the workers forgotten that an injury against one is an injury against all? Have the gay people forgotten how the forty-hour work week was won? I take the opportunity of the twenty-minute bus ride to explain both of these concepts to my three- and four-and-a-half-year-old sons, whose attention is interrupted each time the bus doors open to admit a man in spike heels, fishnet stockings, and sequined cocktail dress or a woman whose leather vest doesn't quite conceal her pierced nipples. Already I can tell that the gay rights movement is gaining favor with my sons.

"I know why the workers had to have a march—so the bosses won't make them work for cheap," Peter says, as across the aisle from us one woman plops into another woman's lap and starts nuzzling her neck. "But why does there have to be a gay march? Why does anyone think it's bad to be gay?" *How quickly my kids are absorbing their political education! What a proud mother I am!* "That's a really good question, honey," I say. "And I honestly don't know the answer."

We get off on the corner of Castro and Market along with every other passenger on the bus. Castro Street is pulsating with legions of banner-waving, bubble-blowing, costume-wearing, tongue-kissing, slogan-chanting gay men and lesbians, transvestites and transsexuals of every ethnic and fashion persuasion. The one category of people that isn't present here is children: Peter and Jesse are the only two I see. *How will I ever get to be a lesbian if gay people don't like children?* We wander into the crowd, holding tightly to each other's hands. Peter is transfixed by a man on stilts dressed as Marilyn Monroe. Jesse stops to gawk at one man leading another by a chain leashed to the ring in his nose. Peter sees a woman selling buttons and asks if I'll buy him one. "Sure," I say.

Peter takes a long time to decide between "Homophobia is a Social Disease," "Thank God I'm Gay," and a pink triangle on a lavender background. Finally he picks the pink triangle; I pay and then ask if he wants me to pin it to his shirt. He nods, and I drop to my knees in front of him. "Do you want to know what the button means?" I ask, and he nods again. Jesse moves in close to hear the story.

"Do you remember a long time ago we talked about Hitler and the Nazis?" I ask.

Jesse pipes up, "They killed all the Jews by burning them in ovens."

"Right, sweetie," I say. *Why does it hurt even more to say this to my children than it does to know it?* "Well, Hitler killed a lot of other kinds of people besides Jews. Including gay people."

"They had gay people back then?" Peter asks.

"As far as we know, there have always been gay people," I answer. "Remember I told you that the Nazis made the Jews wear yellow Jewish stars so everyone could tell who they were?" Peter says "Yeah." Jesse just listens. "The Nazis made the gay people wear pink triangles so everyone could tell they were gay."

"What if the Jews and the gay people didn't want to wear a yellow star or a pink triangle? Couldn't they just take it off? And then nothing bad would happen to them?" Peter asks hopefully. *Am I stealing my kids' innocence, teaching them these horrible bits of history?*

"The Nazis had an army," I say. I put one arm around Peter, the other around Jesse. "They had the power to make people do what they said." The kids are silent, their faces somber.

"But a lot of Jews and gay people fought back against the Nazis," I add. "They were really brave." *There's got to be some hope in here somewhere.* "And people still need to be brave and fight back whenever someone tries to take away their rights. That's why the workers were marching this morning, and that's why gay people are having this parade."

Suddenly applause explodes around me. I look up from where I'm crouched in the street and see that Peter, Jesse, and I are surrounded by a circle of gay men. Bare-chested and beshackled; sequined and polo-shirted; mustached and mascara'ed—thirty or forty men are clapping and beaming down at Peter, Jesse, and me. "Good job, Mom," calls one man, and the crowd breaks into cheers. "That's bringing 'em up right," says another. *Maybe I do have a chance to fit in with this crowd. Maybe I am doing the right thing with my kids.*

Peter and Jesse look around, half-curious, half-scared. I draw them closer to me and smile up at the men. "Trying, anyway," I say.

Snapshot: 1987

I've neglected to memorize the school calendar once again this year, so once again it comes as a shock when I pick my kids up and the teacher "reminds" me that there's no school tomorrow. It's hard enough for a working mother to deal with all the school holidays employers never even heard of—*two* President's Days, Columbus Day, International Women's Day, for chrissake; and whole weeks off for Christmas and Easter. But these damn Student Release Days are the worst, popping up out of nowhere, stretching my emergency child care resources beyond the breaking point. The after-school center is closed whenever school is. (Big help.) The kids' father lives an hour away. Ann and my mother both have full-time jobs. I've already asked Wendy twice this month. And I used up the one sick day I had coming on Peter's last stomach flu.

So—even though I've had my job at Banana Republic for only four months; and even though I've got a really important meeting tomorrow; and even though I'm in the closet at work and my seven- and eight-year-old sons might inadvertently "out" me by mentioning their "Mom Two" to the wrong person; and even though I have no idea what I'll do with them in a downtown San Francisco office building for nine hours—Peter and Jesse are coming to work with me tomorrow.

As I dress them in their least stained T-shirts and most intact jeans, I attempt to impart to my young sons the key tenets of office behavior. "Don't bother people while they're working. Be polite and friendly. Don't make noise. Don't open any doors without knocking first." Peter and Jesse ignore me completely, interrupting to ask if we can sit in the first car on the BART train and whether they can have pizza for lunch. It's hopeless, I know. Banana Republic bills itself as a hip, relaxed workplace, but no workplace could be relaxed enough to put up with these uncivilized ruffians for a whole day. I'll be lucky if I still have a job by five o'clock.

The morning goes surprisingly well. Peter and Jesse are impressed by the tall buildings, the views out my window of suicidal bike messengers careening between taxis, the packets of hot chocolate mix in the office kitchen. I hope they are also impressed by the fact that their mom has big responsibilities and a big office, that my boss and my boss's boss are both women.

On one of our many visits to the bathroom, one boy holding each of my hands, I am mortified to run into Patricia Ziegler, Banana Republic co-founder. But Patricia (who, unbeknownst to me, has recently started trying to get pregnant) doesn't reprimand me for obstructing productivity. She drops to her knees, coos over Peter and Jesse, resolves right then and there to start designing khakis for khids. Saved by the biological clock! Then I luck out again: when it's time for my meeting, a kind-hearted graphic artist sits Jesse at a drawing table with a huge box of markers, and a copywriter digs up a copy of *Pee-wee's Big Adventure* and pops it into the conference room VCR for Peter. I am almost able to concentrate during the meeting. At lunchtime a well-meaning but childless co-worker suggests that we take the kids to Chinatown. We return an hour later toting twenty-two dollars' worth of rubber nun chucks, velvet slippers, wooden puzzles, and Chinese yo-yos.

Just when I'm starting to believe this might work out after all, I look up from the copy I'm editing and notice that Jesse isn't in my office. "Where's your brother?" I ask Peter, who's sipping his fifteenth cup of hot chocolate and slinging his new nun chucks. Peter shrugs. I get up and look around. No Jesse. I knock on the men's bathroom door. No Jesse. *He probably* hasn't *taken the elevator down to the lobby and run out into Financial District traffic,* I tell myself. *He probably* hasn't *stuck his fingers into one of the industrial sewing machines on the second floor.* I want to ask someone to help me look for him, but I'm supposed to be Supermom; I'm supposed to have this kids-at-the-office thing under control. *Where's Jesse?*

Just then a loud clanging sound erupts from somewhere in the building. People look up from their desks, and then, when the clanging goes on, start milling around with their fingers in their ears. No one seems to know what the noise is or how to stop it. The building's maintenance man jumps out of the elevator, looks around, jumps back in. Mel Ziegler comes wandering out of his office, scowling and shaking his head. The noise continues. Jesse is nowhere to be found. Call it mother's intuition; call it Jewish pessimism—but I can't shake the sinking feeling that there's a connection between the two.

Finally the noise stops. A moment or two later, the elevator doors open again. The maintenance man steps out of the elevator. Jesse steps out behind him. "This kid says his mom works in the building," I hear the maintenance man say to the first person he sees—who happens to be my boss. "Any idea who he belongs to?" Just then Jesse spots me, runs to my side. I'm glad he hasn't been flattened by a bike messenger or stitched to an All-Night Flightsuit. I'm also dreading the words I know I'm about to hear—in the presence of my boss and every one of my co-workers, no less.

"Yours?" the maintenance man asks me. I nod. Jesse nestles against me. "He got into the stairwell somehow. Pushed open every emergency door from the fourth floor to the lobby," the man says. "We found him wandering around downstairs. Took us a while to shut off all those alarms." I nod again, my face aflame. "Sorry," I mutter. The man shrugs. "Kids and office buildings don't mix," he says, and gets back into the elevator. I avert my eyes, lead Jesse into my office, shut the door, and do a little Lamaze breathing. Peter watches silently from his Ninja outpost in the corner.

"Jesse," I say as calmly as possible, "do you realize how much trouble you caused? Do you realize how mad my bosses are going to be at me? Didn't I ask you to behave yourself while you were at my office?" Jesse regards me with big, brown, unrepentant eyes.

"I did what you said, Mommy," he says.

"WHAT?" I yelp.

"You told me not to open any doors without knocking first," he explains. "I *did* knock. But no one answered. So I just went in. Then this loud noise started."

I slap my forehead so hard, my ears ring. Jesse bursts into tears. "I was trying to be good," he sobs. Now there's a knock on *my* door. "Meredith?" calls my boss, who doesn't have children and doesn't want children. "Be right out," I say, wondering if there's any way out of my office besides that door and the fourth-story window.

"It's okay, Jess," I sigh. "I probably shouldn't have brought you to work with me. It's really not the best place for kids."

"I like it here, Mom," says Peter. "It's fun. I want to come back next week."

"You'll be in school next week," I say distractedly, wiping Jesse's running nose, wondering whether my boss is on the other side of the door, or whether she's given up on me entirely.

"Not on Tuesday," Peter says authoritatively. A chill runs through me. *Peter is almost never wrong about these things.* "My teacher told me there's no school next Tuesday," he repeats. "Can we come to work with you again then?"

S N A P S H O T :   1 9 9 1

My brother and his wife have separated after sixteen years of marriage. Drew and I are walking back to the park with his joint custodial kids and mine. Nick and Jesse, ages ten and eleven, are dawdling behind, stopping every few feet to see who can throw a pebble farther or balance longer on the edge of the curb. Josie and Peter, both twelve, are walking ahead of us, talking intently as they've done since they said their first words to each other. Drew and I are hanging back just far enough to eavesdrop without being too obvious about it.

"Is your mom gonna get a job now?" Peter asks Josie. Josie shakes her head, staring at the ground. Roberta hasn't worked for pay since she became ill with chronic fatigue syndrome three years ago. Even before that, her jobs and paychecks were strictly supplemental.

"Then how's she gonna pay for her new house and everything?" Peter asks.

"My dad," Josie answers flatly.

Peter stops walking, gapes at his cousin and best friend. "Your *dad*'s gonna pay? Even when they're not even married anymore?" he says.

Josie stares back at Peter. Since these two could talk, they've been finishing each other's sentences. Now they might as well be speaking different languages. *Culture shock,* I think. When our kids were babies, Drew and Roberta, Rich and I were all in the same communist organization. We lived within blocks of each other, sent our kids to the same baby-sitter, kept each other's kids a few nights a week. Then our organization fell apart, ten years ago, and Drew and I chose different paths out: he got a contractor's license and a house in an affluent all-white suburb; I got a divorce and moved to Oakland. Our kids stayed close, but they've grown up worlds apart.

How, I wonder, will Josie explain what makes no sense to Peter: that in her Menlo Park world, fathers "work" and pay the bills; mothers keep house and spend their husbands' (and ex-husbands') money. How will Peter explain what makes no sense to Josie: that in his Oakland world, good fathers pay child support; bad fathers send checks only for Christmas—or no checks at all; mothers leave lunch money and emergency phone numbers on the kitchen table when they go off to work every morning. I try and can't think of even one woman Peter knows who is financially supported by her husband.

Finally Josie shrugs. "Same as always," she says. "My mom stays home, my dad works and pays for stuff." She starts walking again. Peter scurries to catch up to her. *What will he make of this?* I wonder.

"But . . . *why?*" he asks.

SNAPSHOT: 1993

Peter is telling me about his date last night with his new girlfriend, Sara. "We were walking from the stadium to Sara's house," he says. "We passed this lesbian couple hugging and kissing in their driveway, and I got this big smile on my face. . . ."

"Why?" I ask, not wanting to assume anything. It's been a year since Peter has said much to me about his friends. It's been at least that long since he's brought any of them home. Peter swears it isn't because Ann and I are lesbians. We've never quite believed him.

"Why do you *think*, Mom?" Peter says. "It's nice to see two women in love."

"Oh," I say.

"Anyway," he continues, "I said to Sara, 'Were those two women?'— just to see what she'd say. She got kinda mad. She said, 'So? What if it *was* two women? Do you have a problem with that?'

"So I decided to give Sara this letter I wrote her a couple of weeks ago, telling her about you and Ann. She called me first thing this morning. And guess what?"

"What?" I say.

"She called me stupid!" Peter says happily. "Turns out her best friend's aunt is gay. Isn't that great? She called me stupid for thinking it would matter to her that you're gay!"

"That's great, babe," I say, hugging him. *I'm glad your girlfriend isn't homophobic. And I'm glad you've found a way back to your family.*

"Mom, I was thinking . . . ," Peter says. "Could Sara come for dinner tonight? She wants to meet you and Ann."

"Great idea," I say. "I'd love to meet her, too."

SNAPSHOT: 1994

Peter is out with his friends. Ann, Jesse, and I are eating Friday night pizza, talking about what to cook for my ex-boyfriend Paul when he comes for dinner tomorrow night.

"Why did you and Paul break up?" Jesse asks me. Now that Jesse's only a year younger than I was when Paul and I got involved, he's starting to express some interest in my teenage love life.

"We were fifteen when we got together," I say. "And we stayed together for almost five years. I guess we had to break up so we could grow up."

Jesse frowns impatiently. "C'mon, Mom. What's the real reason?"

Chip off the old bullshit detector. "Well, the immediate thing was, I was sleeping with someone else, and Paul didn't like it."

"Mom!" Jesse cries. *"You were cheating on Paul?"* He gawks at me, horrified.

"Mom wasn't cheating on Paul," Ann says. "She never lied to him."

"Paul and I had an agreement that we could sleep with other people," I explain.

Jesse is still glaring at me. "An *agreement?*" he repeats incredulously. "That you could *have sex with other people?*"

"Different couples have different agreements," I say. "Some people believe they can love one person and still have sex with someone else. Or even love someone else. As long as both people are honest, it's not cheating. It's just a different way to be a couple."

Jesse looks miserable. *Is this too much for a fourteen-year-old to take in? How can I be honest about who I've been, who I am without overwhelming him?*

"Mom and I don't have that agreement, Jess," Ann says. "We're monogamous." Jesse seems to consider this for a moment. Then he shakes his head at me, starts to say something, changes his mind. "Can I be excused?" he asks. He carries his half-full plate to the sink without waiting for an answer.

Two days later, a rainy Sunday afternoon, I'm driving Jesse from one sporting goods store to another. We're looking for the special reversible jersey he needs in case he makes it onto the Berkeley High basketball team. ("Irreversible jersey," Jesse keeps calling it, until finally I fall into his trap and correct him—at which point he informs me, "I was *making a joke,* Mom.")

We're having an animated conversation about Jesse's prospects for making the team, about the GPA the coach expects him to maintain if he wants to stay on it, and which position Jesse might play, when suddenly he falls silent. He turns his head away from me, stares out the window. "Jess?" I say. "Is something wrong? Are you worried about making the team?"

Jesse turns to me. His eyes glint with tears. *"Did you cheat on Dad, too?"* he asks.

S N A P S H O T :   1 9 9 4

A few years ago Jesse started going to the Y on Monday and Wednesday nights when the men play pickup games of basketball. At first he was a skinny eleven-year-old watching from the sidelines, shooting a few quick hoops at one basket while the action was centered at the other, darting out of the way just in time as the men came thundering back in his direction. Finally he got good enough and tall enough to be invited in as a player. Now he never sits out a game.

Jesse doesn't want me to watch him playing basketball. He says that would be as embarrassing as having me watch him in his classroom at school. So when I come to pick him up at the Y, I try to restrain myself from peeking into the gym. I'm not always able to do that. I love to watch my son's lean, muscular body darting through the herd of men; love to see the focused determination on his peach-fuzzed face; love to see those hundred-and-twenty-dollar, size-twelve-and-a-half Nikes suspended in the air as he leaps to make a lay-up. Sometimes I even indulge in an NBA fantasy of my own.

In all the Monday and Wednesday nights I've sneaked a peek into the gym, I've never seen a woman in there—until tonight. I can't keep from watching to see if I can tell what motivated her to break the gender barrier: talent, feminism, oblivion? Jesse catches me looking, pushes through the swinging gym doors sweating and scowling. "Oh, come on, Jess," I say. "I was only watching for a minute."

His scowl deepens. "I'm not mad at *you*," he answers. "Did you see that *woman* in there?"

"Jesse!" I snap. "I can't believe what I'm hearing! Do you mean to tell me you're mad because a woman had the guts to play basketball with a bunch of men? How do you expect things to change if you have an attitude like—"

"Exactly, Mom," Jesse interrupts my diatribe.

"Huh?" I say.

Jesse stops at the water fountain for a long, gulping drink, sticks his head under the arc of water, comes up dripping. He swipes at his face with the palm of his hand.

"I'm not mad because she tried to play with us," he says. "I was *glad* to see a woman on the court for once. I was hoping she'd be good, so the guys would accept her and then maybe some other women would have a chance.

"But she played *horribly*. The worst part was, you could tell she could've played better if she tried. I could understand it if she lagged behind the men physically, but not mentally. She wasn't focused—she wouldn't dive for the ball or anything. She played like a stereotype of a woman."

"Maybe she was too nervous to play her best," I say. Can't he see that a men's basketball game could never be a level playing field for a woman? "Don't you think that could have affected her game?"

"As you were saying, Mom," Jesse says pointedly, "whatever bad attitudes any of those guys had before, she made them worse."

"Sorry I jumped down your throat, Jesse," I say. "I just assumed—"

"You just assumed I was sexist," Jesse says, ruffling my hair and grinning at me. "Now think about it, Mom: what kind of attitude is *that?*"

FEMINIST FAMILY VALUES

Eleven P.M., Stapleton Airport, Denver. I climb into a waiting airport van and squeeze past my fellow passenger, a man in a three-piece suit who's taking up the whole middle seat, his wool overcoat on one side of him, attaché case on the other. The driver slams the door shut, and we head north on a deserted highway, the full moon glowing on the snow banked against the road's edge, ice glinting on the naked branches like long, diamond-ringed fingers stroking the black sky. "I'm Johnny," says the driver, a young white man in a plaid flannel shirt and Broncos cap. "Miss Maran, for Dupont; Mr. Burns—Henderson. Right?" "Right," I answer. The man nods. "Those towns are forty-five minutes apart," Johnny says. "I'll need to drop one of you off, then double back to drop the other. So I could take Mr. Burns first, then you, Miss Maran, or—"

"Plan A," Mr. Burns says.

"Or I could drop Miss Maran first," Johnny says deliberately.

"Me first, please," Mr. Burns says. "I've got an early meeting tomorrow."

Johnny looks at me with his eyebrows raised, waiting for me to speak in my own defense. But I'm silenced by the thought that pops into my head. "I'm a woman—they should defer to me." *Where did* that *come from?* A few minutes later Johnny pulls to a stop at a junction. "Maybe we should talk about this," he says. "It's late at night for the lady, too."

"We've already made that decision, haven't we?" Mr. Burns says.

"I do have a meeting at eight o'clock in the morning," I mumble. I'm caught in the headlights—immobilized by Johnny's protectiveness, Mr. Burns's insistence, and my own distinctly unfeminist reaction to both of them. "Look," Mr. Burns says, "one of us is going to get where we're going forty-five minutes later than the other. And I don't see why that should be me." He turns and stares out the window.

What an asshole, I think. But I'm not so proud of the way I'm handling myself either. Johnny turns right toward Henderson. *Is this the future we've been fighting for?* I wonder as the van hurtles away from my destination. When chivalry is truly dead, will men and women treat each other as equals, or will the species be reduced to power struggles between jerks like this guy and doormats like me—the survival of the shittiest? "Sorry," Johnny says as we leave Mr. Burns's hotel. "I should've just dropped you first, no questions asked." "Thanks for trying," I say. "But he was right. We both had early meetings. I had no more right to special treatment than he did."

Johnny shakes his head. "I can't agree with that," he says. "This might sound sexist to you, but I like to put women up on a pedestal." *Sounds good, actually,* I think. *If I'd let you do that for me, I'd be asleep right now.* "It does sound sexist to me," I say. "People put women on a pedestal 'cause they think we can't take care of ourselves." *Like I just did such a great job of that.*

"Naw," Johnny says. "My fiancée looks out for herself just fine. She makes more money than I do, as a matter of fact. I just like to treat her right." In the darkness I roll my eyes, imagining what that might mean. "You know—I clean the house, do the laundry, cook the meals." He chuckles. "*All* the meals. She can't even boil an egg." I stare at him, speechless. "She treats me real good, too," he adds. "When we first started going out, she bought me flowers. No one ever did that for me before. It really hooked me."

"It doesn't sound like either one of you is on a pedestal," I say.

"Oh, it's not what I do or what she does. It's the way I think of her," Johnny says. "Like with my mom. I wouldn't want to treat her the same way I treat my father. My mom deserves more respect. She's a . . . *woman.*"

I wonder what my sons would say about that—if they've ever even heard of "putting a woman on a pedestal." Most of their friends would probably agree with Johnny. But then, most of their friends have been raised by single mothers. I wonder what Peter or Jesse would've done if they'd had Johnny's problem to solve tonight. Probably flipped a coin. *Why didn't I think of that?*

Johnny drops me at my hotel. I give him a generous tip, sleep four hours, and meet Dave, the CEO of Nature's Botanicals, in the hotel lobby at seven-thirty. By eight we're holed up in the conference room with the Nature's Botanicals creative team and a pot of coffee, brainstorming a socially responsible marketing plan. By six we've invented "Scents For The Globe," a program that commits the company to giving environmental groups a nickel for every bottle of shampoo sold. We agree to work out the logistics tomorrow; after high-fives all around, the meeting is adjourned. Dave asks his secretary to call his wife and tell her we're bringing take-out home for dinner, then call the Chinese restaurant and order our meal. "If you give me the number, I'll call the restaurant," I say. His secretary smiles at me. "Oh, no. You two get going. I'll handle dinner." She turns to Dave. "The usual?" she asks him. "Yup. For three people," Dave answers. "Thanks, Linda."

"Linda's great," Dave says as we climb into his shiny new Accord wagon. "But next time I need an assistant, I'm gonna hire a man. That'll set a better example." *He's trying,* I tell myself. "You did a great job today," Dave says. "We all did," I answer. "We got a lot done." My spirits lift as Dave and I drive through the dusk-shadowed Colorado countryside, envisioning the "Scents For The Globe" logo plastered on paper bags and billboards; imagining all the money the program might raise; congratulating ourselves for a day—and my consulting fees—well spent.

"Katy can't wait to meet you," Dave says, pulling into the driveway of a large ranch-style house on a broad suburban street. I've known Dave for years, but I've never met his wife or kids; he's never met mine. Before today we've seen each other only at socially responsible business conferences, which few wives and even fewer husbands attend. Like many of the progressive CEOs I know, Dave founded his company in partnership with his wife, back when they were young you-'n'-me-babe hippies. Then, when the company could afford hired help and the babies started coming, Katy—like most of the other wives—retired to full-time motherhood, running the family instead of the business.

The ghosts of the wives haunt me in my relationships with these men. I work with them, go to activist conferences with them, confront them about their own and their companies' sexism, help them find women to fill their management positions, all the while knowing that their wives are waiting for them at home; all the while knowing that their families replicate the very institution that the hippies, then the feminists, vowed to overthrow: the patriarchal, father-funded, father-absent family. I admire these guys, I love some of them, but sometimes I want to shake them and scream: "How can you call yourself 'progressive' when you're out flying around, getting rich, getting press for changing the world, while your secretary's ordering your dinner and your wife's at home raising your kids?"

Katy greets us at the kitchen door. "Great to finally meet you, Meredith." She hugs me, accepts a kiss from Dave, smiles at the toddler in the high chair. "This is Ben." She picks a few grains of rice off Ben's cheeks. "And this is Ben's dinner. Dave, would you keep an eye on him? I've got to go check on Nicole. She's upstairs in the tub." "That's okay, babe," Dave says. "You stay here and talk to Meredith. I'll take care of Nicole." Katy and I fall into an easy conversation about our kids and our pasts, baby food recipes and friends we have in common, while she finishes feeding her son. Dave comes down to ask if I'll help him read a bedtime story to Ben and Nicole. What I'd really like to do is lie down for about twelve hours, but I follow Dave up the stairs. Nicole is sweet, and her father is sweet with her: stroking her cheeks, answering her high-pitched questions, tucking her in tenderly. "I'm out of town on business most of the time," he whispers as we close the door behind us. "So I try to be with the kids as much as I can when I'm here."

I wonder how Katy feels about that. Last week Timothy, one of my CEO friends, told me his wife of eighteen years had just presented him with a list of nonnegotiable demands. "She wants to take a family vacation once a year and not have me get called away at the last minute. She wants to go somewhere for the weekend, just the two of us. She wants me to get home before Emily goes to sleep at least a few nights a week. She wants to have another kid, but first—she said it just like this—she wants me to get to know the one we already have."

Timothy shook his head, his balding brow furrowed with worry. "She doesn't seem to realize how much I want all those things, too. If it was up to me, I wouldn't have missed a minute with Emily. But keeping the business going isn't optional. I've got other people's lives depending on me, too.

"Before we had Emily, we agreed Marg would go back to homeopathy school when Emily was five. Now she's five, and it's obvious our household would fall apart if one of us wasn't there. I know Marg's tired of handling everything at home by herself. I know she wants to get on with her life. But I can't just drop everything I've spent all these years building. I don't know how we're gonna make it through this."

Over dinner I watch for that kind of tension between Katy and Dave, the tension that was a constant presence between my husband and me during the worst year of our marriage, when he was learning to be a machinist and I was home mothering our two infants. It didn't matter that he was as exhausted as I was when he got home; it didn't matter that he was learning a trade that would guarantee us a steady income someday; it didn't matter that he craved time at home as desperately as I longed to get the hell out of the house. All that mattered to me was that somehow I'd ended up trapped in my mother's life—and for the oldest reason in the book, no less: one of us had to breast-feed the babies and one of us had to earn the money, and it wasn't even worth talking about who was better suited for which job. Intellectually I knew where the blame belonged; in my rational moments I knew this wasn't my husband's fault any more than it was mine. But The Oppression of Women didn't sit down to eat the dinner I'd shopped for and cooked and put on the table every night— Richard did. So I raged at him when he didn't know the pediatrician's name, and I raged at him when he didn't do the laundry, and then I raged at him when he did it and shrank my favorite sweater, until finally my rage—and his—drove us apart.

If that anger exists between Katy and Dave, I can't see it. Katy doesn't seem to care that Dave doesn't know where the serving spoons or the trivets are kept. Dave doesn't seem to notice that Katy is setting the table, filling the water glasses, serving the food. We sit down to eat. Dave and I tell Katy about our exciting day at the office. She tells us about Nicole's doctor visit, Ben's newest word. Each seems equally interested in the other's stories, equally engaged in the news from their disparate separate but unequal lives.

Asking questions about Katy's day with the kids, I can't help but wonder: how could Katy and I have ended up with such different lives when we have so much in common: shared histories in the antiwar and women's movements, shared hope that progressive business will carry that torch forward, mutual friends, motherhood. When Dave puts his napkin down and excuses himself to make a business call, I can't help but ask. "How does this setup work for you?" I ask. "Are you happy staying home with the kids? Do you miss having a job? Do you ever resent Dave for being gone so much?"

Katy smiles serenely. "This is an ideal partnership," she says. She stirs a spoonful of honey into her chamomile tea. "We both get to do exactly what we want. Dave's out building something for all of us. He loves what he does. And for me this is a dream come true: having the luxury of time to raise my children the way I want them to be raised. So few women have that chance. If Dave didn't do what he does, I couldn't do this. I think we're both really lucky."

"You mean this is really your *choice*?" I blurt. "You're not just doing it because Dave can earn more money, or because it's what a mother's supposed to do?"

"I don't know who *you've* been hanging out with lately, Meredith," Katy says. "But this isn't what a woman's supposed to do anymore. Just the opposite." We stare at each other across the table. "I don't know what you mean," I say finally.

"There's a huge value judgment against stay-at-home moms these days," Katy says. "You're making that value judgment yourself. You assume this isn't my first choice, that every woman would rather work outside the home. That assumption is just as pervasive now as the opposite assumption was in our mothers' day. Believe it or not, some of us actually prefer being a full-time parent to having a full-time job and having our kids grow up in full-time child care."

"But—even if your reasons for doing it this way are different from your parents'," I ask, "don't you think you're teaching your kids the same model we rebelled against?"

Katy frowns and sets her cup down. "What I *hope* I'm teaching my children is that men *and* women should do what makes us happy. That's not what our parents taught us. And I hope I'm teaching them how good it feels to be in a healthy, intact family, getting as much attention as they need. That's more than most kids in this country ever get to know." I feel the stab of that familiar double-edged knife: divorce guilt, working mother guilt, slicing right through my conviction.

"You think the way Dave and I run our family is sexist," Katy goes on. "Well, I think it's sexist to assume that the work in the world is more important than the work at home. Dave and I value what each of us does equally. It's not like our parents' families, where the father was the only important person because he earned the money. We're both important here."

Both important *here,* in the bubble of your family, I think. But it's not just politics that makes me question Katy's choice; it's economics. If Katy disappeared from Dave's life, he'd have Linda to order his dinners and hire him a housekeeper; he'd have his stock and his salary to keep him warm. But what if Dave disappeared from Katy's?

Katy pours some tea into my cup, fills her own, and lets out a long breath. "Sorry I got so worked up. It does get to me, what other people think. Even though I know my own work is important, I have to fight to keep from internalizing the message that it isn't."

"I'm sorry, too," I say. "It's not just you I've had this argument with. I have other friends in your situation. Their husbands support the family, and they stay home with the kids. They've given up their careers to be mothers, but their husbands' careers are hardly affected at all by being fathers. And their husbands 'help out' with the kids and the housework when they're not at work, which they almost always are."

I tell Katy about my old friends Sharret and Lee. When they met in 1972, Lee was a hippie and Sharret was a radical feminist anthropology student. When she married Lee, he wore a wedding ring but she didn't. She kept her name, and just to make sure the whole world got the point, she cut her hair short (but didn't shave her armpits) a week before the wedding. Now Lee's a partner in a law firm, and Sharret is the full-time mother of three boys, president of the PTA, and a volunteer at her kids' school.

Sharret has been doing more crafts projects than paintings since her twins were born seven years ago; her canvases now are her three (wildly gifted) children and her modernized adobe house, whose walls, floors, and furniture she paints in the crazy rich colors of her discarded palettes, their splattered luster now gathering dust, packed away in their two-car garage. Lee works long hours six days a week, comes home for dinner, reads bedtime stories to his sons, and often goes back to work when they're asleep. He pays for Sharret's art supplies, pays for the kids' music lessons, pays for the house cleaner, pays the mortgage, pays for everything. Sharret still has her last name. But her kids don't share it.

"I know Sharret's a feminist," I tell Katy. "But it's hard for me to see how her lifestyle advances the cause of women."

A spot of color appears in each of Katy's cheeks. "Maybe her lifestyle serves her family, not some political dogma," she says.

Who am I to judge my more traditionally married friends? My own feminist scorecard is not without its black marks, either. My kids' last name is their father's, plain and simple, without even the requisite hyphen—a decision I made in the heat of postpartum passion and have regretted since the hormone surge subsided. All three of Peter and Jesse's parents work for a living, and all three of us earn about the same amount of money, but the two cultures our children live in differ in the most traditionally gender-appropriate ways. When Richard and I divorced, we made a trade in the interest of our kids' well-being: he gave me his toolbox; I gave him my recipes. But in twelve years of divorce, we've been unable to change what wouldn't budge in ten years of marriage: the kids eat a lot more out of the microwave at his house, and a lot more out of the oven at mine. And Dad can build or fix anything, and Mom and Ann hire men when the water heater's leaking or there's a broken picket in the fence. And Dad's house is messy, and Mom and Ann's house is tidy. And Dad is gruffly affectionate, and Mom and Ann are gushy. "Feelings, feelings, feelings!" Jesse exploded one Sunday night, an hour after he'd arrived from a week at Richard's house. "That's all you guys want to talk about. We *never* have to talk about our feelings at Dad's!"

I have other married fortysomething feminist friends whose husbands barbecue but don't cook; "watch" the kids but don't know what size clothing they wear—or refuse to have kids at all; earn more money and do less housework; must be cajoled or coerced into celebrating an anniversary, taking a family vacation, coming home in time for dinner. I try not to judge these women; I try to stretch my definition of feminism to fit them into it, but still I wonder about the causes and the effects of what they do. Am I dogmatic and inflexible because I wonder if they're selling feminism out, putting the personal above the political; refusing to relinquish primary parenthood; teaching their children the same gender-rigid stereotypes their husbands—and good men everywhere—are struggling to unlearn? Are they sinking into what's comfortable; retreating from the battle that was still, last I checked, in progress? If so, I know these women are doing this, in whole or in part, because they *can:* because unlike the vast majority of American families, theirs can survive with two people doing two jobs instead of three.

The truth is, I feel abandoned on the battlefield. *I turned around one day, and my sisters weren't with me.*

And maybe just a bit jealous. *Being taken care of is politically incorrect. But it sure sounds good.*

On my shelf there's a book, its cover curled, its pages yellowing. "Ma, Can I Be A Feminist And Still Like Men?" the comic strip character Sylvia asked fifteen years ago, when Katy, Sharret, and I were marching against monogamy and the feminist fever was high. Now I wonder, "Ma, can I be a feminist and still be taken care of by a man?" Ma, can I be a feminist and still have a husband who buys me a car, pays my bills, rents me a studio, sends my kids to private school? Can I smash the patriarchal paradigm while earning my keep in the kitchen instead of the job market? Can I make my husband's coffee in the morning wrapped in my feminist beliefs like a worn fuzzy bathrobe, and pick up his suits at the cleaner's without taking on the baggage of my mother's subservient life?

The answer to Sylvia's question was the subtitle of the book: "Sure—Just Like You Can Be A Vegetarian And Still Like Chicken." The answer to my question seems to be, "Sure—you can be a feminist and live any damn way you please."

Or, you can *not* be a feminist—or, more to the point, not *call* yourself a feminist—and still have a more egalitarian family than most of us who claim the label so possessively. What seems to help is being younger—or older.

My neighbor, Alice, is sixty-six; her husband Phil was seventy-four when he died last May. Alice is white; Phil was African-American; she was nineteen and he was twenty-seven when they were married in 1947. Their marriage was so extraordinary—such a source of support and joy for them, such a model of equality for their three children and the interracial community that embraced them—that Alice was pressed into service a few years ago, teaching marriage classes at their church. Sitting with her in her living room just weeks after Phil's funeral, photos of her husband and children smiling down on us, I wonder aloud: how did she and Phil do what they did; how did they get what they had?

"Phil and I both worked outside the home so we could *have* a home," Alice says. "I worked at whatever jobs I could get because black men couldn't get good jobs. Having a career wasn't such a treat in those days— I wanted to stay home. But I only got to do that for a little while after each baby.

"My husband was very supportive of anything I wanted to do. No matter how hard it was financially, whenever I wanted to leave a job, he supported that. When I wanted to go to school to become a dental assistant, he told me to go ahead. He said we'd make it somehow."

"How'd you divvy up the housework?" I ask. Alice smooths the hand-crocheted afghan that's draped over the vinyl couch. "My husband cooked. He cleaned. I cooked and cleaned. We shared." Alice smiles. "But Phil always did the wash. We didn't even have a washing machine, but Phil washed the clothes. My son does that now. When he moved in with his girlfriend, she started doing the laundry one day. He said, 'That's my job.' His girlfriend just looked at him, she was so tickled."

I catch myself feeling skeptical. Alice's glowing description sounds too good to be true. Or maybe there's a bit of second-wave feminist arrogance at work here. Is it possible that even before the missionaries of my generation arrived upon their shores, our foremothers had already discovered the joys of the feminist family?

"Did your family and friends think your arrangement was weird?" I ask. "Not weird—unusual," Alice answers. "More women were homebodies fifty years ago. But I never associated with people who put women down." She stares at the photo of Phil on the end table. "Sometimes I'd put *myself* in the role of the woman who had to do everything. Like on Saturdays I'd be cleaning the house, no matter how tired I was, and Phil would say, Alice, go take a sunbath. I'll sweep."

I know a lot of women my age who'd swoon at the thought of a husband like that. Including, maybe, me. "Phil was a real supporter of women and women's rights," Alice says. "We just never talked about it much."

Oddly enough, Alice and Phil's marriage reminds me most of the couples I know at the other end of the life cycle—people in their twenties and thirties who don't use the word *feminism,* didn't grow up watching *Ozzie and Harriet,* were in diapers while the women's movement was raging, and take equality for granted without the self-consciousness or strife that seems unavoidable in couples my age.

I met Brooke several years ago, when I was an editor and she was a freelance designer at Banana Republic. When Brooke fell in love with George—a public high school teacher; sweet, even-tempered, smart; just the kind of man she'd been looking for—we all noticed a *settled* quality to Brooke, a calm confidence that the biggest question in her life had been answered. A year after they met, George and Brooke bought and renovated a cavernous South of Market loft; two years later, when George was thirty and Brooke was thirty-one, they got married. Eight days ago, with George and her best friend Melody telling her when to push, Brooke gave birth to their daughter, Rebecca.

"We don't use the word *feminism,* but we consider ourselves complete equal partners," Brooke says. "That's true of most of our friends. If their relationships weren't like that, I couldn't stand to be around them.

"We've never fought about whose career matters more. We're both supportive of what the other one does—not just our jobs, but the big picture of our lives. I'm always telling George to take a break, go out and take a bike ride. He makes sure I go swimming and that I see my women friends."

Brooke winces as Rebecca roots at her aching nipple. "Of course we've had to make a few adjustments lately." She kisses her daughter's bald head. "George stayed home the first week after Rebecca came. It was great. We took turns getting up with her at night. He was on diaper duty. He said, 'You put it in, I'll take it out.' " Brooke smiles. "Now he calls five times a day to say he misses us. We made a deal that he'll come right home after work instead of going to the gym the way he used to. We both have to make sacrifices now. We don't want her to grow up more attached to me than she is to him."

"Is that possible?" I ask, remembering how Richard and I made that vow to each other when I was pregnant with Peter—one of many we couldn't keep. Brooke shrugs. "Right now I'm definitely the food source. But she likes it best when he holds her—his arms are big and furry. Anyway, I'm going back to work in three months, and he'll be with her all summer. Then *I'll* be calling *them* five times a day." *Or maybe,* I think, *you'll fall in love with full-time motherhood and let your career slide, the way so many once-ambitious mothers have done.* In the past few years, Brooke has built a great reputation, an impressive clientele—and an income twice as big as her husband's—as a magazine designer. But watching her gazing adoringly at her newborn daughter, it's hard to imagine a page layout or a paycheck ever getting that kind of attention from her again.

"Do you think having a baby'll put a dent in your career?" I ask. "It's definitely going to affect my work as I knew it," she says. "But to tell you the truth, I was kinda burned out anyway. I haven't taken this much time off in ten years. I'm looking forward to doing something different for a couple of months. It may take a while to get back up to speed, but that's okay.

"It's the same for George," she adds. "I think it'll be good for him to slow down. Being a teacher is so overwhelming—he's afraid he won't have time to do a good job and be a good father. But I think it's great that now there's a bigger priority for his life than his work."

Ma, could I *not* be a feminist and have a harmonious, equal marriage?

"Is Rebecca's last name—" "George's," Brooke says. "We didn't really argue about it, but that was more of an issue than the other stuff. A friend of mine had a baby, and her husband left her after a year, so she changed her daughter's name to her own. I'd probably do the same thing. But I didn't want to start out that way. And I didn't want to give her a hyphenated name. So I decided not to make a big deal out of it.

"I don't sweat the small stuff," Brooke says. "I feel really lucky with George. Even when we disagree, he wants to talk things through." "Did you have to train him, or was he this great when you met him?" I ask. Brooke chuckles. "He came this way," she says. "And it's a good thing, too. I wouldn't have wanted to work that hard."

Who would? But it's all hard work, it seems to me: making a marriage, making a family that's good and growthful for each person in it. So we make choices, all of us, for reasons conscious and unacknowledged, exemplary and embarrassing, financial and psychological—choices that are fashionable in one decade and passé in the next, economically necessary to some and unthinkable to others; choices that dilute the bitter brew of gender inequality and choices that serve it up full strength to yet another generation of girls and boys.

"I know I'm in a privileged situation," Katy says, as we're gathering the dirty dishes. "Most women can't afford to stay home and still feed their kids. Most women don't have husbands who provide for them and still treat them as an equal, the way Dave treats me. But it won't help all those other women for me to chuck my happy life and go get a job."

"You're right," I say, meaning it. "The point of feminism was to give women choices, not to dictate what those choices should be."

Dave comes into the dining room with the cordless phone in his hand. "Job?" he asks, looking from Katy to me. I feel like an outside agitator, insinuating my way into heterosexual households, fomenting rebellion amongst the wives just to reinforce my sagging ideology. "We're just talking. Just talking about feminism," Katy says. She and I smile at each other across the table. Dave takes the plates out of Katy's hands. "You must be exhausted," he says. "Why don't you go to bed? Meredith and I'll clean up. We need to talk about tomorrow's meeting anyway."

Katy kisses him on the cheek, then turns to me. "Your towels are in the guest bathroom," she says. "There's an extra blanket at the foot of your bed. Think you'll need anything else?" "No, thanks," I say, trying to remember if any man in any situation has ever told me where my towels were. She gives me a hug and goes upstairs. I carry the empty take-out boxes into the kitchen. Dave is bent over the dishwasher, frowning and muttering to himself. "We just got this thing a few weeks ago," he says. "I haven't figured out how it works yet. Oh, well." He goes to the sink and starts rinsing a pot. I read the instructions on the dishwasher, pour in some soap, start the load, and start wiping off the countertop.

"About tomorrow," Dave says. "We need to figure out how to get the sales department invested in our plan. Those guys tend to care more about the bottom line than they do about the big picture."

"We just need to convince them it's in their own self-interest," I say.

"We can show them some studies that prove investing in social change programs is good for profits." I pick up a note that's lying on the counter. "Keep this or throw it away?" I ask.

Dave peers at the piece of paper and frowns. "Keep it, I guess," he says. He shrugs. "I don't really live here. I try not to touch anything that might be important."

GARBAGE

Jesse was supposed to call or be home by 6:30. It's 6:45 now. Fifteen minutes is late enough, these days, to cause me to get into my car and go look for him. I gather my keys and my wallet, zip up my rain jacket, pull on my boots—willing the phone to ring, straining to hear Jesse's feet pounding up the porch steps. 6:48.

"I'm going to get Jesse," I tell Peter, who's washing the first-shift dinner dishes. Ann, Peter, and I ate before she left for her karate class; there's a plate of spaghetti in the microwave for Jesse. "He's late coming home from practice."

"What about the meeting?" Peter asks. I'd planned to go to the Berkeley High tenth-grade parents' group at seven o'clock tonight—in large part because it's about Peter's class, not Jesse's; and nearly all of my attention lately has been going to Jesse, not Peter.

"Maybe I'll send him home on BART and go to the meeting," I say, "if it works out that way."

Meaning: *if* I find Jesse where he's supposed to be, in the Berkeley High gym, practicing with the freshman basketball team. And if I can convey to him, in five minutes or less—again!—how important it is that he call me when he's supposed to. And if his response convinces me that it's safe to send him home by himself, that he won't run into someone he knows on his way to BART and "forget" to go right home. And, most of all, if I can be reassured that tonight won't be the night Jesse decides that he's been scolded or punished or scrutinized once too often; or that he's fallen too far behind in school and it's just too hard to catch up; or that the pressure is too great and the rewards too intangible for him to do yet again what his mother tells him to.

This is my greatest worry, these days: that the fragile thread that binds Jesse to me—to the things he's supposed to do, the way he's supposed to be—will snap. And then our mysterious contract will be rendered null and void, and he'll have no reason to go to his room when I tell him to, even though he's taller and stronger than I am. No reason to run to the nearest phone booth in the middle of a basketball game and call me, even though he's the only one on the team who has to check in with his mother. No reason to crave my approval, even as he's learning to transfer that authority to himself. No reason not to simply vanish into this dark rainy night, into the parallel universe of teenagers who don't listen to their mothers anymore. No reason for him to come home at all.

My jaw clenches as I approach the gym. *What if he's not there?* Through the foggy window I see a blur of red-and-yellow uniforms, basketballs lofting toward hoops. I pull open the gym door. *Girls. All girls.* "Do you know where the boys' team is practicing?" I ask one of them. She points to another building. "Second floor." I run through the rain, up the stairs. I hear male shouts, the echoing slap of basketballs against varnished wood. Jesse is the first person I see. He's easy to spot; as usual, he's the only white person in the gym. What is it that takes my breath away every time I get my eyes on this boy? The relief of knowing that for this one moment, at least, he is safe? The shock that never softens—how tall he is; how alive, how handsome? How much I love, love, love this manchild of mine?

Jesse frowns at me—I've broken our agreement, invaded his basketball world. I frown back. He looks surprised; then awareness breaks across his face. He tosses the ball to a teammate, runs over to where I'm standing with my arms folded across my chest. "Is it past six-thirty?" he asks breathlessly. "Sorry, Mom."

"Get your stuff," I say. "I'm supposed to be in a meeting that started five minutes ago."

Jesse walks away, his shoulders slumped. *No one could ever be half as hard on this boy as he is on himself.* A handsome young black man approaches me. "I'm Coach McNeil," he says. He transfers his clipboard from one hand to the other, extends the empty one. "Jesse's mom," I say as we shake hands. "Meredith."

"It's my fault he's late," Coach McNeil says. "First week of practice, I get a little carried away."

I shake my head. "I knew practice might run over. It's just that I told him to call me by six-thirty. Look, Coach," I say, "you should know: I've got Jesse on kind of a short leash right now."

I don't say why. *Jesse got arrested for shoplifting two weeks ago. His father got the call; he went to the police station and found our son handcuffed to a chair. I know, I know—teenagers shoplift. I shoplifted. But this is scary: Jesse says he did it because a man he knows from playing basketball in the parks around here, a man who was hanging around outside the sporting goods store, told Jesse to go inside and "Steal me hella stuff." Jesse denies he was afraid of the guy. "I just didn't want to have to deal with him on the bus the next day," he said. "What if he'd told you to go to the corner and get him a couple of rocks of crack?" I asked him. I rarely cry in front of my sons, but I was crying that night. Jesse didn't roll his eyes and accuse me of overreacting, the way he usually does. Instead he nodded gravely. "I just hope I've learned my lesson," he said. We were all left wondering.*

"Jesse lives for basketball," I tell his coach. "I don't want to take that away from him. But he's grounded for the next month. I need to know exactly where he is and what he's doing."

Coach McNeil cups my elbow in his hand, moves his face close to mine. "I understand what you're going through, Mrs. Graham," he says. "I came up in this neighborhood myself. I was a lot like Jesse when I was a kid: popular, big-mouthed, a little out of control. I spent my weekends going from park to park playing street ball, like he does. My mom worried just like you do." He smiles. "I hated her for it at the time—I was the only one of my friends who had to do my homework, had to tell my mom where I was and who I was with, got punished when I messed up. But now most of my old friends are dead or in jail. Or else they sit around getting high. I thank my mom every day for how she raised me. Jesse'll thank you one day, too. In the meantime we'll work on him together."

"I don't need him to thank me," I say. "I just need him to do what he's supposed to do. I realize it's not your job to police these boys, but . . ."

Coach McNeil shakes his head, puts his hand up to stop me. "I'm not just about basketball here," he says. "I'm trying to save these kids' lives."

My chest aches. It's a familiar sadness. Here I am again, having the same conversation I've had with every one of Jesse's coaches in the past five years. Here I am again, hearing a young black man tell me that he grew up on these streets, dodging their temptations and dangers; has somehow come through intact; and hopes, by coaching a boys' basketball team, to pull a few younger black men (and my son in the process) through that narrow crack of light with him. *Why is there so little hope for these children that they need to have their lives saved by a basketball coach? And why is the NBA the only way out they can see?*

Someone's tugging on my arm. I turn and see Tyrone, a kid who played on Jesse's last team, the Oakland Rebels. I have two strong memories of the time Tyrone spent at our house last summer. Once I found him standing next to Jesse in front of our open refrigerator with his mouth agape and his eyes round with disbelief. "Man," he muttered, "I never *seen* so much stuff." Another time I asked Tyrone if he thought it was safe for the Rebels to practice at Bushrod Rec Center. I asked because there'd been a rash of drive-by shootings and a murder near Bushrod recently, but Tyrone misunderstood my question. "You don't need to worry 'bout Jesse," he said. "We don't treat him no different 'cause he white. Jesse fits right in."

"Hi, Missus . . . Missus . . ." Tyrone stammers. The name thing always *was* a problem: Jesse's Rebels friends kept trying to call me Mrs. Something. I kept telling them to call me Meredith. The standoff resulted in most of them avoiding the use of my name entirely.

"Hi, Missus . . ." Tyrone starts again. Then he gives up, throws his arms around me, hugs me tightly. "Tyrone," I say. "It's good to see you." Tyrone releases me, ducks his head, avoids my eyes and his coach's. "Yeah, me, too," he says, and walks away. *I fed that kid maybe three times, really talked to him once or twice. Was that enough to earn such affection?*

Jesse bounds over with his backpack slung across his shoulder. He glances at his coach, then at me. I can read him like a book: he's hoping to get out of here without a lecture from either one of us. The kid is out of luck.

"Listen here, Jesse," Coach McNeil says. "I don't know what you've been up to, but if your mom's got you on a short leash, that tells me you're not taking care of business at home. And you'd better start doing that if you want to stay on my team. Understood?"

Jesse nods sheepishly, his eyes on the floor. "Look at me when I'm talking to you!" Coach McNeil snaps. Jesse whips his head up. *Is* that *what this boy needs?* I wonder. *The discipline he gets from a strict black basketball coach, instead of the hippie-hang-loose mixed messages he's gotten all his life from me?*

"I know you don't like your mom coming here after you," Coach McNeil says. "But let me tell you something, Jesse. You are one lucky young man. You know why?"

Jesse shakes his head, his eyes still fixed on his coach. "Because you've got a mom who cares enough about you to show up. Do you know how many of these kids would give their right arm to have a mom like that? Some mothers think as soon as her son is taller than she is, her job is done. But that's not true, is it? You should be grateful to your mom. And you better do what she says. You hear me?"

"Yes," Jesse says. "Good. Now go on over there and wait," Coach McNeil instructs him. "Your mom and I aren't finished talking."

"Thanks," I say, when Jesse is out of earshot. "I know you've got a hard enough job just coaching. I appreciate what you're trying to do."

"Don't you worry about Jesse," Coach McNeil says. "Some of these boys—well, they may not make it. Never had a chance. But Jesse's a good kid. He's got a mom who looks after him. He'll be all right."

"Thanks again, Coach," I say. I gesture to Jesse, and we walk downstairs together. I'm trying to decide whether to go to the meeting or take him home. I'm a half-hour late for the meeting. I'm not much in the mood to go. But I do have this other son who needs to know I'm paying attention to him, too. "Can I count on you to get right on BART and start your homework as soon as you get home?" I ask Jesse.

"God, Mom," he says. "Just because I messed up once, does that mean you're never gonna trust me again?"

"Yes or no?" I bark at him. Jesse looks at me sharply—this isn't my usual parenting style.

"Yes," he says.

"Okay then. Go," I tell him. I watch him walk off across the dark campus. *It's not just him I have to trust, every time I let him go.*

I turn and enter the C building, climb the stairs to the school library. I notice that the graffiti in the halls has been painted over again since I was here last week, doing my every-other-Tuesday volunteer stint in the principal's office. The head of the English department, a white man, is addressing a group of about forty white and five Asian parents. Aside from the tenth-grade class president, an African-American girl, the only other black person in the room is a father who sits by himself in the back corner. You'd never guess that two-thirds of this school's students are nonwhite, one-third of them African-American.

"I don't know why there aren't any Advanced Placement classes in English, Mr. Edison," a white woman complains.

A white man behind her says, "My daughter's totally bored in her English class. I understand why you wanted to eliminate tracking, but I don't think it's fair to hold the more advanced students back to accommodate the slower ones."

"I won't touch *that* with a ten-foot pole," says Mr. Edison. A murmur of understanding ripples through the crowd. The tracking/no-tracking (aka segregation/integration) controversy has been raging at Berkeley High for years. Given the odds of satisfying both ends of the school's constituency—the wealthiest and the poorest people in Berkeley—it seems likely to rage for many years to come.

"Maybe you should take the kids to see Shakespeare plays," says a gray-haired woman in jeans. She looks familiar—oh, yes: we used to pass out plastic speculums and birth control advice together, twenty years ago, when we both worked at the Berkeley Women's Free Clinic. "That might make Shakespeare more relevant to them."

Another white man raises his hand. "I looked over the semester reading list. Why aren't these kids reading Dickens?"

Dickens. Advanced Placement. Jesus. *And they wonder why the masses of parents don't flock to these meetings.* I'm hoping my younger son won't get kicked off the basketball team for flunking too many classes—or end up in Juvenile Hall. We'll all be thrilled if my older son pulls a few B's. But the wealthy Berkeley liberals in this room—hills people, as they're called by the flatlands folks—have different worries. And no wonder. Odds are, most of these parents have followed the educational tradition of wealthy Berkeley liberals: keeping their kids in private school through the formative years, then enrolling them in Berkeley High for a last-minute diversity experience. Once they get here, they want their diversity experience and their private school standards, too. More power to them, I say. Let them use their time and their money and their determination to get their kids into good colleges to turn Berkeley High into their own public private school. More power to them, that is, as long as it's more power to us all: as long as the benefits of their lobbying are distributed democratically. But—*Dickens?*

The lone African-American man gets up and slips out of the meeting. A few of the white parents' eyes follow him to the door. *These people look like me, and dress like me, and grew up like me. But I'm not a hills person. Their problems aren't my problems. I'm not black or poor, either. But what happens in the gym is a lot more relevant—and at the same time more alien— to me than what's happening here. No wonder it's been hard for my kids to know where they fit. Where do* I *fit?*

Mr. Edison leans forward in his chair. "We're trying to meet a wide range of needs in this school," he says. "And to be perfectly frank, the biggest problem I'm facing isn't tracking, or adding Dickens to the reading list. Since the latest round of budget cuts, I've been trying to figure out who to hit up for donations so we can pay for the bare minimum of books we've already ordered."

"There's two hundred dollars in the tenth-grade parents' fund," says the woman who's been taking notes and chairing the meeting. "We could make that money available for books. On the condition that they'll be used for our kids—I mean, for the tenth grade—only."

Mr. Edison nods. "I can guarantee that," he says.

A father pulls a checkbook from his pocket. "If we want to make personal contributions, who should we write the checks to?"

"The parents' group," Mr. Edison answers. "If it goes to the school, the money'll get lost in the bureaucracy. Also, this way your donations are tax-deductible."

I watch with conflicting emotions as the parents go to the task of bailing out the school. Good for them, I think—writing checks to give their kids (and maybe mine; and those of the black man who just left) a better education. And so affordable, I think cynically—what with the forty thousand or so apiece they're saving on private school. And then I feel the same anger that fills me every other Tuesday when I come to Berkeley High to take my shift (invariably, alongside another affluent white parent) answering phones and issuing hall passes and typing memos. *How did this country's priorities get so screwed up that teachers are turned into beggars and tax-paying parents into volunteer secretaries and charitable donors?*

I'm reminded of all the Back-to-School nights I've attended over the years—first at mostly poor, mostly black Peralta Elementary and then at mostly poor, mostly black Claremont Middle School. As budget cuts sliced away again and again at the paltry resources they were given to begin with, the teachers spent more and more time at those events pleading for contributions and less and less time talking about curriculum. "Scrap paper, film cans, staples, whatever you can spare," Jesse's eighth-grade science teacher begged at the last Claremont meeting I went to, a year ago.

Garbage. The thought struck me that night for the first time. It has struck me many times since. *This society treats kids like garbage.* Especially poor kids. Especially black kids. Or kids—like my kids—who get lumped in with poor and black kids, because their parents can't or won't send them to private school. Public schools, public school teachers, public school kids get "whatever you can spare," whatever's left over after the Lockheed invoices and the senators' salaries have been paid: chitterlings tossed from the Massah's scrap heap to the slaves.

What do we do when the garbage starts to stink? When kids behave like what we have led them to believe they are? Do we think they don't get the message? Do we think they don't understand what it means that they do their homework assignments from ditto sheets because there aren't enough books to go around? Do we think they don't know what it means that their school bathrooms are so filthy that they have to either "hold it in" all day, or risk suspension for going off-campus to use a clean toilet? That the few computers in their classrooms are as old as the students who use them; that their music programs have been eliminated; that their guidance counselors are responsible for four hundred students apiece? Do we think they don't swallow that devaluation right down with the Velveeta-covered french fries they are served as "vegetables" for school lunch?

"We'd really appreciate any help you can give us," Mr. Edison is saying. "We don't like to keep coming to the parents, but the money's getting tighter every year."

It's triage we're doing here, I think bitterly. Coach McNeil in the gym with the black flatlands kids; Mr. Edison in the library with the white hills parents; the teachers in their classrooms trying to serve them all; the parents who are too overworked or too alienated to come to this meeting; me in my car on a rainy night, trying to keep my son from harm. All of us trying to salvage a generation of children from the wreckage of what America has bequeathed them.

I see evidence of triage, too, in the effort Jesse's teachers pour into him. Class clown though he may be, homework evader, test flunker— week after week they spend their lunch breaks giving him retests, their prep periods devising special make-up assignments. They meet with us for hour-long parent-teacher conferences, call us from their homes at eight o'clock at night to report on Jesse's progress and problems. I asked Jesse's Spanish teacher how she finds the time, the energy, to put out so much when she is given so little.

"We try to focus on the ones we think we can actually help," she told me. "Jesse's a great kid. He's bright. He's creative. He's got his parents behind him. Unlike a lot of these kids, he's got a chance. Do you know how many phone numbers I dial every night and never find a parent at home, never get a call back? Do you know how many parents have simply given up on their kids?"

I wonder if this white teacher who is doing so much for my son—a lot of it on her own unpaid time—would see Jesse as equally salvageable if he was black and poor. Or would those extra strikes against him—not in her eyes, necessarily, but in the culture's—cause her to nudge Jesse into that other category: kids who don't seem to have a chance and therefore aren't given one? If Jesse was African-American, would he be left to sink to the bottom of the heap—the heap of garbage this country keeps throwing "away," but there *is* no "away," and so our garbage and our short-sighted priorities are coming back to haunt us. . . .

A few days ago Wendy told us she'd finally found an adoption agency that can help her—as long as she's willing to adopt a baby of color. Because Wendy is unmarried and self-employed, a two-time cancer survivor who lacks the small fortune required for a private adoption, Caucasian infants are not available to her. In Wendy's interview the social worker spelled out the ranking that usually goes unspoken: a two-to-three-year wait for an Asian baby, one year for a Hispanic baby; six months for an African-American girl. But if she's willing to adopt an African-American boy, the social worker said, Wendy can have one right away.

I was thrilled for Wendy—and horrified by the implications. "They made it that clear: the darker the skin, the less desirable the baby?" I said. "You're not good enough to raise a Caucasian girl, but you're good enough to raise a black boy?"

"The agency knows what'll happen to those African-American boys if they don't give them to high-risk people like me," Wendy said. "They'll end up in foster care. There just aren't many people who want them."

Garbage.

The morning after the parents' meeting, I'm driving Peter to school. He's telling me what happened yesterday in social living class between James, a black eleventh-grader notorious for being a troublemaker, and Nancy, a white teacher known for her twenty years of initiating controversial classroom conversations about sex, drugs, and race.

"James came in and slammed his backpack down on the floor really hard," Peter said. "Nancy asked him in front of the whole class if he was mad. James ignored her. Nancy asked him if he wanted to talk about his feelings. James looked at her like she was stupid. She *was* being stupid!" Peter said. "After all these years she acts like she still doesn't know how to relate to people from the ghetto."

"What *is* James's story?" I ask.

"Mom—James isn't so special," Peter says. "He's like a lot of other kids. If anything, he's got his head screwed on more than most. James is mad because of what he's seen and lived through—what's been done to him and his people. I don't blame him a bit."

We drive in silence for a few blocks. Then I tell Peter about my conversation with Coach McNeil last night. "It breaks my heart that kids feel so hopeless. And that teachers and coaches have to do so much parenting and so little teaching. I guess a lot of parents just let go of their teenagers when they start getting into trouble."

Peter shakes his head. "A lot of these kids' parents let go of them a long time ago. Maybe you just didn't notice it before. Jesse should appreciate it that you don't let go of him. But he doesn't, because in his world it isn't cool to have a mom who cares about you."

I'll take them all, I think. The ones whose parents don't call their teachers back; the ones whose apartments and refrigerators are empty when they get home from basketball practice; the ones whose parents are so poor or so strung out or so overwhelmed that the best they can do is cut their teenagers loose and hope for the best.

But I can't take them all, of course. Not really. Even with the full-time, full-bore support of my lover and my children's father; even with my flexible schedule and my relatively abundant resources, I barely have the energy, the patience, the cautious but relentless optimism it takes to give my own two sons—day after difficult day; night after dark rainy night— what they need.

Wendy put herself on a waiting list for an African-American boy. She said that if we wrote letters of recommendation to the adoption agency, she might even get the next baby who came along. As soon as Jesse heard the news, he ran to the computer.

"When Wendy gets a baby," Jesse wrote, "I'll take him to the parks. I'll teach him to play basketball. I'll be his big brother. If he defies Wendy, I'll talk to him, ask him what's wrong.

"I'll tell him I can relate to him, because I used to be just like him."

RACE RELATIONS

The phone was ringing as Ann and I walked into the house after a week-end at the cabin. "Meredith." Richard's voice was grim. "Jesse got into a fight at school. He's okay, but he's suspended for three days." My heart sank. On the way home Ann and I had been telling each other how much better Jesse had been doing, how much more mature he'd seemed, since he was arrested for shoplifting three weeks ago. "The fight was no big deal— some kid named Lamond took a swing at Jesse, Jesse took a swing at him, they fell down, a teacher broke it up. The bigger problem is—what might happen next."

After Richard picked Jesse up from the Berkeley High counseling office, where statements were taken, parents called, and suspensions issued, Jesse confessed to Richard what he hadn't mentioned before: Lamond's friends had been threatening him all week—following him into the locker room before basketball practice, waiting for him in the hall outside math class, spreading the word around campus that Jesse was going to get jumped. Jesse swore he didn't know why. Maybe he'd said something to someone in the wrong tone of voice, made a joke someone didn't think was funny, called someone the wrong name in front of the wrong people.

It wouldn't be the first time. For years Jesse's basketball coaches—in elementary school, in junior high, at the Berkeley Y, in the Oakland league he played in last summer—had been warning Jesse, and us, that one day his mouth was going to get him into trouble. "A lot of white kids think they have to act twice as bad to make it in basketball," his junior high coach told us. "Sometimes people take Jesse's kidding the wrong way," the Y coach said. "And on a basketball court, that's *dangerous.*"

Whatever the original reason, the threat had been issued and now reputations depended on carrying it out. So after school, while his teammates watched, six boys surrounded Jesse in the locker room. They presented him with two choices: go outside and fight Lamond one-on-one, or they'd beat him up. Jesse knew Lamond, liked Lamond, knew Lamond liked him. He was sure he and Lamond wouldn't hurt each other. His teammates told Jesse they'd "get his back," that he might as well get the whole mess over with. Jesse went outside. His friends followed. Lamond was waiting. His friends gathered around. Jesse and Lamond exchanged a nervous look: neither of them really wanted to do this. Then Lamond took the first swing.

"The counselors are worried that this won't be the end of it," Richard told me. "They say the only way these vendettas get resolved is when someone gets beaten up. Since that didn't happen, they think there's a good chance Lamond's friends will go after Jesse again. They overheard one of them talking about bringing in a gang—the East Side Boys."

"A *gang?*"

"I'll bring Jesse over," Richard said. "We can talk to him together."

For the second Sunday night in a month, we sent Peter upstairs, sat in the living room facing our younger son. Jesse sat by himself in the center of the couch. Ann, Richard, and I pulled chairs around him.

"I know I shouldn't have fought Lamond," Jesse said. "But you guys don't know how hard I work to avoid getting in fights. I walk away from at least one fight every day."

"How are you living?" I cried. "Who are you hanging around with, that you have to walk away from a fight every day?"

Jesse shook his head, his jaw clenched. "You don't understand, Mom. You don't play basketball. You don't know who I have to make friends with, what I have to do to live my life."

"I understand this," Richard said. "Your reputation for running your mouth has finally caught up with you."

"Dad: *I'm not a shit talker anymore,*" Jesse said. His voice broke. "If I was, do you think I'd have the whole basketball team and all my friends backing me up? Nobody likes a shit talker. Stuff like this just happens. Kids get jumped at Berkeley High every day for no reason."

"Well, you're not going to be one of them if I can help it," I said. "What can we do so this doesn't get worse?"

"I'll call Lamond," Jesse said. "We don't have a problem with each other. We'll work it out. Then he'll tell his friends it's over, and it'll be over." I realized then how right Jesse was: I don't understand his world. When Jesse drinks Capri Sun, I can tell him that real juice is better. When he goes out in the rain without a jacket, I can tell him he'll get wet. But what do I know about settling a fight between teenage boys—between a *gang* and a teenage boy? For better or worse—without even knowing what *worse* might actually mean—we had to rely on Jesse's judgment.

I said I'd call the counseling office on Monday to get Lamond's number. We extended Jesse's previous punishment—since the shoplifting, he'd been grounded except for basketball—by one month. Jesse went to his room. Richard went home. Peter came downstairs to take the family temperature. Ann and I went into the kitchen, made tea, tried to reassure each other that Jesse would be okay. Eventually.

"I'm sorry, but I can't give you Lamond's number, Mrs. Graham," Ms. Carver, the vice-principal, said when I called her the next morning. "School policy." Okay, I said, not bothering to correct the *Mrs. Graham*. "Then could you give Lamond our number and ask him to call Jesse?"

"Actually," Ms. Carver said, "I don't think Jesse and Lamond should have any contact right now. Mrs. Robinson, Lamond's mother, was in my office first thing this morning. She's extremely upset. It turns out Lamond was rushed to the hospital after the fight. I didn't know this, but his arm was badly injured last summer. When he fell to the ground during the fight, it was reinjured. It seems . . . Lamond may lose his right arm."

I felt like the breath had been punched out of me. *Some fourteen-year-old child might lose his arm because of something my son did.*

"Mrs. Graham?" Ms. Carver said. "Yes," I whispered.

"You need to understand Mrs. Robinson's situation. Her husband was murdered recently. Her older son, James—I'm sure you've heard about James—is in the process of being expelled from Berkeley High. Lamond has always been her hope. Before he put his arm through a window last summer, he was an honor roll student, a talented pianist, a promising basketball player. Now he's likely to be permanently disabled. Mrs. Robin-son is blaming Jesse for that. She says if Lamond loses his arm, she's going to sue."

"Sue?" I said. "Who? The school?"

"You," Ms. Carver said. "So for your own protection, I wouldn't let Jesse call Lamond. Let's just wait and hope the arm gets better and every-one cools down. I'll hold a meeting between both families on Thursday morning when the boys come back to school."

I hung up the phone, put my head in my hands. Jesse came clomping down the stairs. "Did you get Lamond's number?" he asked me.

"No," I said, looking up at him. "Did you know Lamond had a bad arm?" Jesse shook his head. "Which arm? I just played basketball with him last week." "The right one," I said. "And when he fell during the fight, it got worse. Jesse—Lamond might have to have his arm amputated."

Jesse's face turned pale green. He slumped against the wall. "No," he moaned. "I never would've fought him if I'd known. I *need* to get his number. I need to call and tell him I'm sorry."

"You can't," I said. "His mom might be suing us. Anything you say to Lamond could be used against us in court."

"But the fight wasn't my fault any more than it was his," Jesse said.

"I don't think they'd win," I said. "But Dad and I could lose our houses paying for lawyers."

"Mom . . . ," Jesse said. "I feel like I'm gonna faint."

"I know," I said. "Me, too. Go sit down. I need to call Dad and Ann."

"I want him out of Berkeley High," I told Richard. "*Now.* We'll send him to whatever private school we can get him into. And no more basket-ball."

"Meredith, you can't just—"

"We have to do *something*! I can't take this anymore. I can't send him back to Berkeley High not knowing if he'll make it through the day. I can't keep letting him walk out of here with his damn basketball every Saturday morning not knowing if he'll come home in one piece."

Richard didn't even try to calm me down. He made me promise to wait till after the meeting on Thursday to make any decisions. Ann sug-gested that I call Jesse's coach and see if there was anything he could do to help.

"I heard the whole story," Coach McNeil said. "Frankly, I'm disappointed with Berkeley High. They're letting a bunch of little gangsters run the school. They ought to get the cops in there and arrest those kids. But I guess we'll have to handle this ourselves. Lamond's brother James is on the junior varsity team, so this is basketball family business. I've already spoken to James. I think I got him chilled out."

James! I thought wildly. *What if he decides to go after the kid who hurt his little brother?*

"I'll talk to Mrs. Robinson, too," Coach McNeil said. "Maybe I can convince her this wasn't Jesse's fault."

"I appreciate what you're trying to do," I said. "But I'm thinking about taking Jesse off the team. And out of Berkeley High. And out of basketball. I just don't think he's mature enough to be in that world and make good decisions. I want him to have his dreams—but I want him to live to be eighteen, too."

There was a long silence. I wondered if Coach McNeil heard what I heard in it: *Middle-class white woman telling young black man that she doesn't want her white son to become a young black male statistic.* "I'm going to do everything I can to change your mind, Mrs. Graham," Coach McNeil said.

"Meredith," I said.

"Meredith. I know you're afraid for your son. But I also know the best thing for Jesse is to keep him on the team. I'm not just saying this because Jesse's one of my top players—which he is. I'm saying this because I see strength of character in Jesse that you may not see. I put him through a lot of tests before I decided to make an investment in him. He's passed every one of them. Frankly, life isn't easy for a white kid who's as good a basketball player as Jesse is. He has to be twice as good in order to be accepted. And Jesse *is* accepted. The other kids really like him."

"Because he acts out?" I asked.

"Because he's talented, because he cares about other people, because he's *serious,*" Coach McNeil said. "We've helped a lot of kids turn their lives around. If Jesse stays in the basketball program, we can work with him, protect him, discipline him. For starters I'll give him a three-game suspension for fighting. You *know* he'll be thinking about his behavior when he's sitting on the bench watching his team play without him.

"On the team Jesse's part of the family. Cut him loose, and he's just another kid floating through Berkeley High. Another kid on the streets.

"Promise me you'll keep an open mind, at least till Jess goes back to school. In the meantime I'll talk to Mrs. Robinson and the counselors, see what I can do. Do we have a deal?"

"I'll think about it," I said.

The phone rang at seven-fifteen the next morning. It was Coach Mc-Neil. "Good morning, Mrs. . . . Meredith," he said. "I hope you got some rest. How are you feeling today?"

"It's a little early to tell," I said.

"I understand. May I speak to Jesse?"

"He's sleeping," I said.

"Well, would you do me a favor and get him up, please? He's not on vacation; he's suspended. I need to make sure he's using this time off to get his act together." When I knocked on his door and said, "Your coach is on the phone," Jesse didn't grunt at me to come back in five minutes the way he did every other morning. He jumped up and ran to the phone. "Coach?" he said reverently.

McNeil called again that afternoon. And again that night. I overheard Jesse telling him how he'd spent the day: "Cleaned my room, did some chores for my mom, made a list of what I'm gonna do to turn my life around." And again at seven-thirty the next morning. "Mom—you know what Coach told me?" Jesse said, his eyes glowing. "He said the challenge of life isn't the easy times. It's the hard times, like now. He said people are like gold. We have to go through fire to be molded into our final form. He said surviving the fire will mold me into something useful."

I'd read the books, seen the movies about ghetto kids getting recruited by Division One college coaches: stretch limos parked outside housing projects, long-suffering single mothers being wooed with fancy dinners, first-class plane tickets, suburban houses, promises of academic and athletic success for their sons. Now I felt I was in my own version of the movie. I hardly knew this man, Coach McNeil—this stranger in a suit and tie who was offering me what I wanted more than anything in the world; what friends, family members, teachers, and a small army of therapists had been unable to assure: my "at-risk" son's salvation. Was Coach McNeil pursuing Jesse, and me, with such determination because he truly wanted to save Jesse—or to bolster his own career by recruiting a player who could help deliver a winning team? And even if McNeil's intentions were pure, would he be able to deliver on his promise? Or would I be putting my son at greater risk by giving him the chance to try?

In the last month I'd come to understand that I hardly knew my son, either. Was Jesse obsessed with basketball because it gave him an entree into ghetto culture—or was ghetto culture something Jesse had learned to cope with in order to play a sport at which he was truly gifted? If it was the former, I had to wonder why Jesse aspired to join the most discriminated against, most feared and despised, most endangered group in America: young African-American men. If it was the latter, I had to admire him for integrating himself, against all odds, into the culture that could best prepare him to achieve his hoop dreams. Either way: *how could I honor who he was, what he loved, and still keep him safe?*

Listening to me worrying about Jesse, a few weeks ago, Wendy's boyfriend Michael said, "Well, one thing you can be proud of: he certainly isn't drawn to privilege." And how could he be—living the life he lives, being close to the friends he's chosen, seeing the world through their eyes? All season long Jesse traveled with his team in their too-small bus and their too-small, hand-me-down uniforms to the white-flight suburban schools they competed against—where tall, muscular blond boys recruited for their athletic abilities pranced into pristine gyms in matching warm-up suits with their names stitched on the backs, and ran off at half-time to drink Gatorade from flowered Dixie cups while their cheerleaders turned cartwheels across glossy floors.

During half-time at a particularly wealthy private school whose teams go undefeated nearly every year, where Berkeley High Yellow Jackets have been called "nigger" on at least two recent occasions, the freshman Yellow Jackets fell apart in the locker room: yelling at their coach, swinging at each other, arguing about whose fault it was that they were losing so badly. A couple of them broke down in tears. "It was the low point of my coaching career," Coach McNeil told me the next day. "Sometimes it's just too painful for my kids—and for me—to see the differences between what's available to these other teams and what's available to them. My kids run onto that court *worried*, every single time—about their grades, about one of their teammates getting jumped, about their mom losing her job. Their lives are in chaos. These other kids have stable families, safe neighborhoods, tutors, nothing to worry about but winning the game.

"I'd be the last person to deny racism. But it's hard to acknowledge to my kids how pervasive and destructive racism is—and at the same time tell them to believe in themselves, convince them they can succeed. Sometimes it makes them mad, and they fight harder to win. Last night it just made them feel defeated."

After losing a close game at a school like that, while their teammates were getting dressed, Jesse and his teammate Charles went outside to shoot around. There were two little kids on the court—kindergartners, Jesse said, when he told me about the incident later that night. Jesse and Charles started throwing the ball to them, playing with them, giving them pointers. The kids would throw the ball to Jesse, but when one of them started to throw it to Charles, the other one admonished him. "Now, Timmy," he said, "you know we don't give the ball to black people."

"They were like three feet tall!" Jesse told me. "People aren't *born* racist, Mom. Can you believe their parents taught them that while they're still so young?"

The following Saturday night Jesse and seven of his teammates were walking to a downtown Berkeley bus stop at eleven-thirty, after the janitor who'd let them into the UC Berkeley gym finally kicked them out so he could go home. Three cop cars pulled up beside them. The cops jumped out, surrounded the kids, demanded to see their ID. When Jesse asked why they were being stopped, a cop said they matched the description of some juveniles who'd assaulted a woman earlier that night: "A bunch of black kids, one wearing a green jacket, and one white kid." Jesse and his friends were held there for a half-hour, until the woman who'd been assaulted arrived at the scene. Then they were lined up in the street with lights shining in their faces, so their "victim" could see them but they couldn't see her. A neighbor started snapping photographs from across the street; one of the kids called to him, "Get a video camera," and the cops chased the photographer away. Finally the cops told the kids they could go, since the woman had "failed to identify them as the suspects."

As the season went on, as Jesse was wounded again and again by the stray bullets of racism aimed at his friends, I found myself in the unlikely position of trying to convince my white son that not all white people are evil, rich, and racist. But I didn't realize how much I—and our whole family—had come to identify black and poor as "us"; white and rich as "them," until we spent an afternoon sitting on the other side of the gym. Jesse stayed home to watch the Super Bowl the day Peter, Ann, and I went to cheer for my brother's son Nick, who plays on the basketball team of his mostly white middle school in suburban Menlo Park. When we walked into the gym, we instinctively started past the white parents and headed toward the section where all the black parents sat. Then the teams ran onto the court—Nick's team all white except for one biracial kid; the other team all black—and we yelled for Nick's team, and suddenly realized that we were with the white folks, for once.

As I watched Nick playing with much the same focus and talent as his cousin Jesse, I thought about assumptions. I wondered if the black parents on the other side of the gym were making the same assumptions about Peter, Ann, and me that we made about the white parents who sit on the other side of the gym at Jesse's games. I thought about Coach McNeil's assumption—and my own—that kids from rich white neighborhoods have nothing to worry about but winning basketball games. I compared that assumption to the reality of Nick's life at the moment: his parents in the throes of a bitter divorce; his mother living with a new man and his seven-year-old daughter; getting caught with marijuana at school, which caused Nick to be banished from his best friend's life. Nick and his friends don't dodge bullets on their way to school; their uniforms are new and clean; they have doughnuts and 7-Up and employed fathers in brand-new minivans waiting for them after their games. But they are fourteen years old in America. They do have worries on their minds.

In the car on the way home, we talked about how strange it felt, being at Nick's game. Ann said, "I hated the segregation in the gym. I wanted to go talk to the black kids, tell them they played well, too—just to step over that line." Peter said he was rooting for the black team. I said what I'd realized two minutes into the game: that rooting for a white team felt like promoting white supremacy; that having a son who's always played on predominantly black teams has made it possible for me to root for black liberation while rooting for my white son; that part of what I'm screaming for at Jesse's games, part of what I'm contributing to when I slip Coach McNeil a twenty to buy the team a pizza or when I drive Jesse's friends home at midnight to neighborhoods it's not safe for me, or them, to be in, is the ascendancy of the oppressed—or, at least, the right of young African-American men to live to be adult African-American men.

"We need to postpone the meeting," Ms. Carver greeted us on Thursday morning. "Lamond is getting some more treatments on his arm. He won't be back till Monday. We'll meet then instead. Jesse: if you have any problems today—if you even think someone *might* be threatening you— you come directly to my office. Understand?"

Jesse glanced at Richard, then at me. He looked pale and miserable. I put my hand on his shoulder, looked at Ms. Carver. Her hair, her makeup, her green silk dress were impeccable; her smooth face was impassive. "Can't you—" I said.

"I'm going to class," Jesse interrupted me, and walked away, his backpack flopping between his broad shoulders.

"It'll be all right, Mrs. Graham," Ms. Carver said. I stared at her and found nothing reassuring in her eyes. "Really it will. You'll see." She turned and walked into her office. I wondered how many times in her ten years at Berkeley High Ms. Carver had dealt with a mother like me, in a situation like this. Five times a year? Five times a month? Was she so calm because she could predict its outcome better than I could—or because she was too jaded to *care* what happened to Jesse? I wondered if she assumed that Richard and I were rich, racist "hills people." I wondered if she saw what I saw when she and I looked at each other: *middle-class white mother begging middle-class black administrator to protect her white son from a group of poor black kids.*

"Stay by the phone today," Richard said to me. "I'll do the same." I wanted to run after Jesse, snatch all six feet of him up in my arms, carry him home with me. Instead I went to my car, beeped off the burglar alarm, went home to begin my vigil.

The call came at three-fifteen. "Jesse's here," Richard said. "He's okay. Lamond's friends went looking for him during eighth period. Jesse's friends protected him—they lied about where he was so the gang wouldn't find him. Then Tariq got Jesse out of class, told him to get off campus, and ran over here with him. Good thing I live so close to school; otherwise I'm not sure where they would've gone. Anyway—I'm about to drive them to the bus to meet the team and get to the game. We'd better plan on driving out to Vallejo tonight to pick him up. We don't want him getting off the bus at Berkeley High in the dark."

"What about tomorrow?" I said.

"We'll go see Ms. Carver in the morning," Richard said.

"I'm not leaving Jesse at school unless they're sure they can protect him," I said.

"Meredith: be realistic. How *could* they protect him? Do you really think Berkeley High can assign a bodyguard to every little freshman who gets himself into a fight?"

"*I'll* be his bodyguard, then," I said. And then I pictured myself following Jesse around Berkeley High for a day, a week, a month. And then I realized I was powerless to protect my son.

"There's no reason to believe that what happened yesterday won't happen again today," Ms. Carver said when she found us waiting for her the next morning. "I called the police as soon as I heard and told them Lamond's friends were stalking Jesse. An officer visited Mrs. Robinson's house last night. We're all hoping James won't take this matter into his own hands, and that Lamond will call his friends off. But until we meet on Monday with Mrs. Robinson and Lamond, I don't think Jesse's safe at Berkeley High. I have to ask you to take him home."

"Jesse's already missed a week of school. Why don't you call those kids in here and suspend *them* till this blows over?" I said. As the words hung in the air, I imagined Ms. Carver thinking: *rich white woman thinks her son's education is more important than the education of a bunch of ghetto kids.*

Ms. Carver turned to Jesse. "Will you give me the names of the boys who came after you yesterday?"

Jesse shook his head.

"Will your friends give me the names?"

"No," Jesse said.

"*That's* why," Ms. Carver said to me. "I'll see you all on Monday morning."

At two o'clock that afternoon, I delivered Jesse into the arms of Coach McNeil, who escorted Jesse onto the team bus and promised to drive him home after the game. Then I went home and packed a borrowed van full of sleeping bags and vegan groceries for Ann and Peter and his six closest friends, who were going to the cabin for the weekend to celebrate Peter's sixteenth birthday. Hugging them all good-bye at the curb, I found myself taking an ethnicity count: two white boys, one Chilean, one Mexican, one black, one biracial—black and Japanese. *It's not all a failure,* I thought to myself. And then I ran back inside to wait for Coach McNeil to bring Jesse home. "Have you been crying, Mom?" Jesse asked when I met him at the door. I nodded. "I don't want you crying about this. I've been thinking," he said. "I'll just let them jump me on Monday. It's no big deal—they won't use knives or guns or anything. Even if they break my nose or my arm, at least it'll be over with, and none of us'll have to worry anymore."

"*No,*" I said.

On Saturday morning I talked to Jesse about private school. "Just try it for one semester. You can go back to Berkeley High next year if you don't like it." Jesse shook his head at me. "I can't just run away from my problems, Mom," he said. "I have to learn to make it in the real world."

On Saturday night I offered to take Jesse to see *Hoop Dreams.* Normally he wouldn't have considered being seen at the movies—especially a basketball movie—with his mother. But now his punishment, and his security needs, gave him no choice. As we drove into downtown Berkeley, Jesse put his head between his knees. "Are you okay?" I asked him.

"I don't want Lamond's friends to see me," he answered.

So we drove down Shattuck Avenue with Jesse slumped over, hiding, and me nervously eyeing the teenagers on the street. As I pulled into a parking lot on a side street, Jesse looked up at me, his right cheek resting on his left thigh. "You're gonna write about this, aren't you, Mom?" he asked.

I was still raw and terrified—my heart broken wide open by everything that mothering Jesse had caused me to know and to witness and to feel— still seeking solace, when I had breakfast with Aletha, a friend I hadn't seen in a while, to ask how she was doing with her sixteen-year-old son Miles. "He's living with my parents in Mississippi. It's better for him down there," she said, and changed the subject. I was puzzled but determined; I was there to talk about what was happening with Jesse, and that's what I proceeded to do. When I stopped to blow my nose, I saw tears in Aletha's eyes.

"What is it?" I asked.

"I didn't tell you what really happened, why Miles went to Mississippi," she said. "After school one day Miles was running to catch the bus. All of a sudden, with all his friends watching, two cops pulled up, grabbed Miles, threw him up against a wall, and searched him. The cops said he matched the description of a man who'd just robbed a bank. Miles kept saying, 'I'm not a man! I'm a kid! I was in school all day!' Finally the cops realized it couldn't have been Miles so they let him go.

"Ever since we moved to Marin County, Miles has had problems. It was hard on him, being the only black kid in almost every situation. He was just getting himself together, making friends, when this happened. It made him go crazy. He started doing drugs, stealing—he told me it was what the world expected of him, that the world would never let him amount to anything anyway, so why should he try. The night I picked him up from Juvenile Hall, I promised myself I would do whatever it took to save him."

Aletha was crying openly. I put my hand on her arm. "My parents said they'd take him," she said. "So I sent him to Biloxi. It's a relief to know he's safe, but I've been in pain, being without him. I've only seen him once since he left. We talk on the phone, but you know what *that's* like with a teenage boy."

"Yeah," I said. Because that much I did know. And I knew some other things Aletha knew, too: What it's like to sit by the phone on Friday and Saturday nights, hoping when it rings that it's my son and not the police. What it's like to teach my son, raised to fight for justice, to "respect authority" so he won't provoke the cops and endanger himself when he gets picked up for shoplifting, or for being in the wrong place at the wrong time with friends, with skin the wrong color.

But I don't know what it's like to be an African-American mother, raising an African-American boy. I don't know what it's like to live without my son. And most important, I don't know—does *anyone?*—what to do to stop this, change this, so a whole generation of Mileses and Lamonds and Jameses isn't lost to us all.

"Meredith," Aletha cried, "it is the worst thing a mother could have to do—to send her child away to keep him alive."

"Yes," I said. I leaned across the table to hug her. She rested her head on my shoulder. I stroked her dreadlocks with one hand, wiped the tears off my face with the other. "Yes, I know."

.   .   .

On Monday morning Richard, Jesse, and I meet again outside Ms. Carver's office. Her door is locked. A few minutes later a woman my size and a boy Jesse's size come walking down the hall. I'm sure they can see my heart pounding right through my leather jacket. "Mrs. Robinson?" I say. She looks me up and down. I look her up and down. Her hair is straightened, pulled back into a short, nappy ponytail; her skin is blotchy; her eyes deep and intense. I put out my hand. She shakes it. "You must be Jesse's mom."

I turn to her son. "Lamond?" I offer my right hand. He offers his left. I see his right arm hanging limply from his shoulder. I feel ill, remembering. "Sorry," I say. "How's your arm?"

"Better," his mother answers. "Thank you for asking."

Suddenly, inexplicably, standing in that graffiti-splattered hallway with Mrs. Robinson and Lamond—the targets of my fear and empathy and hatred and sorrow every waking moment of this last week—my terror and anger float away from me like a feather in a breeze. Lamond is no longer a faceless gang leader—he is a sweet-faced, scared fourteen-year-old boy, like Jesse. Mrs. Robinson is no longer my enemy, out to take everything I own as reparations for a lifetime of oppression, neglect, and grief— she is a worried, loving mother, like me. For the first time in a week, I can breathe. For the first time in a week, I believe we will all survive this. I feel oddly drawn to Mrs. Robinson and to Lamond. I want to be with them, to see this through with them.

Ms. Carver bustles up to us. I wonder if she planned to arrive late so the two families would have this time alone together. "Boys, can I trust you in my office without supervision?" she asks. Jesse and Lamond smile little half-smiles at each other. "Okay. You two talk in here. When you're through, meet us in Ms. Yee's office." Ms. Carver leads the parents down the hall.

"Mrs. Robinson and I spoke last night," Ms. Carver tells Richard and me. "She says Lamond's arm is improving."

"That's great. Great news," Richard says.

"I'm so glad," I say, looking into Mrs. Robinson's eyes. "Thank you," she says, looking into mine. "He may never have full use of it again. He'll never go to the NBA like he'd dreamed he might. But at least he won't lose it."

Lamond and Jesse appear at the door, squeeze themselves between the filing cabinets and chairs crammed into the tiny room.

"That was quick," Ms. Carver says.

"I told you—we're friends," Jesse says.

"It's a good thing, too," Mrs. Robinson says. She looks intently at me. "You're lucky your son is alive, Mrs. Graham. When I brought Lamond home from the hospital after the fight, James asked me, 'Who did this to my little brother?' He was halfway out of his chair. I thought to myself, 'That child is dead, whoever he is.'

"I told James, 'Some freshman named Jesse.' And James sat back down. *Jesse?* he said. 'Jesse's a good kid. Like Lamond.' That was the moment I knew your son would be spared."

She looks at Jesse. "I remember you now. You helped James that time he got hurt playing basketball at the Y."

"James and I get along fine," Jesse says, and I remember the argument he and I had a few weeks ago, when he mentioned that the infamous James was a friend of his. "Great choice of role models," I'd snapped. Jesse rolled his eyes and told me, yet again, that I just didn't understand.

Mrs. Robinson turns to me again. "Everyone's been telling me to bring charges against Jesse. My grandmother, my friends, my lawyer. But Lamond said, 'Mom, I don't want to do to Jesse what's already been done to James. They've already ruined James's life with all those charges they've put on his record. I want Jesse to have a chance.' "

I inhale a ragged breath. Jesse glances at Lamond, then down at the patched linoleum floor.

"Well, it seems we've resolved the problem between the two of you," Ms. Carver says. "Now, boys, how are we going to make sure this feud stops here?"

"I already told my friends to leave Jesse alone," Lamond says. "They said they would. But Jesse and I made a plan, just in case."

"Lamond and I are gonna meet in the C building after second period," Jesse says. "We'll walk down the hall together. When everyone sees we're friends, they'll know it's over."

"I hope that puts an end to this," Ms. Carver says. "You know the police are involved now. If there are any further incidents—"

"There won't be," Mrs. Robinson says. "Jesse and Lamond are both good boys. This was the first time in his life Lamond's ever gotten into trouble at school. He's on the honor roll, you know. Now that his arm's getting better, he's going right back to studying. No more of this mess."

Everyone stands up. Ms. Carver tells the boys to come to her office for hall passes. Richard follows them. I stay behind with Mrs. Robinson.

"Jesse says no one knew about Lamond's arm until after the fight," I say.

Mrs. Robinson nods. "He went to a lot of trouble to hide it. He'd lift his right hand onto the desk with his left hand, prop a pencil between the fingers, then take notes in his lap with his left hand. But I guess it won't be much of a secret anymore."

"Your son has a lot to deal with," I say.

"We *all* have a lot to deal with," she says.

She holds out her hands. "You see these chewed-up fingernails? *James.* He keeps me awake nights, worrying. Just yesterday some gang was up in his face, trying to get him to go off with them. James is right on that line. I'm trying to keep him from falling off."

"I know exactly what you mean," I sigh.

"No, you don't," she says. She puts her hand on my arm. "Having a child like James, you learn a lot. And I can tell you this, Mrs. Graham— you don't have to worry. Jesse's not like James. Jesse will be all right."

In a few words Mrs. Robinson gives me what I've been unable to find anywhere else. She soothes me. And what can I offer her in return? What makes us different—what makes our sons' futures different—is so much greater than what we share in this moment, mother to mother.

"Thank you," I say.

Mrs. Robinson nods. "I'm sure we'll be seeing each other again." She walks away.

EPILOGUE:
NOW AND THEN

"There's something contagious about demanding freedom, especially where women, who comprise the oldest oppressed group on the face of the planet, are concerned. . . . It is not a small job, and it does seem as if women's work is never done."

FROM THE INTRODUCTION TO
Sisterhood Is Powerful

APRIL 14, 1996

I'm marching to Fight the Right through the streets of San Francisco with my friends Marg and Elaine. Like the thousands of people around us, we're waving signs—in Spanish, Mandarin, and English—printed with the slogans of the march. "No Retreat On Affirmative Action! Fight Racism! Protect Abortion Rights! Stop All Forms Of Violence Against Women! Demand Lesbian, Gay and Bi Rights! End The War On Poor Women!"

The pounding beat of a reggae band belting out Bob Marley freedom songs competes with the chants that echo between the cars and houses. Banner after banner, group after group—I'm surprised by how diverse the march is; especially surprised by how many men and young people are in it. High school and college students from black student unions and NOW chapters all over the West Coast. Mexicanas and Mexicanos in serapes and huaraches. Lesbian Avengers and radical fairies. Native American men, women, and children in tribal costumes. Pro-choice activists and trade union members.

"Our kids should be here," I complain to Elaine, whose son Toby is in Peter's biology class at Berkeley High. *And so should Ann,* I think. But she had to work today, a Sunday. Since her last promotion she never seems to get caught up. "They should've organized a Berkeley High delegation."

Elaine shrugs. "It's not like the old days, when we could buckle 'em into their strollers and drag them along with us." Just then I catch a glimpse of Cathy, whose sons Carlos and Claudio are Peter's and Jesse's oldest friends. Cathy grabs me up in a hug, her face flushed with that familiar demonstration fever.

"Great march, huh?" she says. "Really good," I agree. "But I wish . . . ."

"I know," she says. "I tried to get my guys to come, too. They had soccer practice. Some excuse. Yours?"

"Jesse's playing basketball," I say. "And Peter says he doesn't want to demonstrate *against* anything. He thinks it's negative energy." Cathy and I look at each other and smile. "That's not a bad point, actually," she says. "Well, maybe the next march will be *for* something." We wave good-bye and look around for the people we came with.

As I'm on my way to find Marg and Elaine, I'm almost knocked over by the force of a compact body hurling itself at mine. "Meredith! It's me!" A dark-skinned young woman untangles herself and plants herself in front of me. "Tina! From the China meeting." I'm still peering at her, trying to place her. "The Berkeley High girls' delegation to the UN women's conference! I talked to you after the meeting—remember?"

Tina? I think. The girl who took me aside and told me she was bisexual? But that girl was quiet and uncertain, with conservative clothes and long black hair. "I shaved my head," Tina says, laughing. "I guess I look different now." "You sure do," I say. "You look great." And she does. Her eyes, now fully exposed against the smooth skin of her face, are full of fire. Her body, dressed in torn denim jeans and the T-shirt they're selling at today's march, is pulsing with energy.

"Look!" she says. She points to a purple banner behind her that reads "Lavender Youth Recreation and Information Center." "Right after I came out to you, I joined LYRIC," she says. "It's changed my life. I have so many good friends now—gay friends. We have a speaker's bureau— I've spoken at a bunch of schools already. And we just started an on-line 'zine for gay and bi kids. Do you know anyone who might wanna write for us?"

"Hey, Tina!" calls the young, multiply-pierced woman who's holding up half of the LYRIC banner. "You coming?"

"I gotta go," Tina says. She pulls a pen out of her back pocket, scribbles her phone number on the corner of a leaflet, tears it off, and hands it to me. She nods at the woman holding the banner, then glances at me with a trace of the shyness I remember. "That's my new girlfriend," she says. She grins and gives me a quick hug. "Call me, okay?" She runs back to the LYRIC delegation and throws her arm around her lover. "Gay rights *now*! Bi rights *now*!" she yells along with her group.

I run ahead to meet up with Marg and Elaine, who've bumped into some friends. "This is Pat," Marg introduces me to a woman with short salt-and-pepper hair. "We worked on abortion stuff together a long time ago." "Twenty-five *years* ago," Pat says, shaking her head. "Can you believe we're still at it?" "And this is Sondra," Elaine says. "An AA pal." We step onto the curb for a moment, passing around a water bottle and a bag of dried prunes, watching the marchers go by, their chants ringing in our ears.

"This is great," Elaine says. "All this energy." "It is great," Pat says. "And it makes me feel really old. I mean, look at all these *kids*. Were we really that young when we started with all this?"

I take a long swallow of water and think about how young I was when I started with all this. I think about how much has changed since then, and how much hasn't. So many of the picket signs, so many of the battles are the same. Yet the world that my sons are becoming men in—the world that Tina is becoming a woman in—is so different from the world that shaped me.

There are still plenty of laws and minds to change, still plenty of questions to ask and to answer. But there are also plenty of young warriors to carry on the torch—strong young women like Tina, strong young men like Cathy's sons, and Elaine's, and mine.

"Hey, there's LYRIC," Sondra says as the purple banner goes by.

"Those kids are so brave. Can you imagine any of us being out like that when we were fifteen?"

I search the crowd and see Tina, smiling and waving at me. "Meredith!" she calls. I wave back.

"Who's that girl?" Marg asks me.

"That girl," I answer, "is the future."

POSTSCRIPT

As I was finishing this book, Ann and I broke up. I can't say why. I certainly can't say—here, or anywhere, coherently—how it feels.

I can only turn these pages, turn the pages of our twelve years together, looking for clues and wondering how our relationship might have been different if her woman's life, if my woman's life, had been different: less evocative of our wounded, fearful selves; more reinforcing of our trusting, loving selves.

And I can only hope that the damage stops and the healing starts here—for Ann, for me, for girls, and for women.

Oakland, California
September 1996

ABOUT THE AUTHOR

MEREDITH MARAN was an anti-Vietnam War protester, a New Mexico hippie, a women's health care worker, and a labor organizer in Bay Area factories. She now works as a consultant to socially responsible businesses and writes for publications as diverse as *Parenting, Utne Reader, New Age Journal,* and *New Woman.* She lives in Oakland with her two teenage sons.